Policy Implications of Research in Education

Volume 2

For further volumes:
http://www.springer.com/series/11212

Policy Implications of Research in Education

Scope of the Series

In education, as in other fields, there are often significant gaps between research knowledge and current policy and practice. While there are many reasons for this gap, one that stands out is that policy-makers and practitioners may simply not know about important research findings because these findings are not published in forums aimed at them.

Policy Implications of Research in Education aims to clearly and comprehensively present the implications for education policy and practice drawn from important lines of current education research in a manner that is accessible and useful for policy-makers, educational authorities and practitioners.

Kara S. Finnigan • Alan J. Daly
Editors

Using Research Evidence in Education

From the Schoolhouse Door to Capitol Hill

Springer

Editors
Kara S. Finnigan
Warner School of Education
University of Rochester
Rochester, NY, USA

Alan J. Daly
Department of Education Studies
University of California, San Diego
La Jolla, CA, USA

ISBN 978-3-319-04689-1 ISBN 978-3-319-04690-7 (eBook)
DOI 10.1007/978-3-319-04690-7
Springer Cham Heidelberg New York Dordrecht London

Library of Congress Control Number: 2014935864

Printed on acid-free paper

Springer is part of Springer Science+Business Media (www.springer.com)

Foreword

The editors and authors of this volume are asking readers to rethink the connection between research in the social and behavioral sciences and the work of practitioners. No more research *to* practice. If we hope to connect research *and* practice, then our efforts must reflect an ongoing and reciprocal relationship between the two communities. To make that possible, we need a lot more information about practitioners' work. I agree with this message and believe it productively challenges many of the current practices of researchers and research funders.

It is difficult to determine how much money and effort is devoted to research meant to improve policy and practice, but it is a lot. The Census Bureau's 2012 Statistical Abstract notes that the federal government proposed spending $26.3 billion on applied research in 2009,[1] much of it related to defense and health. A fair amount of federally supported applied research focuses on technology and communication, and the pace of change in those areas suggests that the funding is producing results. For example, the Defense Advanced Research Projects Agency (DARPA) is widely credited with giving us two innovations that pervade our daily lives, the internet and GPS. It is less clear that the research and development (R&D) expenditures in education and related fields are having similar effects on how we live and work. (Admittedly, DARPA's budget alone is about $2.8 billion annually. The Department of Education spent a relatively modest $353 million on R&D in 2010.) Contrast the changes in communication with the experience of walking into a high school. Before breakfast I might scan my email, check the weather on my smart phone, and get a bit frustrated when a new book will not download on my e-reader. If I then visit a school, I'll see rhythms, practices, and outcomes that look very much like they did 50 years ago when I was in high school. When the bell rings, each teacher closes the door with 25–30 students for 45–50 min. Those teachers are likely to see 150 students in six hours, for 180 days. Much of the work is didactic, and large amounts of time are spent on noninstructional activities such as managing the transitions between class periods. This consistency in how school work is structured might be fine if our

[1] 2009 is the most current year for which the total is available.

young people were doing well and our education, health, and other human services were robust. Few, though, would make that argument.

For the past 10 years, I have been the president of the William T. Grant Foundation, an institution dedicated to the proposition that research can help policy makers and practitioners improve the lives of young people. When I joined the Foundation in 2000 as Senior Vice President for Program, I had a fairly conventional view about the role of a research funder—support researchers to do good work, help them communicate findings effectively, and work with policy makers to encourage evidence-based reforms. To accomplish the latter, I assumed the need to influence the voting public's attitudes by getting research evidence covered in the public media. It seems to me that most researchers and research funders hold these ideas today. During my tenure, my colleagues and I have revised most of these assumptions in light of subsequent experience, and the type of empirical work featured is in this volume. We think it is time for others to do the same. Here is a brief account of our journey.

In 2000, our program documents said that we wanted to understand how different members of the public (e.g., corporate leaders) regarded youth and how communication efforts could influence the views of such people. It was a big, broad aspiration that exceeded our limited resources, and we felt that we needed to get more focused. Following conversations with influential advocates—from both sides of the political spectrum—in 2003, we changed our target audience from the general public to influential policy makers, practitioners, advocates, and members of the media. We also stated a special interest in their social networks, and when and how research evidence affected their knowledge, views, and behaviors. In retrospect, the shift was a modest one that left the underlying paradigm intact. We were still interested in sending research to practice; we just wanted to be more efficient about it. It was all moot because despite stating our interests, we received few fundable proposals to study any of this.

Vivian Tseng joined the Foundation's program group as a postdoctoral fellow in late 2004, and by 2007 we decided to "fish or cut bait" on our interest regarding how research is used. Vivian and I led an internal effort to understand why we received so few research proposals to examine how policy makers and practitioners use research findings. As a research funder, it seemed like a fundamental question for our work, but if we could not stimulate competitive applications, we would need to move on.

Vivian and I formed an internal reading group to master the iconic literature on research use, which was mainly developed in the 1970s and 1980s. She also had many conversations with researchers and funders trying to understand why the literature—by Nathan Caplan, Carol Weiss, and others—had not been followed by a second generation of scholars and studies. One hypothesis was that no academic discipline owned the terrain of research use, particularly use in practice as opposed to policy, and thus it was hard to train scholars for a field with an uncertain future. In addition, there were no federal agencies or private foundations funding such empirical work, and thus it was not possible to build a successful and sustained research program in academia. There were some signals, however, that institutions and incentives were changing in what might be promising directions. As the standards movement grew in the 1990s in most human service areas and budgets tightened in the twenty-first century, policy makers began to call for the use of "evidence-based" programs and practices and to build that exhortation into law. This made it more important to understand how and when research use occurred. The rise of evidence-based requirements was paralleled by the growth of professional schools in education, law, public health, public policy, and social work that could create an academic home for scholarly work on research utilization.

Our Board authorized us to make a concerted effort to develop a portfolio on research use in late 2007. In 2008, we commissioned Lisa Towne, now principal and research director at Education First, to interview influential education scholars as to their interest in doing such research. We then asked scholars Sandra Nutley and Huw Davies to write a white paper on how to develop an empirical agenda that built on prior work. Throughout, we had two goals in mind. Our first aim was to figure out what the Foundation might do to be useful in this field. We also wanted to create some excitement about the topic so that we could attract strong applicants and other funders.

In early 2009, we released the first of a series of annual Requests for Proposals (RFPs) seeking projects that would advance our understanding of the acquisition, interpretation, and use of research evidence in policy and practice. In the RFP, we acknowledged the dominant paradigm—there are many gaps between research and policy and research and practice. And researchers, research funders, and intermediaries have tried to eliminate those gaps by encouraging more rigorous research evidence, better research syntheses, and improved approaches to disseminating research evidence. For the first time, though, we also questioned whether such efforts would ever suffice. Our thinking, subsequently developed in essays and articles, was that the research community has made great progress in line with its assumptions about why research and practice were so disconnected. But policy makers and practitioners were telling us, through some small projects we commissioned, that research was too often irrelevant to the decisions they needed to make. They also reported that findings rarely penetrated the networks they drew upon when trying to make decisions about ongoing work or possible changes. This raised the possibility that the dominant model for thinking about the research-practice connection was amiss.

Based on what we were hearing, and because research use is so often "tactical" in the legislative process (i.e., used after the fact to justify a predetermined position), we expressed a particular interest in mid-level decision makers in executive branch agencies at the federal, state, and local levels (e.g., assistant superintendent in a school district or the head of a county welfare agency). Our goal was to understand how people in these roles acquire, interpret, and use evidence of any type—including research evidence, which we defined as empirical findings derived from systematic research methods and analyses. In calling for such studies, we argued that very little was known about such research users, and work was needed to help us and others build stronger conceptual models or theories to explain—or at least predict—acquisition, interpretation, and use. We also had the idea that these were not processes that varied solely because individual decision makers have different tastes and abilities when it comes to research. Rather, we thought that research acquisition, interpretation, and use might vary because those decision makers were in different organizations, and variations in organizational culture and connections would make a difference. In addition, we thought that intermediary organizations, such as trade, professional, and advocacy groups, were probably important. We also signaled an interest in understanding how the larger political, economic, and social contexts affected decision makers. Is research more or less important when resources are severely limited? Does it make a difference if the decision involves an issue that is severely contested versus one that is less heated?

In addition to our novel focus on potential users of research, we worked to fund studies that were methodologically stronger than what had come before. While not wanting to paint all prior work with a broad brush, much of it was retrospective, done with one wave of data (i.e., cross-sectional), and reliant on interviews or surveys with policy actors to understand how research had been used in the past or might be used in hypothetical situations. This work had illuminated that any linear model of research to practice or research to policy was misplaced. But the research suffered from the possibility that respondents' recollections and therefore the storylines were much clearer in retrospect than they would have been in prospect. In addition, it was difficult to assess how much findings were a product of the data collection strategy and method used. For example, would the inferences about the findings have been different if interviews had complemented observations and document reviews? What if data had been gathered over time?

Given our interest in theory building and our belief that the research community knew too little about the decision makers they were trying to reach, we understood that we'd start with close-in studies comparing various case examples. In any study, the cases needed to contrast along dimensions that might be important, such as the political context, organizational culture, or policy issue at hand. And to provide stronger information, the studies needed to be prospective and longitudinal and use multiple forms of data collection to be able to "triangulate" the information on any part of the enterprise that was presumed to be important. For example, if practitioners' social networks are seen as important, then they should be understood using multiple sources of data such as surveys, observations, and interviews.

Four years later, we have made important progress. By seeking projects through an annual RFP and our regular process of investigator-initiated grants, we have funded 25 studies, most of which meet the standards described. Not surprisingly, given the press for using evidence-based programs and practices in education, about half of the studies are in education. But we also have a growing portfolio in other areas such as child welfare and mental health. The education portfolio is highlighted in this volume, in part because it is the furthest along. Across the studies, it is clear that strong senior, mid-career, and junior scholars from a wide range of disciplines are interested in understanding if, how, and when practitioners acquire, interpret, and use research, and they are capable of producing fresh insights. Their work is starting to appear in journals and at refereed conferences. In addition, other funders are starting to notice, notably the federal research arm of the Department of Education, the Institute of Education Sciences. What is less clear is that we have launched a renewed area of inquiry that will sustain itself and endure. Will these scholars, their students, and their colleagues stay with these questions over time? Will other funders enter the fray? Will academic departments and institutions hire and promote scholars working on research use?

One measure of the ability of the topic to sustain itself might be if it passes the test that motivated us to begin. That is, will policy makers and practitioners see the findings as relevant and begin to demand more? While it is too early to tell, this possibility remains real because the findings from the early studies are drawing attention from such audiences. For example, the federal legislative staff involved in reauthorizing the Institute of Education Sciences have asked for briefings on the work, and practitioners including leaders in state departments of education and school districts are doing the same.

The initial findings from this work are covered by the editors and authors in this volume, particularly in the integrative chapters by Alan Daly, Kara Finnigan, and my colleague Vivian Tseng. It appears that many of the questions important to practitioners too rarely get attention in research and evaluation as currently funded and practiced. Yes, these decision makers want to know about the effects of programs and policies. But they want much more information than is available about what it takes to put those programs or reforms into practice, and the degree to which they have been tested in organizations and situations similar to theirs. They also distrust much research, worrying that a study can be found to support any recommendation. Thus, they draw on their trusted networks and want reliable ways to synthesize evidence from any study with evidence from their personal experience and peers. How can that sort of synthesis be done in a useful and timely way? Decision makers are also increasingly open to working with researchers in order to make progress on enduring problems of practice. This is leading to new arrangements that look very different than the research to practice models, which still underlie too much of our discourse and activities.

With that brief preview, I invite readers to this volume, which contains new studies and ideas about the connections between research, practice, and policy. Taken together, the studies only scratch the surface, and others need to examine the questions that motivated this work. But the scratch may be so deep that the current paradigm cannot be refinished. Rather, in order to make intellectual and practical progress, it needs to be scrapped in favor of new models and methods for connecting research and practice.

New York, NY, USA Robert C. Granger, Ed.D.

Author note: Robert C. Granger retired from the Foundation on August 31, 2013.

Acknowledgements

We would like to thank Bob Granger and Vivian Tseng of the WT Grant Foundation for their early recognition and continued commitment to our work. In addition to the feedback and support they have each provided individually along the way, we are deeply appreciative of the knowledge community they have developed through the ongoing meetings of grantees from various fields and disciplines. We have not only strengthened our scholarship as a result of these connections but also enjoyed the collegial relationships that have developed over the years. By breaking through strongly defended silos in the academy, you have both crafted something extremely special—thank you!

We are also extremely grateful to our friends and colleagues who have strengthened our ideas and provided feedback and support along the way. We stand on the shoulders of giants in doing this work and are indebted to all of you who provided support big and small over the course of the journey.

We would like to thank Nadine Hylton for her assistance behind the scenes in making sure everything was moving forward as scheduled and providing editorial support for the book.

Finally, Kara would like to provide special thanks to Kelly, not only for his unwavering support but also for his commitment through his own work to a more just world. And special thanks to Maya and Hugh for reminding me of what is important every day through your stories and laughter. Alan would like to acknowledge his family, particularly his parents who have worked hard their entire lives in making a difference in the world. May the next years of your lives be filled with the ease, peace, and joy you so often bestowed on others.

Contents

About the Editors

Kara S. Finnigan, Ph.D., is an Associate Professor of Education Policy at the University of Rochester's (UR) Warner School of Education. She has conducted research and evaluations of K-12 educational policies and programs at the local, state, and federal levels for more than 20 years through her work at the UR as well as several prominent research organizations, including the Wisconsin Center for Education Research at the University of Wisconsin-Madison, SRI International, RPP International, and the George Lucas Educational Foundation. She teaches courses on educational policy, sociology of education, and research methods. Finnigan has written extensively on the topics of low-performing schools and high-stakes accountability, district reform, principal leadership, and school choice. Her research blends perspectives in education, sociology, and political science; employs both qualitative and quantitative methods, including social network analysis; and focuses on urban school districts. She recently served as Associate Editor of the *American Educational Research Journal* (AERJ). She has published articles in prominent academic and practitioner-oriented journals. Finnigan received her Ph.D. in Education Policy from the University of Wisconsin-Madison, her M.A. in Administration and Policy Analysis from Stanford University, and a B.A. in English from Dartmouth College.

Alan J. Daly, Ph.D., is an Associate Professor and Vice Chair of the Department of Education Studies at the University of California, San Diego. He graduated from Clark University with a Bachelor of Arts in Psychology and received a Master of Science in Counseling from San Diego State University and a Master of Arts and Ph.D. in Education with an emphasis in Educational Leadership and Organizations from the University of California, Santa Barbara. Prior to coming to the university, Alan had over 16 years of public education experience in a variety of positions ranging from classroom teacher to district psychologist to site administrator. His research and teaching primarily focus on the role of leadership, educational policy, and organization structures and the relationship between those elements on the educational attainment of traditionally marginalized populations. Alan draws on his methodological expertise in social network analysis in his work and has a book on the topic published by Harvard Press entitled *Social Network Theory and Educational Change* and a second under contract with Harvard entitled *Networked Systems: Improving Educational Systems in the 21st Century*.

About the Contributors

Robert Asen is a Professor in the Department of Communication Arts and an affiliate at the Institute for Research on Poverty at the University of Wisconsin-Madison. His research explores the relationship among social, economic, and political inequalities and public deliberation and includes developing theoretical models of public deliberation that may promote inclusive interactions, affirm diversity, and promote justice as well as studying social policy debates. Asen is the author of *Visions of Poverty: Welfare Policy and Political Imagination* and *Invoking the Invisible Hand: Social Security and the Privatization Debates* and numerous journal articles and book chapters and coeditor of two books. He is currently working on a book titled *Democracy, Deliberation, and Education*, which examines school board deliberations.

Carol A. Barnes, Ph.D. is a recently retired Research Scientist at the University of Michigan and Senior Researcher at the Consortium for Policy Research in Education (CPRE). She uses mixed methods to understand macro and micro influences on school improvement in high-poverty settings, especially the relationship between policy, research, and instructional or leadership practice. Barnes' research ranges from close examinations of teachers and principals incorporating research or policy principles into their practice to evaluations of federal or state policies aimed at school improvement. She is currently analyzing how research-based programs affect school organization, leadership, and instructional practice in 30 high-poverty schools. Barnes recently completed a study of how state education agencies are organized to manage and use evidence in their policies or practices to improve low-performing schools.

Jing Che, Ph.D. from the Warner School of Education of the University of Rochester, is an Educational Data Strategist at the Rochester City School District and a Data Fellow at Strategic Data Project, Center for Education Policy Research. Her areas of focus include research and teaching in fields of English to Speakers of Other Languages, quantitative research, and educational policy analysis.

Cynthia E. Coburn is a Professor at the School of Education and Social Policy at Northwestern University. Coburn studies the relationship between instructional policy and teachers' classroom practices in urban schools. In a series of studies, she has investigated critical issues facing public schools, including the relationship between reading policy and teachers' classroom practice, the scale-up of innovative mathematics curricula, the implementation of Common Core State Standards, and the relationship between research and practice for school improvement. In 2011, Coburn was awarded the Early Career Award from the American Educational Research Association in recognition of her contributions to the field of educational research in the first decade of her career.

Elizabeth DeBray is an Associate Professor in the Department of Lifelong Education, Administration, and Policy in the College of Education, University of Georgia. She received her Ed.D. from Harvard University. Her research interests are the politics of federal education policy, policy implementation, and interest group politics, including the role of intermediary organizations in disseminating research and information about education reforms.

Margaret E. Goertz is a Professor Emerita of Education and a Senior Researcher at the Consortium for Policy Research in Education in the University of Pennsylvania's Graduate School of Education. She specializes in the study of education finance and governance policy and has conducted research on state and local implementations of Title I and the No Child Left Behind Act; the design and implementation of standards-based reform by states, school districts, and schools; federal and state accountability policies; and state and local district resource allocations. She is currently studying how state education agencies search for and use research in their school improvement strategies.

Deb Gurke has over 25 years of experience in public education. Currently, she is the Director of the Research and Development Department for the Milwaukee Public Schools. She has a Ph.D. in Educational Policy Studies from the University of Wisconsin-Madison where she studied school organizations and rhetoric—specifically the role that the community plays in policy decisions. As the Director of Governance and Leadership Development at the Wisconsin Association of School Boards, Gurke worked with school board members to help them understand how the changing world requires relationship-based leadership. She also served on the Stillwater, Minnesota, Board of Education.

Ron Haskins is a Senior Fellow in Economic Studies at the Brookings Institution, where he codirects both the Center on Children and Families and the Budgeting for National Priorities Project, and is a Senior Consultant at the Annie E. Casey Foundation. He is the author of *Work Over Welfare: The Inside Story of the 1996 Welfare Reform Law*, coauthor of *Creating an Opportunity Society* and *Getting Ahead or Losing Ground: Economic Mobility in America*, and senior editor of *The Future of Children*. In 2002, he was the Senior Advisor to the President for Welfare Policy at the White House. Haskins was a Senior Researcher at the Frank Porter Graham Child Development Center at the University of North Carolina, Chapel Hill. He holds a Ph.D. in Developmental Psychology from UNC.

Meredith I. Honig is an Associate Professor of Educational Leadership and Policy Studies at the University of Washington (UW) where she also directs the Leadership for Learning (Ed.D.) program. Her research, teaching, and district partnerships focus on policy, leadership, and organization change in urban educational systems. Her most recent studies have examined the participation of school district central office administrators in the implementation of reforms that challenge the status quo in central offices including school-community partnerships, new small autonomous school initiatives, data-informed decision-making, and efforts to improve teaching and learning districtwide. Dr. Honig's many publications include the edited book *New Directions in Education Policy Implementation: Confronting Complexity*. Dr. Honig recently launched the District Leadership Design Lab (DL2) to bring together leadership scholars, learning scientists, and district leaders in support of improved central office performance.

Huriya Jabbar is a Doctoral Candidate in Education Policy in the Graduate School of Education at the University of California, Berkeley. She studies the social and political dimensions of market-based reforms in education, including school choice and incentive pay, and how policy makers at the local, state, and federal levels use research on such reforms. Her dissertation research on marketization and competition in New Orleans, Louisiana, was awarded a 2013–2014 National Academy of Education/Spencer Foundation Dissertation Year Fellowship.

Christopher Lubienski is a Professor of Education Policy and Director of the Forum on the Future of Public Education at the University of Illinois, where he studies the political economy of education reform. He is also a Sir Walter Murdoch Distinguished Adjunct Professor at Murdoch University in Western Australia. His most recent book *The Public School Advantage: Why Public Schools Outperform Private Schools* (with Sarah Theule Lubienski) was published by the University of Chicago Press in 2013.

Greg Margolis is a Research Analyst in the Center on Children and Families at the Brookings Institution. Since coming to Brookings, his research has focused on the use of evidence in the development and enactment of social policy. Margolis holds a Bachelor's degree in Political Science from the University of North Carolina. He resides in Washington, DC.

Diane Massell (Ph.D., Stanford University, 2000) focuses on the impacts of government education policies and their influence on schooling practices. Her research has examined the implications of policy and program interventions on changing practices in districts, schools, and classrooms (e.g., From Congress to the Classroom, Study of Instructional Improvement). Her recent research and evaluation studies focus on state efforts to create systems of support for low-performing schools, federal efforts to intervene in state education agencies with research-based practices, and state education agencies' use of research for school improvement. She served on several education advisory boards and journal review teams and in Division L Leadership for the American Educational Research Association.

Lorraine M. McDonnell is a Professor of Political Science at the University of California, Santa Barbara. Her research has focused on the design and implementation of K-12 education policies. In several studies, she examined the politics of student testing, particularly the ideas and interests underlying state assessment and accountability policies. In her current work, she is comparing the use of research and other types of evidence in the Common Core State Standards movement. She is the past president of the American Educational Research Association and a member of the National Academy of Education.

Patricia McNeil is a Ph.D. student in educational leadership and policy studies at the University of Washington. She is a former Assistant Secretary at the U.S. Department of Education. Her research interests focus on improving learning opportunities for all students. She is particularly interested in high school reform and more recently on how small district central offices transform their work to support the improvement of teaching and learning district-wide.

Nienke M. Moolenaar, Ph.D. is a postdoctoral researcher at the University of California, San Diego, funded by the Netherlands Organisation for Scientific Research (NWO). Her work focuses on the co-evolution of social networks and educational change. Drawing on complexity theory and social network theory, she uses longitudinal social network analysis and multilevel modeling to understand how elementary schools' social networks change during educational reform. She has published about social capital theory, a social network perspective on collaboration, school leadership, innovation, and teacher beliefs.

Jenee Myers Twitchell is a Ph.D. student in educational leadership and policy studies and is the director of the Dream Project at the University of Washington. Her research interests focus on collective impact efforts to increase postsecondary education attainment. She aims to understand how adult learning within regional college access networks affects individual organizational change.

Sandra Nutley is a Professor of Public Policy and Management at the University of St Andrews, Scotland. She is also the Director of the Research Unit for Research Utilisation (www.ruru.ac.uk), which investigates the use of social science research in public policy and service delivery settings. She has published widely on this topic, and she has been active in supporting efforts to improve research use and impact. In 2011 she received the Campbell Collaboration's Robert Boruch Award for her distinctive contribution to research that informs public policy.

William R. Penuel is a Professor of Educational Psychology and Learning Sciences at the University of Colorado Boulder. His research focuses principally on the design, implementation, and evaluation of policies and programs to improve science and mathematics education. As part of this research, he is collaborating with Cynthia Coburn (Northwestern University) and colleagues at the University of California at Berkeley and the University of Colorado Boulder on a study of research use within research-practice partnerships focused on the design of policies and programs to improve mathematics teaching and learning in three large urban districts.

Janelle Scott is an Associate Professor at the University of California at Berkeley in the Graduate School of Education and African American Studies Department. Her research explores the relationship between education, policy, and equality of opportunity through three policy strands: (1) the racial politics of public education; (2) the politics of school choice, marketization, and privatization; and (3) the role of elite and community-based advocacy in shaping public education. She was a Spencer Foundation Dissertation Year Fellow and a National Academy of Education/ Spencer Foundation Postdoctoral Fellow.

Vivian Tseng is the Vice President of Program at the William T. Grant Foundation, a US Foundation that supports research to improve the lives of young people. Dr. Tseng leads the organization's grantmaking and spearheads its initiatives on understanding the uses of research and improving research-practice connections. Dr. Tseng has a deep interest in mentoring young researchers and is committed to strengthening the career pipeline for scholars of color, overseeing the William T. Grant Scholars Program for promising early-career researchers and enhancing the program's mentoring components. Her recent publications focus on evidence-based policy and practice and mentoring for young scholars. She has published articles in *Child Development, Journal of Marriage and the Family, American Journal of Community Psychology, SRCD's Social Policy Report, the Handbooks of Parenting, Asian American Psychology*, and *21st Century Education*, among others. Previously, Dr. Tseng was an Assistant Professor in Psychology and Asian American studies at California State University, Northridge. She received her doctorate in community psychology, with a minor in quantitative methods and a concentration in developmental psychology, from New York University.

Nitya Venkateswaran is a Ph.D. student in educational leadership and policy studies at the University of Washington. Her research interests focus on the professional learning of administrators in K-12 public schools. She specially aims to understand schools as workplaces and how social interactions among adults in schools impact adult learning and ultimately student learning.

M. Stephen Weatherford is a Professor of Political Science at the University of California, Santa Barbara. His work focuses on policy history and political leadership, including how local activists and parents mobilized in response to school desegregation, the emergence of citizen deliberative forums in school politics, and the use of scientific research in formulating and advocating education reform policies.

Elliot H. Weinbaum is the Senior Program Officer in the Education Program at the William Penn Foundation. In that capacity, he oversees efforts to improve educational opportunities for children in Philadelphia. Elliot previously served as an Associate Commissioner at the Institute of Education Sciences of the US Department of Education; was a Research Assistant Professor at the University of Pennsylvania, Graduate School of Education; and was a Senior Researcher at the Consortium for Policy Research in Education.

Chapter 1
Beginning the Journey: Research Evidence from the Schoolhouse Door to Capitol Hill

Alan J. Daly and Kara S. Finnigan

Educational inequities remain despite decades of attention at all levels of the educational system by practitioners, policy makers, and researchers. A contributing factor in not making greater progress on these issues is that components of our educational system, from early childhood educators to policy makers, often operate as independent units drawing on inconsistent types and quality of evidence that, in fact, may continue to create and replicate unequal outcomes for students and communities. While districts, states, and governmental agencies are experiencing a multitude of educational reforms, these reforms are typically enacted in a reactive rather than proactive way, with a limited understanding of available evidence and a focus on short-term survival at the expense of long-term solutions. Furthermore, a failure to recognize and embrace the idea that decisions, actions, inactions, and the evidence used in making decisions are mutually influential and consequential has perhaps inhibited our collective ability to address pressing issues that have for far too long plagued educational systems. It is in the context of increasing pressure to identify ways to create a more equitable system, a press for educational improvement, and a resulting increasing attention to available evidence that we situate the studies in this book.

This unique volume presents the best of a new generation of studies on the topic of "research evidence" foregrounding the examination of the definition and use of research evidence in US education from the schoolhouse door to Capitol Hill. Through a collection of chapters and thoughtful commentaries by leading scholars, readers are provided with a diverse set of studies and perspectives that examine and

---

Authors "Alan J. Daly" and "Kara S. Finnigan" contributed equally to both the overall book as well as this chapter.

A.J. Daly (✉)
Department of Education Studies, University of California,
San Diego, La Jolla, CA, USA
e-mail: ajdaly@ucsd.edu

K.S. Finnigan
Warner School of Education, University of Rochester,
414 LeChase Hall, Rochester, NY 14627, USA

K.S. Finnigan and A.J. Daly (eds.), *Using Research Evidence in Education: From the Schoolhouse Door to Capitol Hill*, Policy Implications of Research in Education 2,
DOI 10.1007/978-3-319-04690-7_1,

explore the definition and use of research evidence in education. In this opening chapter, we provide a general background on the increasing role of research evidence followed by an overview of the contents of the book.

1.1 Background

When No Child Left Behind (NCLB) was passed in the USA more than a decade ago, it oriented educators and policy makers toward alignment between federal dollars and the use of research-based evidence. With the onset of the Common Core State Standards (see Chap. 9) and i3 grants (see Chap. 10), there is an increased federal push toward the use of "evidence" in instructional decision making. This emphasis has remained central in both the Bush and Obama administrations. In fact, the U.S. Department of Education (2010) issued its *Blueprint for Reform* a few years ago, retaining many of the cornerstone features of NCLB including a focus on standards and accountability and an emphasis on the need for a solid evidentiary base in education. Like NCLB, the *Blueprint* also exhibits a lack of clarity about what counts as evidence as well as what types of evidence should be accessed and used in improving America's school.

In recent years, due to in large part from a push from the aforementioned policies, a renewed interest in understanding the extent to which research-based practices are central to practitioners' work has emerged from inside and outside of the field of education (Nelson et al. 2009). While referred to as "evidence-into-practice" (Nutley et al. 2003), "evidence-based decision making" (Coburn et al. 2009; Honig and Coburn 2008; Nutley and Davies 2008), or "research-based evidence" (Tseng 2009, 2012), all refer to the use of research in some form of decision making. This is not to suggest that the use of research evidence has moved easily into educational policy or practice. In fact, emerging research suggests that educators tend to recycle approaches and base decisions on an array of "evidence" including: anecdote, popular press, social contagion, personal experience, empirical data, and local context (Finnigan et al. 2012). Thus, at the local and policy level, how evidence is accessed and used for decisions varies widely, and as a field, we lack a solid empirical base in understanding what is meant by "evidence" and how that "evidence" is acquired and used. This lack of conceptual and practical clarity and an underdeveloped empirical base is particularly concerning when we consider the number of individuals that are impacted by educational systems, with many of those systems perpetuating long-standing inequities.

Renewed interest in the research community about evidence use follows from increased attempts to disseminate research information with limited success, and the recognition that educational practitioners draw upon evidence in limited ways, often relying on informal or tacit information (Finnigan et al. 2012; Honig and Coburn 2008). From a research, and for that matter a practical standpoint, understanding the process of defining and using evidence requires knowledge around a particular problem or set of problems, understanding the policies or strategies to address these issues, clarity regarding what needs to be done to implement these policies or strategies, and finally a grasp of who must be involved to implement these policies or strategies and an understanding of why action is required. Nutley et al. (2003) refer to these as "know-about," "know-what," "know-how," "know-who," and "know-why," emphasizing that currently only "know-what" is emphasized while the other types of "knowing" are critical to understanding processes regarding research evidence. An important and foundational aspect of the research evidence story is that research is rarely used in a linear way, but rather the process of transferring research into practice occurs in a multidimensional, complex way that is social and interactive as well as "…unfolds within a social ecology of relationships, organizational settings, and political and policy contexts" (Tseng 2012, p. 16).

1.2 Overview

As we see the work of using evidence in support of improvement as requiring all stakeholders, we intend this text to be useful for researchers, policy makers, and practitioners who work at a variety of levels in the educational endeavor. Typically, texts focus solely on the school or the policy level. As we view the improvement of America's schools through research evidence as an interconnected and interdependent system, the chapters in this book examine multiple levels of the educational system while focusing on the core idea of the definition and use of research evidence. This approach accomplishes multiple goals including: opportunities for chapters representing different levels of the system to "speak" to one another, creating a common text targeted at multiple levels simultaneously to create the potential for cross-system dialogue, and providing a broader understanding about the comprehensive and interconnected nature of the system and how changes at one level may affect another level.

In taking a more systems perspective on the scope of the work, we are able to draw cross-cutting themes that have implication for multiple levels of the educational endeavor. In beginning the journey into how research evidence flows and is used across the educational system, we start with a prologue written by Robert Granger, the former president of the WT Grant Foundation, whose foundation's work has been instrumental in understanding the research evidence space. The book is then divided into three core parts: Part I is focused on research evidence at the local level, Part II is focused on state and federal policies/policy makers, and Part III summarizes and integrates the chapters. The volume does not have to be read in any particular order, as each chapter within a specific part, although connected, stands on its own. Together, the chapters in the text capture important theory, salient research, and connections to practice. Given the text can be read either in its totality, parts, or chapters, we offer a general overview of the landscape each chapter will cover.

1.3 Contents

Penuel and Coburn, both scholars in education and learning sciences, begin by framing the four chapters in Part I. Their thoughtful commentary is followed by Chap. 3 by Daly, Finnigan, Moolenaar, and Che, which uses social network analysis to illuminate how evidence is diffused and moved by the educational leaders (central office, area superintendents, and school site administrators) in a large urban system, with a particular focus on low-performing schools. Results suggest limited relationships around the use of research evidence, specifically in underperforming schools that are arguably in most need of evidence for improvement. Moreover, this work underscores the social and interactive nature of the use of evidence, as well as a misalignment between the formal and informal connections around evidence.

Chapter 4 by Honig and Venkateswaran examines six school districts drawing on sociocultural learning theory to understand evidence use. The work highlights both the role of intermediaries and the importance of educational leaders in facilitating the integration of research into practice. Similar to the previous chapter, this work situates research use as a learning process requiring intensive support and connectedness.

In Chap. 5 Asen and Gurke shift to the role of evidence in school board deliberations, finding that the use of evidence by board members was conditioned on individual background and training and exhibited a preference for more "local" evidence. This work builds on the previous chapters by implicating the role of context as well as the group dynamics and quality of relationships related to the use of evidence.

For the final chapter in Part I by Scott, Lubienski, DeBray, and Jabbar, the authors direct our attention to the role of intermediary organizations in evidence use. The authors call attention to the growing and increasingly influential sector of intermediary organizations that frame, package, and deliver research on education policies and programs that typically support a particular agenda. This chapter illuminates the ways in which intermediary organizations are assuming a growing political role in research creation and dissemination.

Part II, which is focused on research evidence use at the state and federal level, begins with a framing chapter by Elliot Weinbaum, former Associate Commissioner of the Knowledge Utilization Division of the Institute of Education Sciences (IES) at the U.S. Department of Education. His insightful chapter is followed by Chap. 8, written by Barnes, Goertz, and Massell, which focuses on evidence use at State Education Agencies (SEA), finding that staff actively sought research from both external and internal sources resulting in connectedness among SEA staff that has not been uncovered in past research. Like Chap. 3 at the district level, this chapter involves social network analysis to highlight the movement of research evidence across the SEA.

McDonnell and Weatherford in Chap. 9 discuss the role of research evidence in the development of the Common Core State Standards (CCSS), noting that the standards were the product of a complex interaction of multiple stakeholders that require an expanded idea of what is meant by evidence. This chapter highlights the different types of evidence used at distinct points in the policy process and suggests the importance of policy coalitions in the communication and exchange of knowledge.

Chapter 10 written by Haskins and Margolis brings us to the "top" of the educational system by examining the federal government, including the president, in shaping evidence use. Haskins and Margolis uncover the political and conceptual process involved in the development, creation, legislative process, and ultimate enactment of the Investing in Innovation (i3) initiative at the Department of Education. This work suggests a fundamental shift in how evidence is used as a major factor in the federal grant-making process and highlights the involvement of foundations through i3, reinforcing the earlier work of Scott, Lubienski, DeBray, and Jabbar.

In the final part, Part III, two chapters provide a synthesis of the contributions of the book. In Chap. 11, Tseng and Nutley summarize the chapters, arguing that a core challenge to researchers, policy makers, and practitioners is to bridge a host of differing goals, expectations, and demands in crafting a stronger infrastructure that can better link research evidence with policy and practice. They discuss the importance of high-quality relationships in realizing better linkages between the development of research evidence and its use in policy and practice. In the final chapter, Finnigan and Daly further synthesize the various studies, providing the fundamental meta-themes which cut across levels and contexts, including the current emphasis on strategic use, the importance of rebuilding trust systemwide, the role of research mediators and policy coalitions in evidence access and use, and the importance of a systemic understanding of evidence use.

1.4 Final Thoughts

This is potentially a transformative time in education. There are many changes underway in terms of standards, assessments, and modalities through which education will be delivered. The importance of evidence in all its varied configurations will be even more important in the coming decades, and a better understanding of how it is defined, accessed, and used holds potential to addressing seemingly intractable problems we have faced in education for years.

After years of reductionism, we are embracing the idea that educational institutions are complex systems situated in networks of interactions and interdependence. The question to be asked as we move further into the next decade of this century and beyond is how to create, nurture, and sustain these networks through which research evidence flows, is modified, and is enhanced. As we move toward the future, we will require those in our educational system to redefine what is valued and recognized as evidence, perhaps requiring fundamental shifts from the lone individual (from the teacher to the researcher) to leveraging connected networks of experimentation, reflection, and refinement; moving from the idea that the generation of knowledge and evidence is the purview of the university to embracing collaborative generation of research evidence; and a movement that challenges the notion that information and knowledge is the property of traditional forms and outlets that often limit access to recognizing the need for more open-sourced and well-translated research-based materials available to a wider audience beyond the halls of the academy. These shifts suggest that we need to redefine what is recognized and rewarded in educational systems and move to new dynamic systems that incentivize the formation and spread of collaborative knowledge networks comprised of the muscle of individual human capital and the connective tissue of social relationships.

References

Coburn, C. E., Toure, J., & Yamashita, M. (2009). Evidence, interpretation, and persuasion: Instructional decision making at the district central office. *Teachers College Record, 111*(4), 1115–1161.

Finnigan, K. S., Daly, A. J., & Che, J. (2012). *The acquisition and use of evidence district-wide.* Paper presented at the annual meeting of the American Educational Research Association, Vancouver, Canada.

Honig, M. I., & Coburn, C. (2008). Evidence-based decision making in school district central offices: Toward a policy research agenda. *Educational Policy, 22*(4), 578–608.

Nelson, S. R., Leffler, J. C., & Hansen, B. A. (2009). *Toward a research agenda for understanding and improving use of research evidence.* Portland: Northwest Regional Educational Laboratory.

Nutley, S., & Davies, H. (2008). *Using research to provide stronger services and programs for youth: A discussion paper for the William T Grant Foundation.* Unpublished manuscript.

Nutley, S., Walter, I., & Davies, H. T. O. (2003). From knowing to doing: A framework for understanding the evidence-into-practice agenda. *Evaluation, 9*(2), 125–148.

Tseng, V. (2009). Focusing on demand: Studying research use in policy and practice affecting youth. *William T. Grant Foundation 2008 annual report.* New York: William T. Grant Foundation.

Tseng, V. (2012). The uses of research in policy and practice. *Social Policy Report, 26*(2), 3–16.

U.S. Department of Education. (2010). *ESEA blueprint for reform.* Washington, DC: Author.

Part I
Using Research Evidence at the School and District Level

Chapter 2
Introduction to Part: Research Use at the School and District Level

William R. Penuel and Cynthia E. Coburn

The chapters in this part all focus on the use of research in districts and schools. Local educational systems are important settings for studying research use because actors in district offices and schools have responsibility for programs and policies intended to improve teaching and learning. As such, they have the potential to directly impact teachers' practice and students' opportunities to learn. If one wants to understand the role research can play in influencing instructional improvement, it is therefore important to understand when and under what conditions decision makers at these levels use research. These chapters help to illuminate some of these conditions.

Taken together, the chapters suggest that research use at the local level is not simply the product of bureaucratic rationality or individual leaders' action, but rather is embedded in a dynamically changing ecology of actors and organizational units and connections among them. When policy makers and others encourage school and district leaders to use research in their ongoing work, they often envision that they should use research directly and centrally to make decisions related to policy or practice (Johnson 1999; Sharkey and Murnane 2006; Weiss 1980). Weiss (1980) describes this image, which she calls instrumental use, in the following way:

> A problem exists; information or understanding is lacking either to generate a solution to the problem or to select among alternative solutions; research [or other forms of evidence] provides the missing knowledge; a solution is reached (pp. 11–12).

In fact, educational decision making at the local level rarely happens in an instant; rather, as Weiss (1980) argues, decisions "accrete" over time, through interactive processes that include contention, negotiation, and sensemaking.

W.R. Penuel (✉)
Educational Psychology and Learning Sciences, University of Colorado Boulder, Boulder, CO, USA
e-mail: william.penuel@colorado.edu

C.E. Coburn
School of Education and Social Policy, Northwestern University, Evanston, IL, USA

K.S. Finnigan and A.J. Daly (eds.), *Using Research Evidence in Education: From the Schoolhouse Door to Capitol Hill*, Policy Implications of Research in Education 2, DOI 10.1007/978-3-319-04690-7_2, © Springer International Publishing Switzerland 2014

As the chapters in this part and other studies highlight, research use, too, involves these same interactive processes (Amara et al. 2004; Contandriopoulos et al. 2010; Earl 1995). It entails leaders making sense of conclusions from research, deliberating about their relevance to the current context, and creating policies that reflect agreements about what the research suggests they should do in that context. As the part authors point out, local actors often contest the conclusions of research and their relevance, and the translation of research into practice requires significant learning on the part of local actors.

Furthermore, these chapters highlight the fact that decisions are not made by isolated individuals, but involve actors across, and even outside, districts and schools. Decisions related to teaching and learning are stretched across multiple organizational divisions (i.e., curriculum and instruction, assessment, zone or areas, special education) and levels of the system (county, district, school) (Coburn et al. 2009; Spillane 1998). They also involve and implicate actors outside of the formal system, including a range of consultants, vendors, and advocates seeking to change the system from partway outside it (Burch and Thiem 2004; Burch 2009; Welner et al. 2010).

Despite their commonalties, each chapter makes a distinctive contribution to our understanding of research use. They focus on different actors: two chapters focus on district administrators (Chap. 1 by Daly and Finnigan, as well as Chap. 4 by Honig and Venkateswaran), one on members of school boards (Chap. 5 by Asen and Gurke), and the fourth on intermediary organizations who can play a consequential role in policy making (Chap. 6 by Scott, Lubiensky, Debray and Jabbar). They also differ in the purpose of research use they investigate: Asen and Gurke (Chap. 5) focus on use of research for decision making, while Honig and Venkateswaran (Chap. 4) focus on the role of research in changing work practices of educational leaders. Daly and Finnigan (Chap. 1) focus on data use, rather than research use. And, Scott and her colleagues (Chap. 6) focus on the role of research in advocacy for particular policies and programs. Finally, the chapters vary in the conceptual frameworks the authors draw upon, which, in turn, prompt them to focus on different aspects of the research use phenomenon. Daly and Finnigan use social network analysis to investigate the social structure within which research and data use is embedded, while Honig and Venkateswaran foreground the learning demands or cognitive aspects of making use of research. The chapters by Asen and Gurke (Chap. 5) and by Scott and her colleagues (Chap. 6) focus more on the political dimensions of use.

Daly and Finnigan's chapter (Chap. 1) investigates patterns of advice seeking among central office staff and school principals. Rather than focusing on use of research, they attend to data use, a practice that is explicitly promoted within most of today's accountability systems as an important guide to educational decision making. They make use of social network analysis, which illuminates the ways that information flows through specific ties among local actors and how these flows are constrained in part by the structure of the network. It contrasts sharply with a "rational actor" perspective that presumes information and research flow freely within systems and are readily taken up when findings dictate (cf., Dynarski 2008). As Daly and Finnigan's chapter (Chap. 1) implies, the social structure of advice giving shapes how and where information related to specific studies is likely to flow, and it also points to the potential constraints on information flow when ties are sparse.

Honig and Venkateswaran's chapter (Chap. 4) focuses on when and how district leaders use research related to central office transformation to change their own work practice. The chapter offers a cognitive perspective that frames research use as a learning problem for district leaders from the perspective of sociocultural learning theory. Sociocultural learning theory, the authors argue, helps researchers move beyond binary distinctions between "use" and "nonuse" of research that characterize many policy debates. The authors offer instead a more nuanced way to characterize *how* district leaders engage with ideas from research when they do. The cognitive perspective also brings into focus the importance of prior knowledge in shaping leaders' use of assistance strategies suggested by research.

Asen and Gurke's chapter (Chap. 5) focuses on the forms of evidence that school board members use in public deliberations with one another. By focusing on different forms of information rather than on use of research alone, the chapter authors are able to situate research use relative to other forms of information and investigate the conditions under which research findings persuade others in the course of deliberations. Asen and Gurke's analysis also underscores the critical role that trust plays in shaping when school board members see research findings as persuasive and when colleagues take up others' invocations of research findings. This particular finding connects to Daly and Finnigan's observations about the importance of social networks, in that we might expect to see more evidence of trust where there are frequent interactions among members of the network than where there are less frequent interactions.

Finally, Scott, Lubiensky, Debray, and Jabbar (Chap. 6) focus on intermediary organizations and their role in synthesizing and promoting select research findings for the purposes of advocacy. Scott and her colleagues (Chap. 6) argue that intermediary organizations are not neutral "brokers" of research findings. Instead, they often advocate for the use of some findings over others, packaging findings in forms and sharing them in venues outside the peer review system for traditional social science research. In their analysis, intermediary organizations work nimbly and quickly to fill a void for research that is locally relevant and useful to decision makers that researchers themselves do not fill. It is important to note that the intermediary organizations depicted in Scott and colleagues' chapter are portrayed quite differently from the partners depicted in Honig and Venkateswaran's chapter (Chap. 4), whose aims are to assist local actors with internal transformations of work practices. Their chapter reminds us that research use is situated within and framed by larger policy debates about governance and instruction in schools and that brokering access to findings is often an agenda-driven activity, rather than a neutral effort to bring evidence to policy.

In our view, these chapters are complementary emphasizing different aspects of the complex and interactive processes associated with research use. For example, research findings that appear on the surface to have clear implications for practice may be linked to particular political positions and advocacy groups (Chap. 6 by Scott and colleagues). Actors who agree with their relevance to their own practice, moreover, are still likely to face challenges when learning how to make use of recommendations to change their practice (Chap. 4 by Honig and Venkateswaran). Issues of trust among different actors (Chap. 5 by Asen and Gurke) are likely implicated in all deliberations regarding research use for decision making. And, some actors may have differential access to research findings in the first place, and advice on how to use them, depending upon the nature of their ties to their colleagues and to the range of actors involved in educational policy issues outside the system (Chap. 1 by Daly and Finnigan).

The field is only beginning to understand the nature and dynamics of research use in local educational systems. We need to understand far more about the interactive processes involved in research use or what Tseng (2007) has called "the demand side" of research use before we can improve district and school leaders' research use as many policy makers would like. These chapters help define some of the territory we must traverse to get to that point.

References

Amara, N., Ouimet, M., & Landry, R. (2004). New evidence on instrumental, conceptual, and symbolic utilization of university research in government agencies. *Science Communication, 26*(1), 75–106.

Burch, P. E. (2009). *Hidden markets: The new educational privatization*. New York: Routledge.

Burch, P. E., & Thiem, C. H. (2004, March). *Private organizations, school districts, and the enterprise of high stakes accountability*. Paper presented at the University of Chicago Harris School of Public Policy's conference on Developmental, Economic and Policy Perspectives on the Federal No Child Left Behind Act, Chicago, IL.

Coburn, C. E., Toure, J., & Yamashita, M. (2009). Evidence, interpretation, and persuasion: Instructional decision making at the district central office. *Teachers College Record, 111*(4), 1115–1161.

Contandriopoulos, D., Lemire, M., Denis, J.-L., & Tremblay, E. (2010). Knowledge exchange processes in organizations and policy arenas: A narrative systematic review of the literature. *The Milbank Quarterly, 88*(4), 444–483.

Dynarski, M. (2008). Bringing answers to educators: Guiding principles for research syntheses. *Educational Researcher, 37*(1), 27–29.

Earl, L. M. (1995). District-wide evaluation of school improvement: A system partners approach. In J. B. Cousins & L. M. Earl (Eds.), *Participatory evaluation in education: Studies in evaluation use and organizational learning* (pp. 21–32). London: Routledge.

Johnson, B. L., Jr. (1999). The politics of research-information use in the education policy arena. *Educational Policy, 13*(1), 23–36.

Sharkey, N. S., & Murnane, R. J. (2006). Tough choices in designing a formative assessment system. *American Journal of Education, 112*(4), 572–588.

Spillane, J. P. (1998). State policy and the non-monolithic nature of the local school district: Organizational and professional considerations. *American Educational Research Journal, 35*(1), 33–63.

Tseng, V. (2007). *Studying the use of research evidence in policy and practice*. New York: William T. Grant Foundation.

Weiss, C. H. (1980). Knowledge creep and decision accretion. *Knowledge: Creation, Diffusion, Utilization, 1*(3), 381–404.

Welner, K. G., Hinchey, P. H., Molnar, A., & Weitzman, D. (2010). *Think tank research quality: Lessons for policy makers, the media, and the public*. Charlotte: Information Age Publishing.

Chapter 3
The Critical Role of Brokers in the Access and Use of Evidence at the School and District Level

Alan J. Daly, Kara S. Finnigan, Nienke M. Moolenaar, and Jing Che

3.1 Context

The No Child Left Behind (NCLB) Act enacted a series of large-scale reforms targeted at eliminating the persistent achievement gap in US public schools. This federal legislation contained clear-cut language that reoriented educators and policymakers toward alignment between federal dollars and the use of research-based evidence, or "scientifically based research." Despite the law's emphasis, scant empirical research exists regarding the systematic definition, use, access, and flow of research evidence in schools and across districts (Honig and Coburn 2008).

This research was supported by an award from the W. T. Grant Foundation (Grant #10174). All opinions and conclusions expressed in this article are those of the authors and do not necessarily reflect the views of the W. T. Grant Foundation.

Authors "Alan J. Daly" and "Kara S. Finnigan" contributed equally to this work.

A.J. Daly (✉)
Department of Education Studies, University of California,
San Diego, La Jolla, CA, USA
e-mail: ajdaly@ucsd.edu

K.S. Finnigan
Warner School of Education, University of Rochester,
414 LeChase Hall, Rochester, NY 14627, USA

N.M. Moolenaar
Department of Education Studies, University of California, San Diego, CA, USA

University of Twente, Enschede, Netherlands

J. Che
Rochester City School District and Center for Education Policy Research,
Rochester, NY, USA

K.S. Finnigan and A.J. Daly (eds.), *Using Research Evidence in Education: From the Schoolhouse Door to Capitol Hill*, Policy Implications of Research in Education 2,
DOI 10.1007/978-3-319-04690-7_3,

During the same time period, educators have experienced an increasing national and international push to systematically collect, interpret, and use data for instructional decision making (Finnigan et al. 2013). In this process of data use, district office staff mediate state and federal policies by playing a critical role in selecting evidence, developing knowledge, and supporting the use of data (Coburn et al. 2009b; Datnow et al. 2007; Hamilton et al. 2007; Ikemoto and Marsh 2007). In addition, school-level leaders play key roles in disseminating evidence, directing new learning efforts, and aligning new activities to existing efforts (Datnow and Park 2009; Kerr et al. 2006; Knapp et al. 2007). This suggests the importance of the social interaction between educational leaders in district offices and school sites for these educators to co-construct and make sense of evidence and its use (Coburn 2001, 2005; Datnow et al. 2002; Parise and Spillane 2010; Spillane et al. 2002).

In this exploratory case study, we describe and analyze the structure of a social system by examining the social interactions among district office and school site leaders. Specifically, we utilize social network theory and methods to examine how evidence is "brokered" by educational leaders across a large urban district, focusing particularly on whether evidence reaches leaders in low-performing schools. The term "broker" refers to those individuals who connect otherwise disconnected individuals or groups in the movement of a relational resource (e.g., advice). Social network theory provides insight into how evidence moves across individuals and levels of the educational system. Examining the social network of these district leaders allows us to better understand the more dynamic supports and constraints of the larger social infrastructure (Borgatti and Foster 2003; Cross et al. 2002; Daly 2010; Wellman and Berkowitz 1998).

The evidence "users" in our study are central office leaders and school site leaders. While all leaders comprise the structure of relationships of district leaders, our study specifically focuses on leaders of the low-performing schools given the policy pressures in the United States to improve these schools through increased sanctions and evidence-based reform. Although a growing number of research evidence and data use studies imply the influence of social processes on evidence use, with brokers playing particularly important roles (e.g., Daly 2012), the empirical work and theory building on this topic have not kept pace. In response to this gap, we examine the social network of a large US school district and the role of brokers in the use of data. Our exploratory study is guided by two overarching questions: (1) To what extent do educational leaders in the district broker advice/information regarding research evidence between and among central office administrators and principals? (2) To what extent are low-performing school leaders connected to other district leaders around evidence?

3.2 Frameworks

In recent years, a renewed interest in understanding the extent to which research-based practices are central to practitioners' work and district and school improvement has emerged from inside and outside of the field of education. Several strands of research indicate the need for additional research to better understand the extent to which decisions are affected by research, the ways in which research evidence is shaped or adapted at the local level, and the factors that support or constrain the use of research. "Evidence-into-practice" (Nutley et al. 2003), "evidence-based decision making" (Coburn et al. 2009a; Honig and Coburn 2008), and "research-based evidence" (Tseng 2012) all refer to the use of research in local decision making and follow from increased attempts to disseminate research information with limited success (Nutley et al. 2003). In addition, all seem to imply that the use of evidence is in some ways stretched over people in a web of relationships (Daly 2012; Tseng 2012). Therefore, rather than trying to understand the use of evidence based on the attributes of an individual (e.g., gender or years of experience), in this chapter, we focus on the influence and outcome of an actor's "position" vis-à-vis social ties with others, as well as the overall social structure of a network (Borgatti and Ofem 2010). In more carefully unpacking this idea, we draw on social network theory.

In understanding the use of evidence through social network theory, it is useful to examine its underlying assumptions. First, social network theory assumes actors in a social network are interdependent rather than independent (Daly 2010; Degenne and Forsé 1999; Wasserman and Faust 1994). Second, relationships are regarded as conduits for the exchange or flow of resources (Burt 1982, 1997; Kilduff and Tsai 2003; Powell et al. 1996). Third, the structure of a network has influence on the resources that flow to and from an actor (Borgatti and Foster 2003). Fourth, patterns of relationships, captured by social networks, may present dynamic tensions as these patterns can act as both opportunities and constraints for individual and collective action (Brass and Burkhardt 1993; Burt 1982; Gulati 1995). It is this constellation of relationships that surround an actor and form a social network across a district and school that can both support or constrain the use of research evidence. Our work suggests that this network structure is consequential to the movement of research evidence (Daly and Finnigan 2011; Finnigan and Daly 2012).

In this study we focus on the use of data, which is often conflated with research evidence in the current policy context (see Finnigan et al. 2013). Recent studies of data use invoke a number of themes related to network theory to explain key evidence/data use processes such as the role of district and site leaders in supporting a data-oriented culture (Honig 2006; Wayman and Stringfield 2006), the use of intermediaries in developing capacity and brokering skills (Atteberry and Bryk 2010; Honig and Coburn 2008; Marsh et al. 2010), the nested and interdependent nature of evidence and data in a coherent system (Datnow et al. 2007; Finnigan et al. 2013; Halverson et al. 2007; Kerr et al. 2006; Levin 2008; Marsh et al. 2006; O'Day 2002, 2004; Supovitz and Klein 2003; Young 2006), and the presence of organizational structures and opportunities to collaborate in a high trust environment (Confrey and Makar 2005; Copland 2003; Daly and Finnigan 2012; Datnow et al. 2007; Halverson et al. 2007; Hammerman and Rubin 2002; Ikemoto and Marsh 2007; Wayman and Stringfield 2006).

In addition, a growing number of scholars aim to increase knowledge on evidence and data use by examining central office-school relationships in school improvement processes (e.g., Daly and Finnigan 2011; Honig and Copland 2008).

Fig. 3.1 Visual representation of broker

Their insights underscore the importance of social relationships among educational administrators, both horizontally (within district and school) and vertically (across district and school). These vertical and horizontal ties can be conceptualized as a social network between and among leaders that may support and constrain the flow of evidence across a system (Daly and Finnigan 2010; Finnigan and Daly 2010, 2012; Finnigan et al. 2013; Finnigan, Daly and Stewart 2012). This social network comprised of horizontal (within group) and vertical (cross group) ties also represents an opportunity for leaders to exploit existing information (within their primary group) and explore new information (beyond their immediate group). As such, depending on the network position of leaders within the overall social network, these leaders may be in the position to act as resource boundary spanners or "brokers" as discussed further below.

3.2.1 Brokers

From a social network perspective, an individual is considered a broker when that actor "bridges" a structural hole (Scott 2000; Stovel and Shaw 2012) (see Fig. 3.1). A broker occupies a position that may provide benefits for the overall system in terms of connecting otherwise disconnected others and that may benefit the actor personally in terms of access to resource diversity (Burt 2000, 2005; Obstfeld 2005). The idea of brokers is often examined through an actor's "betweenness," or how often an actor is positioned "in between" two people in the network who themselves are disconnected (Wasserman and Faust 1994). Betweenness has been argued to support the flow of resources in a social network by creating bridging ties between disconnected actors (Burt 1992). These individuals have increased influence and power within a system due to the social control over resources as they "determine" who receives what particular resource and in what form (Ahuja 2000). In this sense, brokers may filter, distort, or hoard resources, which may provide benefit in the form of control or power to the broker, but which may simultaneously inhibit overall individual and organizational performance (Baker and Iyer 1992; Burt 1992).

Studies of evidence and data use have often identified the key position of boundary spanners in brokering access to data (Finnigan and Daly 2012; Honig and Coburn 2008). These studies highlight the role of a range of different actors (e.g., the district office, intermediary agencies, leaders, and coaches) in bringing evidence, information, and support for evidence use to schools. For instance, district office leaders can play a key boundary spanning role by clearly articulating and supporting the development of shared understanding and alignment with respect to goals and practices, enabling a more coherent system around evidence and data collaboration (Finnigan and Daly 2012; Kerr et al. 2006; Supovitz and Klein 2003;

Wayman et al. 2007; Wohlstetter et al. 2008; Young 2006). Case studies of data use suggest that in creating a more coherent system, district office culture and knowledge related to the use of evidence may also have a substantial influence on the practices of principals in the interpretation and use of data (Firestone and González 2007; Louis et al. 2005, 2010). For example, as standardized data do not usually come in manageable formats, district leaders may "repackage" the data for school consumption. However, in repackaging the data, studies suggest that leaders often do so in "simple" terms that align with their previous knowledge and beliefs as to what is important and valued (Coburn et al. 2009a; Honig 2003; Spillane 2000). In this sense, the movement of resources from the district office to the sites goes through a filtering process at the district office before it is brokered out to the schools (Weick 1985).

3.3 Methods

We used exploratory case study methods to allow us to understand and open up the phenomena of brokering for investigation and theory development (Yin 2003). In examining the diffusion of evidence, we used a social network survey to explore both the general pattern of relationships between leaders around "advice for the use of data" and the presence of brokering relationships in the La Urbana Unified School District (LUUSD). An exploratory case study approach is most appropriate when there is a level of complexity that requires an in-depth understanding of the phenomenon of interest and when attempting to add to theory (Yin 2003).

3.3.1 Context

This study takes place within a large district in the Western United States, named La Urbana[1] Unified School District (LUUSD), which serves more than 130,000 students from 15 ethnic groups and well over 60 languages in preschool through grade 12. The district includes more than 140 schools including elementary, middle, high, K-8, and other schools. The approximate ethnic breakdown of LUUSD is 46 % Hispanic, 24 % White, 12 % African American, 5 % Indo-Chinese, 3 % Asian, Native American, Pacific Islander, and multiracial/ethnic students. The district employs 7,500 educators and nearly 900 pupil services employees (such as bus drivers, grounds, facilities, etc.). LUUSD was identified by the State Board of Education (SBE) as requiring corrective actions due to failure to meet Adequate Yearly Performance (AYP) under No Child Left Behind. This designation required the

[1] Pseudonym.

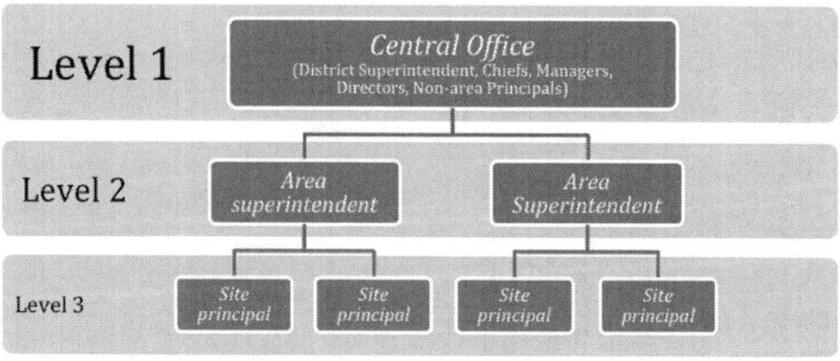

Fig. 3.2 Formal hierarchical levels in the La Urbana District

district to undergo a needs assessment by a national research, development, and service agency. The report noted the need for the district to more directly focus on data-driven decision making and support communication, particularly *within* areas as principals identified inconsistent interactions in their clusters.

In 2012, the district was organized into eight "areas," with each area comprising up to three high school clusters (including elementary and middle schools that feed the high school). These areas were loosely organized by geography and were served by an area superintendent who was responsible for approximately 20–25 schools. La Urbana's website describes the role of the area superintendent as:

> Serving as the ultimate point of contact for the schools in their areas. An Area Superintendent is responsible for all schools and issues in his/her area. Academic, discipline and other issues can be handled by the Area Superintendent's office.

Through this formal role, the area superintendent is the primary point of contact for principals in their cluster, and, as such, also responsible for connecting the central office to the school sites and coordinating action within their cluster. In other words, area superintendents are in the position to broker resources to low-performing schools by way of the relationship between central office leaders and the area principals.

In exploring the idea of brokerage in LUUSD, we examine three distinct levels in our dataset, namely, the central office (Level 1), the area superintendents[2] (Level 2), and the site principals (Level 3) (see Fig. 3.2). In essence, the area superintendents (as the focal actors in our study) are intentionally positioned as brokers mediating the flow of information and resources from the central office to the site administrators in each of their areas.

---

[2] It is important to note that the area superintendents are central office administrators, but given the unique role they serve as a connection point to the schools and oversee the principals, and as such we have separated them out into their own administrative "level" for these analyses.

Table 3.1 Sample demographics

	Min	Max	M	Sd
Experience as educator	1	40	23.5	8.8
Experience in district	1	39	18.3	9.8
Experience in administration	1	36	11.5	6.4
Experience in current position	1	22	5.2	3.9
Experience in current site	1	30	5.4	5.3
Female	62.9 %			

Table 3.2 Distribution of respondents over positions ($n=256$)

	N
Central office	*94*
Area superintendents	*8*
Site principals	*(154)*
From Area 2	24
From Area 3	20
From Area 4	15
From Area 5	13
From Area 6	28
From Area 7	14
From Area 8	14
From Area 9	26

3.3.2 Sample

We collected data from educational leaders in LUUSD regarding the frequency of social interactions around the use of data in improving student outcomes. For this analysis, we included educators who served in formal leadership positions in the district, such as the superintendent, deputy superintendents, area superintendents, directors, assistant directors, and managers from the central office and principals at the school sites. We administered an online survey during the spring of 2012, and 256 respondents completed the survey (98 % response rate). Tables 3.1 and 3.2 provide details regarding the respondents including the high proportion of female leaders (63 %) and the average years of experience as an educator (23.5 years), in LUUSD (18 years), in administration (11.5 years), and at the current site (5 years). Our study included 94 central office administrators, 8 area superintendents, and 154 site principals located in 8 areas (see Table 3.2).

3.3.3 Data Collection

In order to assess the social network structure of advice around evidence use in La Urbana, we developed an online survey that included social network and demographic questions. Our instrument is grounded in the literature on district improvement processes and practices (see, e.g., Coburn and Russell 2008; Chrispeels 2004; Honig 2006; Supovitz 2006; Spillane 2000; Togneri and Anderson 2003), data use (Daly 2012), and network studies (Cross and Parker 2004; Cross et al. 2002; Daly and Finnigan 2009, 2011, 2012; Finnigan and Daly 2010, 2012; Hite et al. 2005; Penuel et al. 2009). We piloted our questions with practicing administrators before collecting these data. Although we asked about a number of relationships, in this study we focus on the exchange of "advice regarding data (evidence) use." Specifically, respondents were asked to quantitatively assess their relationships with other administrators (school and central office) on a 4-point interaction scale ranging from 1 (within the past 2 months) to 4 (1–2 times a week). The evidence/data use network data was taken from the prompt, "Please select the administrators in La Urbana to whom you turn to for assistance in using data for student achievement … and at what frequency?" Our study involves a bounded/saturated approach (Lin 1999; Scott 2000), which includes all members of the LUUSD leadership team (central office and site administrators). We utilized this strategy because it, coupled with high response rates, provides a more complete picture and more valid results according to Lin (1999) and Scott (2000).

3.3.4 Data Analysis

We analyzed network measures using the UCINET software (Borgatti et al. 2002) to better understand the structure of the "Data Use" network. First, we examined the "Data Use" network to reflect advice seeking that occurred at least once within the past 2 months. This network can be regarded as reflecting infrequent, occasional advice seeking among the leaders in La Urbana. Second, we analyzed the same network to reflect advice seeking that occurred at least once a week. This network can be regarded as reflecting more stable, ongoing, and frequent advice seeking among the leaders in the district. Given the extensive literature on the importance of tie intensity in networks (Carley and Krackhardt 1999; Krackhardt 2001; Wasserman and Faust 1994), this approach provides a rich description and understanding of the depth and breadth of the exchange of advice among leaders in La Urbana.

We ran graphic representations of the evidence use network using Netdraw (Borgatti et al. 2002), which provides a visual image of the network and which illuminates overall structural patterns. We also ran a *density* measure, which is the number of social ties between actors divided by the number of total possible connections and can be thought of as how tightly knit a network is. A dense network, meaning one with a high percentage of relationships, is thought to be able to move resources more quickly than a network with more sparse ties (Scott 2000). We also conducted analyses of the amount of brokerage that took place in the district by calculating the *betweenness* score for all leaders in our sample. Betweenness is a measure of how often an actor is positioned "in between" two people in the network who themselves are disconnected (Wasserman and Faust 1998).

3.4 Findings

Our findings suggest that overall interactions regarding the use of data are quite sparse across the district with high variability within specific areas of the district, despite a district-wide push for the use of evidence for improvement. We also find important differences between the underlying informal ties and the structures one would expect based on district's formal lines of authority and communication in regard to the use of data, with area superintendents engaging in differing brokerage roles. Moreover, and perhaps most troubling, our data suggests that principals of underperforming schools, who are arguably in most need of evidence for improvement, are often disconnected from the overall data use structure. General findings suggest that the lack of connections between and among district leaders overall, and out to principals of underperforming schools in particular, may significantly inhibit the coherent flow of evidence. In the remaining paragraphs, we provide the evidence to support these findings.

3.4.1 Sparse Relationships and Varied Brokering Across the District

When we focus on interactions around evidence use that occurred within the past 2 months (Fig. 3.3a), we find that this network (while appearing densely connected) is actually quite sparse with an overall density of 4.4 %, meaning that only 4.4 out of 100 potential advice relationships actually occurred within the past 2 months. On average, leaders in LUUSD sought or were sought for advice around data use by about 11.1 other leaders within the past 2 months. The network that reflects more frequent advice seeking around evidence use as exhibited by data use (Fig. 3.3b) is even more sparse with an overall density of only 0.7 % and on average 1.7 advice relationships for each leader on a bi-weekly basis.

In Fig. 3.4a, b, we graphically display the most frequent relationships around data (at least every 2 weeks), with graphs colored and organized by area. Figure 3.4a

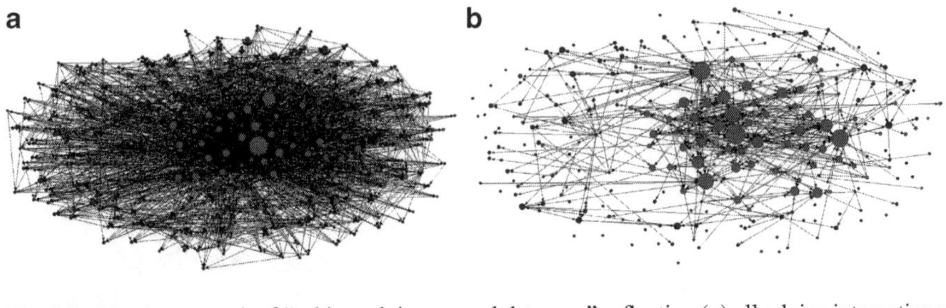

Fig. 3.3 District network of "asking advice around data use," reflecting (**a**) all advice interactions within the past 2 months and (**b**) at least every 2 weeks, sized by indegree

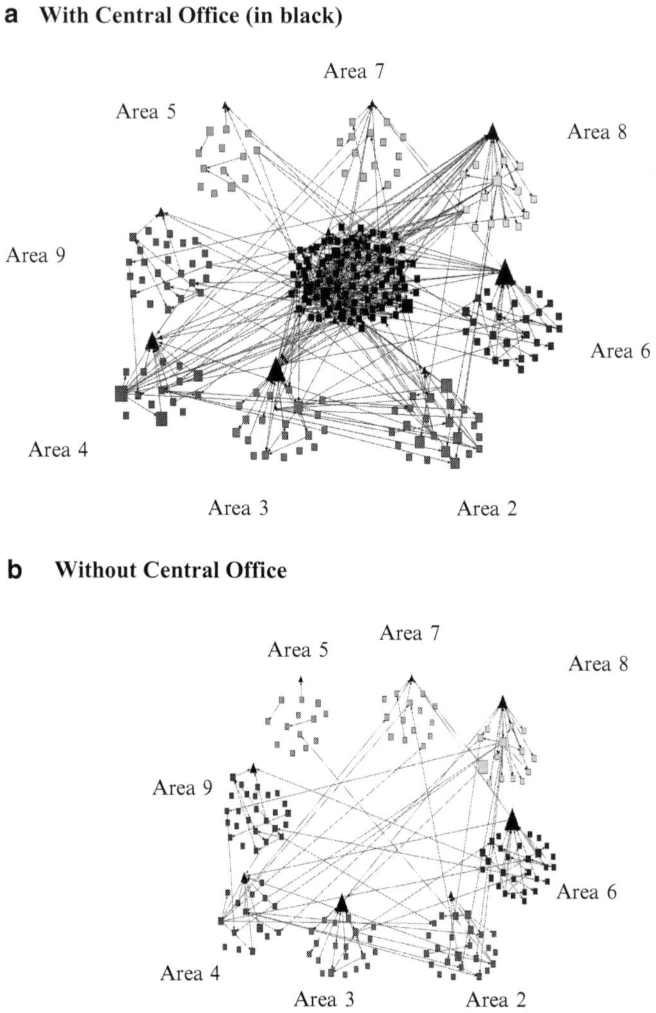

Fig. 3.4 District evidence/data use network, frequency at least every 2 weeks, nodes sized by betweenness, area superintendents in *black triangles*, separated by the eight areas, (**a**) With central office (in *black*) and (**b**) without the central office administrators (in *black*)

includes all areas and the central office, and Fig. 3.4b shows the same network without the central office administrators. The nodes are sized by betweenness brokerage, meaning that larger nodes are more often "between" others who are themselves disconnected, thus reflecting their brokerage role.

These network maps reveal, again, that bi-weekly advice seeking around data is limited. Figure 3.4a shows that advice about data appears to be sought both within and across the central office and the areas, with many ties to and from the central office. Central office leaders tend to be more sought for advice around data, with area superintendents engaging in more betweenness brokerage, which aligns with their formal position in the district in terms of brokering resources to schools.

When we examine the areas without the central office (Fig. 3.4b), we find variation between the areas in terms of their density, the extent to which they are predominantly externally and internally focused, and the betweenness brokerage played by each area superintendent. For instance, the network of Area 6 seems to be more densely connected than other areas, has both internal ties within the area as well as external ties to others outside the area, and has an area superintendent who is strongly connected to both the central office and two other areas and who is a major broker in terms of betweenness (as displayed by the large node). In contrast, the network of Area 4 appears to be much less densely connected, has fewer internal ties compared to external ties (mainly to the central office), has an area superintendent who is connected to the central office but not to other areas, and who does not occupy a major brokerage position in the district (as displayed by the small triangle).

As the bi-weekly exchange of advice among district leaders on evidence use is rather sparse, meaning there are few opportunities to broker relationships, we shift our analysis to those relationships that occur within the past 2 months to a daily basis. In this way we are effectively "capturing" all of the reported advice relationships between and among leaders in LUUSD.

Findings indicate that LUUSD leaders differ considerably in terms of their brokerage roles as measured by betweenness ($M=0.6$ %, $sd=2.2$ % with a range of 0–27 %). This means that of the maximum possible betweenness that a district leader could have, only 6 out of 1,000 times this relationship actually is a brokerage relationship where an individual connects two other administrators *who are themselves disconnected* (Hanneman and Riddle 2005). At first glance, we see that central office leaders broker slightly more than the overall sample average ($M=1.1$ %, $sd=3.4$ %) whereas the site principals broker less ($M=0.2$ %, $sd=0.4$ %). Site principals also broker more within their own areas than within the whole district (1.7 % and 0.2 % respectively). This is not surprising, as the density of advice seeking within areas is higher than the overall district density, which increases opportunities for brokerage within areas compared to the whole district.

Results also indicate that area superintendents, in line with their position, have the highest number of brokerage relationships within the overall district in general. Perhaps not surprising, area superintendents generally exhibit brokerage (betweenness) roles in connecting educators *within* their own areas ($M=24.2$ %, $sd=26.5$ %). In effect, out of all the theoretically possible brokerage opportunities, our data indicate that area superintendents broker in nearly 1 out of every 4 potential "betweenness" situations.

3.4.2 *Diffusion of Evidence and Low-Performing Schools*

Beyond the sparse connections around data district-wide, we found that principals at the lowest-performing schools were least likely to ask advice of others (or be

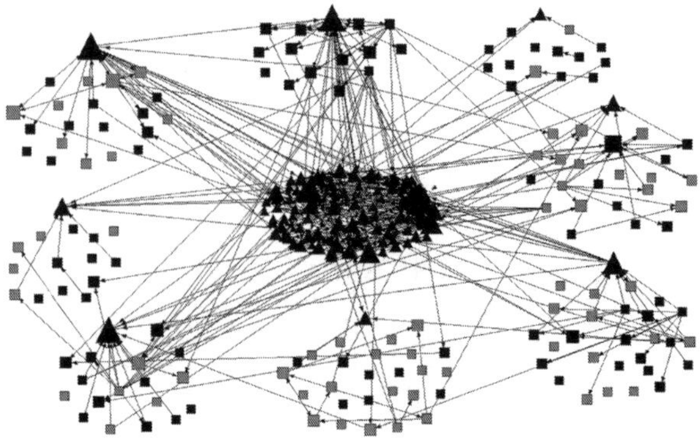

Fig. 3.5 Advice on data and program improvement schools (sized by indegree)

asked for advice) regarding the use of data. Moreover, it also appears that the lowest-performing schools were not evenly distributed throughout the district and, instead, concentrated in a few areas.

In Fig. 3.5 above, we provide a visual display of the groupings of principals and area superintendents by area and illustrate the density of ties within and across areas. In this figure, the squares are principals, and lighter color squares are the principals of program improvement (PI—underperforming) schools under accountability policy sanctions. The black triangles at the top of each area represent area superintendents, and black triangles in the center cluster are other central office staff. The nodes are sized by indegree, meaning that larger nodes were more regularly sought for advice about data. As this graph indicates, while some principals are connected to other district leaders, those in low-performing schools have fewer ties in most of these areas (both to one another and to the area superintendents and other central office leaders), despite the fact that the leaders of underperforming schools are likely to need advice around the use of data for student achievement. Furthermore, this is particularly evident in the area at the very bottom middle of the graph. As can be seen in this area, there is the greatest concentration of principals of underperforming schools, but this area has the least amount of interaction around the use of data for student achievement.

While we might not expect the same amount of ties within each area, certainly the formal structure and emphasis of the district would lead one to believe that there should be a significant amount of exchanges regarding data in schools that are the most underperforming. This can be contrasted with the area at the top middle of the graph that has no underperforming schools, but is the most densely connected. In some ways, this indicates that the "rich get richer" in a data exchange sense, while those in most need have fewer exchanges and as such may reinforce existing performance levels.

While area superintendents were formally tasked with being the "source" of advice for data, it is important to note that they were not always the most sought leaders within their areas (meaning that some of the area superintendents, represented by triangles within an area in the graph, were relatively small in

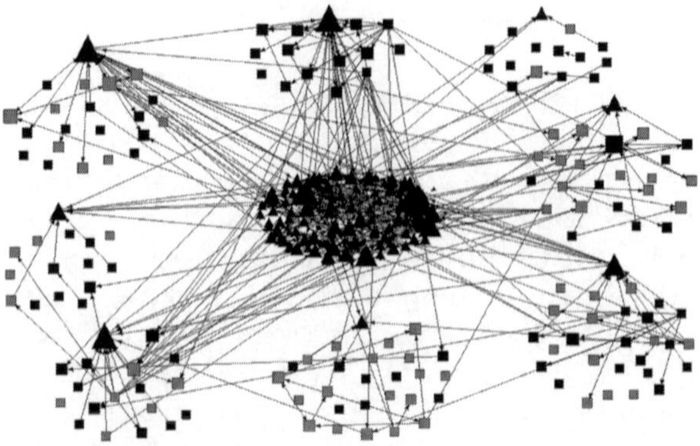

Fig. 3.6 Advice on data and program improvement schools (sized by betweenness)

comparison to others). As is evident in Fig. 3.5, a number of principals were viewed as sources of advice regarding data far more than the formally designated area superintendents who were serving in this "brokering" role. This suggests that while the district may be attempting to set up exchanges with those with formal positional authority to diffuse evidence, it may well be the case that those "outside" the formal exchange system are much more active. This may result in less coherent and consistent messages being sent across the system.

The previous analysis was about actors who were the "source" of advice. In this section we turn our attention to those who "broker" evidence across a system. In Fig. 3.6 we graphically display the most frequent interaction network regarding data. In this graph the nodes are sized by betweenness brokerage, meaning that larger nodes are more often "between" disconnected others on a shortest path. As can be seen in the graph, most connections regarding data were between central office leaders, and yet the data initiative was meant to be engaged at the school level and, in particular, within the underperforming schools. In addition, while some area superintendents engage in comparatively high levels of brokers (bigger size nodes), others enact significantly less brokerage (smaller nodes). The result is a very uneven distribution of brokerage within areas with some area superintendents connecting disconnected principals and others doing significantly less brokerage.

If we again examine the area with the most underperforming schools, discussed above, we see that, in fact, the area superintendent of that zone is engaging in relatively less brokerage activity than, for example, the one in the area on the top of the graph that does not have any underperforming schools. Therefore, not only are there limited "sources" of data available in the area with the most underperforming schools, the area superintendent is providing less brokerage into those underperforming schools. The combined effect may be limited sharing of knowledge within the area, as well as a lack of advice around data from outside the area being moved in to support principals of underperforming schools. This suggests a misalignment between the formal and informal organization within LUUSD that may, in fact, reinforce low performance rather than help these most challenging schools in their improvement efforts.

3.5 Conclusion and Implications

LUUSD, like many educational systems across the globe, initiated a district-wide effort on data use that was meant to be diffused to the schools primarily through the area superintendents. Our results suggest that overall there were very sparse data use ties across the entire district. Although the limited number of ties may be expected in the early stages of an effort, one might expect much more brokerage as a way to get out information about the effort. Unfortunately, our results suggest very few brokerage ties taking place across the system. In fact, those who were formally tasked with brokering this initiative to the schools were not consistently the ones playing the top broker roles. We also found tremendous variation in terms of network structure and the types of brokerage roles that were enacted. In addition, those underperforming schools also seemed to be even more adversely affected by the lack of advice around data exchanges as well as limited brokering. We unpack the main findings and implications from our overall study below.

3.5.1 Sparse Ties, Isolated Administrators, and Varied and Limited Brokerage

One of the first findings from this study is the sparse ties between and among educational leaders in La Urbana. Examining the most frequent ties between leaders in terms of data use suggests that there are limited exchanges, which may negatively influence the overall coherence in the district. Further, a number of principals are isolated and do not have individuals from whom they indicate they seek, or are sought, for advice. Given the limited number of relationships, it may be difficult for the larger system to engage with the use of evidence with consistency and coherence. In addition, we may have expected more brokering relationships to be in place in the district, but there was actually relatively limited brokering taking place across the district, and that brokerage was inconsistent and often fragmented and certainly was significantly different across areas.

3.5.2 Potential Influence of Indirect Connections

Brokers connect otherwise disconnected others in a network. In this case, it means that the advice that actor A received from broker B around data originated in part from the advice that broker B obtained from C. In this way, A was indirectly influenced by C through B. As such, individuals who are two steps away (meaning you have to go through another individual to reach them) potentially influence the advice one receives. Consequently, when seeking advice each person makes some assessment of the potential advice giver. However, at least part of the result of the decision is out of a person's control, as one rarely knows from whom the broker gets his or her advice. Is that person reputable? Are they moving "useful" advice about data? Is their advice reflective of the larger system's goals and interpretation? To achieve coherence, central office leaders may find it necessary to reduce the game of telephone by ensuring that those in brokering positions are providing common understandings.

3.5.3 Advice Seeking Outside Areas

We found that within an area principals will seek out an area superintendent for advice and that area superintendent will go outside the area to a different area to obtain advice—as such the advice a principal receives from an area superintendent is influenced by another area. In contrast, the principals who also play important brokerage roles within their areas tend to seek advice from outside of their areas. In this way principals are actually engaging in advice from a "broader" section of the network. An area superintendent may be less likely to seek advice within his/her own area as that may be interpreted to be a sign of "lack of knowledge" to individuals within their own area. This may also be the case for the principals that do not want to necessarily "expose" their lack of knowledge.

3.5.4 Limited Advice Around Data for Low-Performing Schools

Current accountability policy mandates the use of research-based evidence in overall improvement efforts. Our work would suggest that in school systems evidence is often defined as "data." In fact, many systems across the country, including LUUSD, have taken up "data use" as a mantra for improvement particularly for those underperforming schools. However, despite the district's formal emphasis on this type of evidence, our study indicates very limited exchanges between and among principals of lower-performing schools and between those principals and either principals of better performing schools or district leaders who have the formal authority and mandate to support their work. Without the opportunity to engage with others around the use of data, it may be difficult for individual leaders to break free of existing patterns of use and as such performance may stagnate.

However, perhaps the most troubling part of the findings is that the "rich get richer" in this system. Our analysis suggests that low-performing schools are concentrated in a few areas. Interestingly, in the area that had the highest proportion of principals of underperforming schools, there were both the least amount of exchanges regarding the data and less brokerage activity of the area superintendent. This results in both a lack of exchange within the area and fewer exchanges happening outside the area as would be indicated by high amounts of brokering.

Consequently, although one might not expect principals of low-performing schools to seek other principals of low-performing schools for the use of data, one might expect that these principals could be connected to other principals outside their area for fresh strategies on the use of data. These "outside" connections need to be brokered by those who are in the formal position to do so, area superintendents, but our study suggests that was not happening. This may ultimately leave the principals of underperforming schools to either reach out to other principals of underperforming schools for advice around data, which may limit new successful approaches, or continue to do what they have been doing, which may hinder improvement. As such this situation portends a continued lack of improvement, as limited information makes its way into the hands of the educators who need it the most.

References

Ahuja, G. (2000). Collaboration networks, structural holes, and innovation: A longitudinal study. *Administrative Science Quarterly, 45*(3), 425–455.

Atteberry, A., & Bryk, A. S. (2010). Analyzing the role of social networks in school-based professional development initiatives. In A. J. Daly (Ed.), *The ties of change: Social network theory and application in education* (pp. 51–76). Cambridge, MA: Harvard Press.

Baker, W. E., & Iyer, A. (1992). Information networks and market behavior. *Journal of Mathematical Sociology, 16*, 305–332.

Borgatti, S., & Foster, P. (2003). The network paradigm in organizational research: A review and typology. *Journal of Management, 29*(6), 991–1013.

Borgatti, S. P., & Ofem, B. (2010). Overview: Social network theory and analysis. In A. J. Daly (Ed.), *The ties of change: Social network theory and application in education* (pp. 17–30). Cambridge, MA: Harvard Press.

Borgatti, S., Everett, M., & Freeman, L. (2002). *UCINET for Windows: Software for social network analysis*. Harvard: Analytic Technologies.

Brass, D. J., & Burkhardt, M. E. (1993). Potential power and power use: An investigation of structure and behavior. *Academy of Management Journal, 36*(3), 441–470.

Burt, R. S. (1982). *Toward a structural theory of action*. New York: Academic.

Burt, R. S. (1992). *Structural holes: The structure of competition*. Cambridge, MA: Harvard University Press.

Burt, R. S. (1997). A note on social capital and network content. *Social Networks, 19*(4), 355–373.

Burt, R. S. (2000). The network structure of social capital. In R. I. Sutton & B. M. Staw (Eds.), *Research in organizational behavior* (pp. 1–83). Greenwich: JAI Press.

Burt, R. S. (2005). *Brokerage and closure: An introduction to social capital*. Oxford: Oxford University Press.

Carley, K., & Krackhardt, D. (1999). Cognitive inconsistencies and non-symmetric friendship. *Social Networks, 18*(1), 1–27.

Chrispeels, J. (2004). *Learning to lead together: The promise and challenge of sharing leadership*. Thousand Oaks: Sage.

Coburn, C. (2001). Collective sensemaking about reading: How teachers mediate reading policy in their professional communities. *Educational Evaluation and Policy Analysis, 23*(2), 145–170.

Coburn, C. E. (2005). Shaping teacher sensemaking: School leaders and the enactment of reading policy. *Educational Policy, 19*, 476–509.

Coburn, C. E., & Russell, J. L. (2008). District policy and teachers' social networks. *Education Evaluation and Policy Analysis, 30*(3), 203–235.

Coburn, C. E., Honig, M. I., & Stein, M. K. (2009a). What's the evidence on district's use of evidence? In J. Bransford, D. J. Stipek, N. J. Vye, L. Gomez, & D. Lam (Eds.), *Educational improvement: What makes it happen and why?* (pp. 67–86). Cambridge, MA: Harvard Educational Press.

Coburn, C. E., Touré, J., & Yamashita, M. (2009b). Evidence, interpretation, and persuasion: Instructional decision making in the district central office. *Teachers College Record, 111*(4), 1115–1161.

Confrey, J., & Makar, K. (2005). Critiquing and improving the use of data from high-stakes tests with the aid of dynamic statistics software. In C. Dede, J. P. Honan, & L. C. Peters (Eds.), *Scaling up success: Lessons learned from technology-based educational improvement* (pp. 198–226). San Francisco: Jossey-Bass.

Copland, M. A. (2003). Leadership of inquiry: Building and sustaining capacity for school improvement. *Educational Evaluation and Policy Analysis, 25*, 375–395.

Cross, R., & Parker, A. (2004). *The hidden power of social networks: Understanding how work really gets done in organizations*. Cambridge, MA: Harvard Business School Press.

Cross, R., Borgatti, S., & Parker, A. (2002). Making invisible work visible: Using social network analysis to support strategic collaboration. *California Management Review, 44*(2), 25–46.

Daly, A. J., & Finnigan, K. (2010). A bridge between worlds: Understanding network structure to understand change strategy. *Journal of Educational Change, 111*, 111–138.

Daly, A. J. (Ed.). (2010). *Social network theory and educational change*. Cambridge, MA: Harvard Education Press.

Daly, A. J. (2012). Data, dyads, and dissemination: Exploring data use and social networks in educational improvement. *Teachers College Record, 114*(11), 1–38.

Daly, A. J., & Finnigan, K. (2009). A bridge between worlds: Understanding network structure to understand change strategy. *Journal of Educational Change, 11*(2), 111–138.

Daly, A. J., & Finnigan, K. (2010). A bridge between worlds: Understanding network structure to understand change strategy. *Journal of Educational Change, 111*, 111–138.

Daly, A. J., & Finnigan, K. (2011). The ebb and flow of social network ties between district leaders under high stakes accountability. *American Education Research Journal, 48*(1), 39–79.

Daly, A. J., & Finnigan, K. (2012). Exploring the space between: Social networks, trust, and urban school district leaders. *Journal of School Leadership, 22*(3), 493–530.

Datnow, A., & Park, V. (2009). Conceptualizing policy implementation: Large-scale reform in an era of complexity. In D. Plank, B. Schneider, & G. Sykes (Eds.), *Handbook of education policy research* (pp. 348–361). New York: Routledge.

Datnow, A., Hubbard, L., & Mehan, H. (2002). *Extending educational reform: From one school to many*. London: Routledge/Falmer.

Datnow, A., Park, V., & Wohlstetter, P. (2007). *Achieving with data: How high-performing school systems use data to improve instruction for elementary students*. Los Angeles: University of Southern California, Rossier School of Education, Center on Educational Governance.

Degenne, A., & Forsé, M. (1999). *Introducing social networks*. London: Sage.

Finnigan, K. S., & Daly, A. J. (2010). Learning at a system level: Ties between principals of low performing schools and central office leaders. In A. J. Daly (Ed.), *Social network theory and educational change* (pp. 179–195). Cambridge, MA: Harvard Education Press.

Finnigan, K. S., & Daly, A. J. (2012). Mind the gap: Organizational learning and improvement in an underperforming urban system. *American Journal of Education, 119*(1), 41–71.

Finnigan, K., Daly, A. J., & Stewart, T. (2012). Organizational learning in schools under sanction. *Education Research International, 2012*(16), 1–10.

Finnigan, K. S., Daly, A. J., & Che, J. (2013). Systemwide reform in districts under pressure: The role of social networks in defining, acquiring and diffusing research evidence. *Journal of Educational Administration, 51*(4), 476–497.

Firestone, W. A., & González, R. A. (2007). Culture and processes affecting data use in schools. In P. A. Moss (Ed.), *Evidence and decision making* (pp. 132–154). Malden: Blackwell.

Gulati, R. (1995). Does familiarity breed trust? The implications of repeated ties for contractual choices in alliances. *Academy of Management Journal, 35*, 85–112.
Halverson, R., Prichett, R. B., & Watson, J. G. (2007). *Formative feedback systems and the new instructional leadership*. Madison: University of Wisconsin.
Hamilton, L. S., Stecher, B. M., Marsh, J., McCombs, J. S., Robyn, A., & Russell, J. (2007). *Implementing standards-based accountability under no child left behind: Responses of superintendents, principals, and teachers in three states*. Santa Monica: RAND Corporation.
Hammerman, J. K., & Rubin, A. (2002). Visualizing a statistical world. *Hands On!, 25*(2), 1–7.
Hanneman, R. A., & Riddle, M. (2005). *Introduction to social network methods*. Riverside: University of California.
Hite, J., Williams, E., & Baugh, S. (2005). Multiple networks of public school administrators: An analysis of network content and structure. *International Journal on Leadership in Education, 8*(2), 91–122.
Honig, M. I. (2003). Building policy from practice: District central office administrators' roles and capacity for implementing collaborative education policy. *Educational Administration Quarterly, 39*, 292–338.
Honig, M. (2006). Street-level bureaucracy revisited: Frontline district central-office administrators as boundary spanners in education policy implementation. *Educational Evaluation and Policy Analysis, 28*(4), 357–383.
Honig, M. I., & Coburn, C. (2008). Evidence-based decision making in school district central offices: Toward a policy research agenda. *Educational Policy, 22*(4), 578–608.
Honig, M. I., & Copland, M. A. (2008). *Reinventing central offices to expand student learning. An issue brief of the center for comprehensive school reform and improvement.* Washington, DC: Learning Point Associates.
Ikemoto, G. S., & Marsh, J. A. (2007). Cutting through the "data driven" mantra: Different conceptions of data-driven decision making. In P.A. Moss (Ed.), *Evidence and decision making* (National society for the study of education yearbook, Vol. 106, Issue 1, pp. 105–131). Chicago: National Society for the Study of Education.
Kerr, K. A., Marsh, J. A., Ikemoto, G. S., Darilek, H., & Barney, H. (2006). Strategies to promote data use for instructional improvement: Actions, outcomes, and lessons from three urban districts. *American Journal of Education, 112*(4), 496–520.
Kilduff, M., & Tsai, W. (2003). *Social networks and organizations*. London: Sage.
Knapp, M., Copland, M., & Swinerton, J. (2007). Understanding the promise and dynamics of data-informed leadership. In P. A. Moss (Ed.), *Evidence and decision making* (pp. 74–104). Malden: National Society for the Study of Education.
Krackhardt, D. (2001). *Network conditions of organizational change*. Paper presented at the Academy of Management Annual Meeting, Washington, DC.
Levin, B. (2008). *How to change 5000 schools: A practical and positive approach for leading change at every level*. Cambridge, MA: Harvard Education Press.
Lin, N. (1999). Building a network theory of social capital. *Connections, 22*(1), 28–51.
Louis, K. S., Febey, K., & Schroeder, R. (2005). State-mandated accountability in high schools: Teachers' interpretations of a new era. *Educational Evaluation and Policy Analysis, 27*(2), 177–204.
Louis, K. S., Leithwood, K., Wahlstrom, K. L., & Anderson, S. E. (2010). *Learning from leadership: Investigating the links to improved student learning*. Retrieved from The Wallace Foundation website: http://www.wallacefoundation.org/KnowledgeCenter/KnowledgeTopics/CurrentAreasofFocus/EducationLeadership/Documents/Learning-from-Leadership-Investigating-Links-Final-Report.pdf
Marsh, J. A., Pane, J. F., & Hamilton, L. S. (2006). *Making sense of data-driven decision making in education: Evidence from recent RAND research* (OP-170). Santa Monica: RAND Corporation.
Marsh, J. A., McCombs, J. S., & Martorell, F. (2010). How instructional coaches support data-driven decision making: Policy implementation and effects in Florida Middle Schools. *Educational Policy, 24*(6), 872–907.
Nutley, S., Walter, I., & Davies, H. T. O. (2003). From knowing to doing: A framework for understanding the evidence-into-practice agenda. *Evaluation, 9*(2), 125–148.

O'Day, J. (2002). Complexity, accountability, and school improvement. *Harvard Educational Review, 70*(3), 293–329.
O'Day, J. (2004). Complexity, accountability, and school improvement. In S. Fuhrman & R. Elmore (Eds.), *Redesigning accountability systems* (pp. 15–43). New York: Teachers College Press.
Obstfeld, D. (2005). Social networks, the Tertius Iungens orientation, and involvement in innovation. *Administrative Science Quarterly, 50*, 100–130.
Parise, L., & Spillane, J. (2010). Teacher learning and instructional change: How formal and on-the-job learning opportunities predict change in elementary school teachers' practice. *The Elementary School Journal, 110*(3), 347.
Penuel, W. R., Riel, M. R., Krause, A., & Frank, K. A. (2009). Analyzing teachers' professional interactions in a school as social capital: A social network approach. *Teachers College Record, 111*(1), 124–163.
Powell, W. W., Koput, K. I. V., & Smith-Doerr, L. (1996). Interorganizational collaboration and the locus of innovation: Networks of learning in biotechnology. *Administrative Science Quarterly, 41*, 116–145.
Scott, J. (2000). *Social network analysis* (2nd ed.). London: Sage.
Spillane, J. P. (2000). A fifth grade teacher's reconstruction of mathematics and literacy teaching: Exploring interactions among identity, learning, and subject matter. *Elementary School Journal, 100*(4), 273–307.
Spillane, J. P., Reiser, B. J., & Reimer, T. (2002). Policy implementation and cognition: Reframing and refocusing implementation research. *Review of Educational Research, 72*(3), 387–431.
Stovel, K., & Shaw, L. (2012). Brokerage. *Annual Review of Sociology, 38*, 139–158.
Supovitz, J. A. (2006). *The case for district-based reform: Leading, building, and sustaining school improvement.* Cambridge, MA: Harvard Education Press.
Supovitz, J., & Klein, V. (2003). *Mapping a course for improved student learning: How innovative schools use student performance data to guide improvement.* Philadelphia: Consortium for Policy Research in Education.
Togneri, W., & Anderson, S. E. (2003). *Beyond islands of excellence: What districts can do to improve instruction and achievement in all schools.* Washington, DC: The Learning First Alliance and the Association for Supervision and Curriculum Development.
Tseng, V. (2012). The use of research and evidence in policy and practice. *Social Policy Report, 26*(2), 1–16.
Wasserman, S., & Faust, K. (1994). *Social network analysis: Methods and applications.* New York: Cambridge University Press.
Wasserman, S., & Faust, K. (1998). *Social network analysis: Methods and applications.* New York: Cambridge University Press.
Wayman, J. C., & Stringfield, S. (2006). Technology-supported involvement of entire faculties in examination of student data for instructional improvement. *American Journal of Education, 112*(4), 549–571.
Wayman, J. C., Cho, V., & Johnston, M. T. (2007). *The data-informed district: A district-wide evaluation of data use in the Natrona County School District.* Austin: The University of Texas.
Weick, K. E. (1985). Cosmos vs. chaos: Sense and nonsense in electronic contexts. *Organizational Dynamics, 14*(2), 50–64.
Wellman, B., & Berkowitz, S. D. (1998). *Social structures: A network approach.* Cambridge, MA: Cambridge University Press.
Wohlstetter, P., Datnow, A., & Park, V. (2008). Creating a system for data-driven decision making: Applying the principal-agent framework. *School Effectiveness and School Improvement Journal, 19*(3), 239–259.
Yin, R. K. (2003). *Case study research: Design and methods* (3rd ed.). Newbury Park: Sage.
Young, V. M. (2006). Teachers' use of data: Loose coupling, agenda setting, and team norms. *American Journal of Education, 112*(4), 521–548.

Chapter 4
Leaders' Use of Research for Fundamental Change in School District Central Offices: Processes and Challenges

Meredith I. Honig, Nitya Venkateswaran, Patricia McNeil, and Jenee Myers Twitchell

Across the country, a growing number of school districts have launched efforts to significantly reform their central offices to support districtwide teaching and learning improvement, and they are using various strands of research—here defined as formal social science studies of school district central office performance—to guide their reform designs and processes. Unlike other district reform efforts that focus on schools as the sole target, these reforms aim to shift *central office* policies and practices so that central offices operate as support systems for teaching and learning improvements in schools. Such efforts are theoretically promising, since a growing body of research and other evidence is beginning to suggest how central offices might operate differently to support districtwide improvement school goals (Hightower 2002; Honig et al. 2010). However, the research typically calls for fundamental shifts in central office administrators' work—radical departures from the status quo in central offices—and such changes are notoriously difficult to implement. What happens when central office administrators engage with research that calls for fundamental shifts in central office work practices? Under what conditions, if any, do central office administrators buck predominant trends and actually use the research to engage in fundamental shifts in their own practice at the central office level?

We explored these questions with an in-depth qualitative analysis of six school districts engaged in fundamental central office change aimed at strengthening their central offices' capacity to support districtwide improvements in teaching and learning. All the districts intended to use various forms of research to guide their process. For our conceptual framework, we drew on several strands of learning theory, based on the research-based hypothesis explored below that when practitioners such as central office administrators take up research-based ideas in ways that lead to fundamental changes in their practice, they engage in processes of professional

---

M.I. Honig (✉) • N. Venkateswaran • P. McNeil • J. Myers Twitchell
Educational Leadership and Policy Studies, College of Education,
University of Washington, Seattle, WA, USA
e-mail: mihonig@u.washington.edu

K.S. Finnigan and A.J. Daly (eds.), *Using Research Evidence in Education: From the Schoolhouse Door to Capitol Hill*, Policy Implications of Research in Education 2,
DOI 10.1007/978-3-319-04690-7_4,

learning (Collins et al. 2003; Brown et al. 1989; Lave 1998; Levitt and March 1998; Rogoff et al. 1995; Tharp and Gallimore 1991; Weick 1995; Wenger 1998). These strands of learning theory also emphasized that practitioners tend to learn in ways that result in fundamental changes in their practice when they have access to intensive assistance relationships in which assistance providers, knowledgeable about the new target practices, engage in high-leverage teaching moves that support learners' depth of understanding of challenging ideas. We used these theories to frame our investigation involving 116 interviews, 499.25 h of observations, and reviews of approximately 300 documents. In this chapter we summarize some of the main findings that have emerged during our first phase of analysis.

In sum, we discuss that central office administrators used particular research-based ideas to shift district-level policies and their own practice, but to varying degrees. We found that particular conditions enabled research use such as administrators' prior experiences with ideas consistent with the research and their engagement with intermediary organizations that engaged in teaching practices consistent with our conceptual framework. However, such conditions seemed necessary but not sufficient for research use at deep levels. More often, central office administrators tended not to take up research-based ideas at deep levels absent central office leaders who themselves engaged in high-leverage teaching moves to help their colleagues and staff integrate challenging research into their practice. These findings support the hypothesis that internal central office leadership is essential to fundamental central office change.

4.1 Policy Context

School district central office leaders across the country face unprecedented demands to help all students achieve at high levels and to use research to inform the process. For example, the No Child Left Behind Act of 2001 requires that district central offices provide professional development to schools that includes "instructional materials, programs, strategies, and approaches based on scientifically based reading research" (No Child Left Behind Act [NCLB] 2002). Educational research chronicles how districts have been turning to ideas from research, here defined as formal social science studies, to inform such decisions about school-level supports and change strategies (Coburn et al. 2009; Corcoran et al. 2001). But central office leaders are also looking to research to guide their own practice at the central office level (Honig and Ikemoto 2008; Marsh et al. 2004, 2006). For example, central office administrators partnered with the Institute for Learning (University of Pittsburgh), to learn how to observe for high-quality instruction using a research-based practice called Learning Walks in order to build administrators' knowledge of instruction and to develop supports for principals and teachers (Honig and Ikemoto 2008).

Central office staff have new opportunities to use research to inform how they work, in part because a wave of relatively recent formal academic research has begun to take up the question of what forms of central office work might support school improvement (e.g., Augustine et al. 2009; Honig et al. 2010). For example, studies in New York City's Community School District #2 have shown how the implementation of school reform efforts hinged in part on the continual efforts of central office administrators to support principals in building their capacity to help teachers improve the quality of instruction (Elmore and Burney 1997; Fink and Resnick 2001). In our own such research we have elaborated how central offices can significantly build schools' capacity for improved teaching and learning through new partnership relationships with school principals and by reorganizing and reculturing central office functions to provide high-quality, relevant support services to schools (Honig 2012; Honig et al. 2010).

The use of research to reform how central offices work to support teaching and learning improvement in schools holds promise for realizing educational improvement goals. As research on school improvement has shown for decades, school-level efforts to strengthen teaching and learning lumber, plateau, or outright fail in part because central office administrators do not participate productively in their implementation (Bryk et al. 1998; Chubb and Moe 1990; Malen et al. 1990; Ravitch and Viteritti 1997). Educational research has begun to suggest that central office administrators' participation involves remaking central office policies and work practices in particular ways (Elmore and Burney 1997; Honig 2008; Hubbard et al. 2006).

However, central office administrators likely face significant obstacles when shifting policies and practices in ways the actual application of the research would require. For example, the conclusions from a San Diego study mainly show that central office administrators struggled and largely failed to shift their work in ways that the research suggested (Hubbard et al. 2006). Across multiple studies, Spillane found that central office administrators routinely misinterpret or misappropriate ideas about what instructional improvement entails, viewing the ideas as reinforcing their current policies and practices even when such policies and practices depart starkly from what research recommends (Spillane et al. 2002; Spillane and Thompson 1997. See also, Coburn et al. 2009; Kennedy 1982; O'Day 2002).

Such results are not surprising. The kinds of changes that this research demands run counter to school district central offices as institutions. School district central offices were established at the beginning of the last century mainly to carry out limited business and regulatory functions, not to address or centrally support improvements in the quality of principal leadership and, in turn, teaching and learning in schools (Cuban 1984; Elmore 1993; Tyack and Cuban 1995).

Broader research on decision-making in central offices delineates various challenges with changing business as usual in central offices. For example, Hannaway (1989) showed that central office administrators approached their professional decisions with particular biases that led them to favor the status quo rather than consider or implement deeper changes in their policies and practices. Such patterns were especially true of mid-level central office staff members other than superintendents or other central office executives. Coburn and colleagues (2009) confirmed earlier findings by Kennedy (1982), by showing how central office administrators tend to interpret new ideas in ways that reinforce rather than disrupt their prior knowledge and decision frames. Across a series of studies, Honig (2004, 2009) found that even new central office employees fell back on long-standing central office routines that curbed their engagement with new challenging ideas.

Are policymakers expecting the impossible when they require that central offices engage with research fundamentally challenging their status quo in an effort to spark central office reforms for districtwide improvements in teaching and learning? Under what conditions, if any, might central office administrators buck predominant trends and make significant shifts in their work and capacity that the emerging research calls for?

4.2 Conceptual Framework

We explored these questions in a study of six districts that aimed to fundamentally reform their central offices to support districtwide teaching and learning with an emphasis on how they engaged with research to guide the process. Our conceptual framework came from several strands of literature on organizational and sociocultural learning. These theories elaborate that when people engage deeply with new ideas in ways that lead to fundamental changes in their work practices, they engage in a process of learning. As part of that learning process, practitioners such as central office administrators grapple with what new ideas mean and how to integrate these ideas into their ongoing practice. They compare the new ideas against their past experiences and their sense of what constitutes appropriate professional practice. Learners also may edit the new information, amplifying certain parts and downplaying others (Levitt and March 1998; March 1994; Weick 1995).

According to Argyris and Schon (1996), during single-loop learning processes, learners stick with a single conception of the underlying problem motivating their action and use feedback from their actions only to inform how they go about their action taking. During double-loop learning, learners use feedback to scrutinize their understanding of the problem they aim to address. Such double-loop processes lead to deeper understandings of new ideas and more profound changes in practice than single-loop learning which typically involves a learner engaging in different variations of the same general type of practice.

For example, a central office staff person might tackle the problem of a school principal not spending enough time working with teachers on the quality of their classroom instruction by conducting school visits themselves and writing reports directing the principal to visit classrooms more. Over time, the central office staff person might find that despite the reports, the principal still is not visiting classrooms frequently enough. In response, they increase the frequency of their own school visits and the consequences they associate with the principals' failure to comply—marginal changes in their practice. However, another central office staff person might use the feedback that the principal's practice remains unchanged to more fundamentally rethink their approach. They might hypothesize that the principal would like to spend more time in classrooms but they lack the capacity to shift their schedule to allow them the time to do so and they do not have the know-how to feel confident about the efficacy of their observations. That central office staff person might reframe the problem posed by that principal not as one of their lack of compliance but their weak capacity and, in turn, decide to fundamentally shift their own practice to put them in the school building more often working side-by-side with the principal to adjust how they allocate time and sharpen their skills at classroom observations.

Sociocultural learning theories further distinguish outcomes that represent first- vs. second-order changes (Grossman et al. 1999), and we used their distinctions to help us gauge central office staff's shifts in practice. During first-order change processes, practitioners might not appropriate new ideas at all, continuing to engage in their work as they have always done. Practitioners might also "appropriate a label" or engage with the ideas at only a superficial level and not realize the deeper levels of understanding of the ideas that lead to significant shifts in practice. For instance, a central office leader might change the title of certain central office staff from "associate superintendent" to "instructional leadership director" to signal that those staff now focus on helping schools strengthen instruction. But this leader has only appropriated a label if she has not changed the actual work practices of these staff to support such results.

When practitioners "appropriate surface features" they intend to engage in the practices reflective of the new ideas more deeply than when they appropriate a label. But because they do so without grasping what the features mean or why they engage in them, they are likely to engage in these activities only temporarily or in certain contexts, not transferring the ideas to new contexts as is true of deeper change processes (Pea 1987).

Sociocultural learning theorists distinguish two dimensions of second-order change. Practitioners might engage with new ideas by "appropriating conceptual underpinnings." When they do so, practitioners have developed a relatively deep, internalized understanding of the new ideas, they attempt to use them in ways consistent with the research-based ideas, and they are likely to apply them in new situations. Those who have "achieved mastery" are able to fully engage in practices consistent with the new ideas. They deeply understand what the new ideas involve and why engaging in them is important, they frequently demonstrate the new practice, and they are able to improvise, creating new extensions of the practice in ways that create new knowledge.

Various factors mediate such levels of appropriation. Among them, through particular kinds of learning assistance relationships, practitioners may receive support for disrupting their usual ways of thinking and acting and engage in fundamental change of either or both (Tharp and Gallimore 1991; Wenger 1998). Across a wide range of settings, "assistance" strategies have such effects when someone continuously (1) models or demonstrates modes of acting and thinking consistent with the new ideas; (2) develops and uses tools that help practitioners engage with the new ideas; (3) helps practitioners adopt the identity of people on a trajectory toward deepening their engagement with the ideas; (4) creates and sustains social opportunities—including challenging conversations—through which practitioners grapple meaningfully with what new ideas mean for their own work; and (5) bridges practitioners to and buffers practitioners from outside resources both to support practitioners' sustained engagement in the new ideas (Honig 2008).

The so-called intermediary organizations may be particularly well suited to support such assistance relationships (Honig 2004). Intermediary organizations, because of their partial-outsider status, may be able to dedicate the time and other resources that assistance relationship requires; because of their partial-insider status, they may garner a trust with their partners also essential to such relationships (Coburn and Stein 2010).

4.3 Methods

We used our conceptual framework to help us strategically select six study districts based on their likelihood to engage in fundamental changes in their central offices consistent with emerging research-based ideas about how central offices might support improved teaching and learning in schools. We looked for districts that (1) aimed to reform their central office in service of improved teaching and learning districtwide, (2) understood that such reform would mean significant changes in their central office, (3) appeared to be drawing on various strands of social science research about central office performance to ground their approach, and (4) had access to intermediary organizations to support with the process who ostensibly understood their role as assisting administrators' professional learning.

Our data sources include 116 in-depth interviews of central office staff and school principals, observations of meetings and coaching sessions involving central office staff totaling 499.25 h, and over 300 documents related to the central offices' efforts to improve their performance in service of improved districtwide teaching and learning. We invited to participate in the study all central office staff who were engaged with the intermediary and who intended to use research to transform their central office, including the superintendents and central office executive staff members (i.e., Assistant Superintendent of Teaching and Learning, Director of Curriculum, etc.) and in two of the districts, those in the newly created instructional leadership director role.

We analyzed our data using NVIVO8 qualitative software in several phases. During our initial phase of analysis, we sorted our data into low-inference categories such as "outcomes" of central office change processes and topics of research that central office staff aimed to use (e.g., "superintendent role"). We also used our conceptual framework during this phase to code for various, broad potential influences on research use including the role of intermediary organizations. In the second stage of our analysis, we went back into our data by code and refined our analysis using higher-inference codes from our conceptual framework. For example, we recoded our "outcomes" data by degrees of appropriation. We also distinguished the work of intermediary organizations as more or less consistent with the assistance relationship practices highlighted in our conceptual framework.

4.4 Findings

In this section, we share emerging findings from our initial analysis. Specifically, we discuss that we could distinguish central office administrators' use of research-based ideas by the degrees of appropriation highlighted in our conceptual framework. We demonstrate how we made these distinctions by discussing examples from administrators' use of one out of the three main sets of research-based ideas with which our respondents engaged: research on how to develop and execute the role of principal supervisor or what the research calls "instructional leadership director." The distribution of examples related to this strand of research reflects our overall data set which revealed instances mostly of first-order change or low levels of appropriation. Fewer examples indicated degrees of appropriation with conceptual understanding. By contrasting these examples and examining changes in levels of appropriation in some cases over time, we identified several conditions that seemed necessary for central office administrators' engagement with ambitious research ideas at any level but not sufficient for second-order changes. These include individual's prior knowledge and experiences and the nature of intermediaries' assistance strategies. Those central offices and central office staff with little prior experience with or knowledge about the research-based ideas generally did not develop much if at all beyond their initial levels of understanding. While their intermediaries did engage in the kinds of practices our conceptual framework suggested would help central office staff significantly shift their own practice in ways consistent with the research, the intermediaries' efforts seemed promising but not sufficient to realize such results given staff's low levels of appropriation starting out. Those staff and systems whose work seemed to reflect progressively deeper practice shifts consistent with the research also worked with intermediaries, often the same ones as the other staff who showed more growth, but from the outset reported prior knowledge consistent with the research-based ideas. In addition, in those systems, leaders did not rely solely on intermediaries but themselves assumed teaching roles with other central office staff, assisting them with their engagement with the research. Our findings underscore other research on the importance of prior knowledge or experience, what leaders might operationalize as "readiness," to engagement in fundamental practice changes. However, they suggest that intermediary organizations may be viable levers of change when prior knowledge and experience are relatively high, but that internal leadership, particularly that which proceeds from a teaching stance, may be essential to realizing deeper levels of appropriation, particularly in systems without substantial relevant prior knowledge and experience.

4.4.1 *Appropriating Research on the Role of the Principal Supervisor*

As one illustration of how our examples ranged by degrees of appropriation, we found that all six districts aimed to use research on a particular central office position referred to in the research as "instructional leadership director" (Honig et al. 2010).

Those findings described the importance of districts eliminating their traditional principal supervisor position and replacing it with ILDs—executive-level staff charged with working as close to 100 % of the time as possible helping principals grow as instructional leaders, leaders who supported teachers in improving their instructional practice. ILDs worked with principals one-on-one as well as in principal professional learning communities which the ILDs convened. Research on ILDs called for second-order changes in central office practice in several respects. Among them, unlike some traditional principal supervisors such as area or assistant superintendents, ILDs did not also manage central office programs or carry out other functions; rather, they were dedicated to supporting principal growth, jobs typically left to retired principals or coaches deep in the central office hierarchy. The findings on ILDs thus flipped traditional arrangements for principal professional development on their heads, elevating support for principals' growth as instructional leaders to a cabinet-level responsibility. The research also showed that ILDs who were successful in supporting principal growth did not lead in traditional central office fashion, with accountability or top-down directives. Instead, successful ILDs engaged in partnership relationships with school principals and aimed to teach rather than tell principals how to improve (Honig 2012).

While all the districts aimed to adopt the research findings about the ILD function, they varied in how they appropriated that idea across districts at two levels of analysis: (1) between districts, how central office leaders constructed the role, and (2) within districts, the extent to which individual ILDs appropriated ILD practices named in the research.

For example, in one of our mid-sized districts, in several interviews and conversations over time, those hired into the ILD positions reported that, in the words of one, "supporting instructional leadership" among principals was their primary charge. However, when we probed their understanding of what such support work entailed, they described their charge as providing general support to principals. In one ILD's words,

> Of all the experience I've had as a…school principal, there's nothing that any one of these people is going to face that I haven't faced two or three times before. So if I could help problem-solve something rather than have them working it through completely on their own, if I could help problem-solve it and get to solution quicker, then it enables them to have more time for the instructional piece.

Our interviews with and observations of the individual ILDs in this system suggested that none were engaged in the kinds of intensive teaching practices that the research emphasized. Instead, the ILDs typically worked with principals to help them understand and stay in compliance with various policies including those related to personnel. For example, one ILD described their work by saying,

> So where they've [principals have] asked for advice and support has been in dealing with teachers struggling. So…if they've got a teacher that they're concerned about, asking for me to review their observation summary before they send it…Another example would be something like a…kid wants to drop one of their seven courses because they're a high-level tennis player…But there's a district policy that says that a full-time student is seven classes. So working with the principal to try and meet the needs of the kids, but also make sure that we're following district policy.

When we shadowed ILDs in this district, we most commonly saw them helping principals, assistant principals, and teacher leaders develop a shared understanding of the new teacher evaluation system, with an emphasis on following proper procedures when placing teachers on probationary status or helping teachers exit the system. While tasks such as these focused on instructional matters and related to principal needs, they did not involve the intensive focus on helping principals grow their instructional leadership practice as elaborated in the research.

In the other mid-sized district, we found adoption of the research on the ILD role at the level of appropriating surface features, a step deeper than in the other similarly sized district. At the level of individual ILDs, we found a broad range from adopting a label to adopting conceptual underpinnings.

To elaborate, a leader in this district initially set out to retrain her team of principal supervisors so they functioned as ILDs rather than as more traditional area superintendents. This leader reported that these staff would no longer operate as the principals' single point of contact for various central office matters such as assisting with the redesign of school websites, helping principals determine of particular students met graduation requirements, and managing the installation of portable buildings on school campuses. Instead, they would be dedicated to supporting principals' growth as instructional leaders. However, the first year of implementation reflected appropriation of a label because throughout the year these staff operated with a new title but essentially went about their work as they had under their previous title. The next year, that leader rewrote the job description to focus on principals' growth as instructional leaders and turned over 80 % of those staff with people she believed came with a ready understanding of the new conception of the ILD role consistent with the research.

Through broad districtwide communications as well as in principal meetings and community forums, this leader frequently indicated that ILDs were to spend 75 % of their time in schools supporting principal instructional leadership. She created new processes within the central office so that any requests for ILD time from central office departments had to be run by her first so she could help teach others in the system about the new role. For example, in one meeting in which ILDs were discussing various requests for their time from central office staff that seemed inconsistent with their focus on principals instructional leadership, this leader responded, "When stuff like that comes along, forward it to me. You need to forward it to me. I don't know who will do it. So forward it to me and I will figure it out."

However, the research-based conception of the ILD role was not deeply adopted throughout the central office, reflecting a surface-level adoption of the role across the central office. For example, nearly 2 years after the creation of this role, a top cabinet official reported that there was still, in the words of one, a "misunderstanding" about the role and how ILDs supported principals differently than before. In one discussion, he/she reported that the head of the facilities department wanted ILDs to be involved in school openings, "They want more frequent interaction with you [ILDs] on what the community wants and the principals' reaction to this. I've heard them say, 'I wish I had more time with the [ILDs].'" In multiple settings throughout the duration of our study, we observed ILDs receiving requests from central office staff to engage in activities that did not align with the research-based redesign of their role, such as handling transportation mishaps at various schools or managing teacher displacement.

Among individual ILDs in this district, we found that levels of appropriation ranged significantly from appropriating with conceptual underpinnings to little or no appropriation over time. Similarly in our study's other mid-sized school district, one of the ILDs appropriated the role with a label and spent time on instructionally related issues without a focus on principal learning. For example, this ILD spent significant time in schools but typically engaged in tasks that were the principals' responsibility, rather than helping the principal engage in those tasks—a choice that was not only inconsistent with research findings about the ILDs' instructional leadership focus but one that directly conflicted with a finding that ILDs lead through principals and not step in for principals or otherwise become integrally involved with school-level functions. For example, this ILD reported observing classrooms with one of his/her principals and identifying problems related to the quality of instruction such as teachers' failure to use state standards. The ILD then described how he/she followed up on those issues by checking teachers' lesson plans and otherwise working with the teachers himself/herself—rather than coaching the principal through next steps, as indicated by the research. Another ILD commented that this ILD acted as a "super principal," handling responsibilities that the research suggested he/she should have supported the principals in leading.

This ILD presented his/her work with principals as "working intensively with [principals] so that they can elevate teacher practice," but his/her interactions did not reflect the teaching approach consistent with research. For example, during one session where the ILD discussed his/her work with a particular principal, the facilitator from an intermediary organization directly asked him/her during a meeting of ILDs, "I hear you monitoring and setting some priorities but how are you *teaching* the principal how to do a better job?" The ILD responded to this question and similar probes by sharing numerous reasons why this particular principal did not follow his/her directions including the principal's lack of experience and confidence and not being held accountable for following through in the past. He/she described various ways he/she was monitoring the extent to which this principal followed what he/she told them to do such as visiting the schools to check that the principal was providing the professional development as directed.

Two ILDs in this district who displayed surface level of appropriation reported in interviews that they understood their role as maximizing their time on principal instructional leadership. However, they still spent significant time responding to requests from other central office units that took their time away from their school principals and did not directly contribute to helping their principals grow as instructional leaders. One reported that he knew doing so ran counter to their charge, but he was worried about tasks formerly assigned to his role falling through the cracks.

The work of two other ILDs in this district reflected their adoption of research on the ILD role with conceptual underpinnings. In the case of one of these ILDs, we found through interviews, meeting observations, and reviews of e-mail exchanges, this ILD frequently declined requests for his/her involvement in tasks that took time away from her direct work with principals focused on their growth as instructional leaders. During our second year of data collection, this ILD reported that any time he/she received a request from a central office staff, he/she filtered it through the question, "What does this have to do with instructional leadership?" Also in the second year, he/she trained his/her secretary to screen phone calls so that noninstructional issues, such as school lunches, would be directed to someone else and restructured his/her one-on-one meetings with principals so the meetings started with instructional issues and not principals' operational crises.

Over multiple meetings with this ILD's principals, we observed this ILD engaging in the teaching practices highlighted as high leverage in the research, sometimes explicitly using terms from the research to name that she was engaged in modeling or brokering principals as learning resources for each other. For example, this ILD described that one of his/her principals did not seem to understand that their teachers were performing poorly in mathematics across grade levels. The ILD organized a meeting with that principal during which she brought a data coach from the central office to model for the principal how to analyze school-level data, in the ILD's words, to help the principal learn to "generate questions from data" that would help the principal understand how to make inferences about the level of instruction using data. The ILD shared that such support for the principal extended beyond that one event to a series of meetings with the math coach to help with classroom observations to build the principal's knowledge about high-quality math instruction. During a meeting of ILDs at which this ILD presented his/her work with this principal to colleagues for feedback, this ILD articulated a clear rationale for his/her approach, rooted in the research-based ideas about the importance of taking a teaching rather than directive or monitoring approach with principals:

> I'm not using the conversation to turn up the heat. I'm trying to teach [the principal] because I'm still hoping that... [the principal will understand what the issues are in her school and take action.] I've told [principal] that..."I'm going to hold you accountable to the learning" but I am trying to teach [the principal] how to do it. "Let's put the data in a bar graph so we can understand the numbers of the page." I don't think it is negative. I think the tone of the meetings is pretty positive because it's not about the gotcha, it's about, "We have to understand the data in order to move forward." The data holds the secret. I'm trying to make [the principal] understand so we can make the achievement plan.

We also considered this ILD at the deep end of appropriating this research because he/she demonstrated an ability to apply the research to new situations not directly discussed in the research but consistent with the research. For example, in one meeting, the ILDs in this district were discussing whether or not they should all use the same form when providing feedback to principals after site visits. During the discussion this ILD asked, "Why does it make a difference?" probing the other ILDs to articulate the connection between using a similar format and their charge to operate as master teachers of principals instructional leaders. This ILD contributed that he/she believed that the manner in which they provided feedback to principals—and that they did so from a teaching rather than evaluative stance—mattered more to principals learning than what form they used.

In the smaller central offices in our sample (i.e., those with between 9 and 20 central office staff), central office leaders at first questioned the applicability of the research on ILDs to their systems. They generally argued that given their small size, the creation of a team of ILDs did not seem relevant to them. However, by the end of our study period, all districts had appropriated the research-based ideas, some at a surface level and others with conceptual underpinnings, by redesigning parts of the superintendents' and other top-level positions.

For example, in one of these districts, the superintendent seemed to have begun to engage in ILD practices in ways often reflective of appropriation with conceptual underpinnings. The superintendent took on functions of the ILD role and reportedly dedicated approximately 40–50 % of his/her time to supporting principals' growth as instructional leaders, compared to his/her previous interactions with schools that mainly focused on operational issues such as facilities repairs. Furthermore, when probed on the nature of his/her work with individual principals, the superintendent explained how he/she visited all the district's schools every 3 weeks to conduct classroom visits with principals focused on observing specific aspects of the instructional framework. As he/she described,

> A typical meeting [at a school] is I would go in--the principal needs to have a schedule prepared. The schedule will first have kind of an agenda around teaching and learning that addresses the initiatives that we're currently working on and currently added professional development…We then go visit for an hour a number of classrooms. We come back and talk through it. We may pick a question…[for example] we saw this learning target in this classroom. Let's try to interpret quickly what standard that teacher was teaching to.

The superintendent reported that through his/her one-on-one visits with principals, the superintendent aimed to deepen both his/her own and the principals' collective understanding of instruction, as opposed to monitoring instruction and directing principals toward certain actions.

At the start of our data collection period, this superintendent reported in interviews that he/she struggled to observe classrooms himself/herself let alone in the role of teaching principals how to conduct them due to lack of experience with high-quality instruction:

> I've used [my coach from an intermediary organization] pretty much exclusively this year kind of in a modeling role so I can learn from him. And I've partially done that with him because he has more experience…he's been doing this coaching thing with principals for a long time. And so I can listen to how he asks questions, how he focuses in on information.

A year later, we observed this superintendent attempting to take a far more active role as the principals' coach. For instance, during an hour-long discussion with one principal, the superintendent probed how the principal differentiated supports for teachers who varied in instructional quality. Consistent with taking a teaching stance, the superintendent framed his/her intent to approaching this conversation as an opportunity for the principal's learning, not as an evaluative one, reflecting the superintendent's conceptual understanding of how the ILD functions differed from a traditional principal supervisor position:

> I'll follow up with you and we'll talk some more and we will set a time for me to come over and we can look at [what you've been working on] in more depth…We're looking at this from a growth perspective, not from what can I find that you are doing wrong…what we're trying to do is make an extraordinary difference.

4.4.2 *Conditions that Mediate Appropriation of Research-Based Ideas*

Our conceptual framework helped us identify conditions in each district that may help explain the different levels of appropriation between and within districts. While our methods do not allow us to claim a causal connection between these conditions and the levels of appropriation, they do suggest that these conditions theoretically correlate with the outcomes we observed.

4.4.2.1 Intermediary Assistance Strategies

Our conceptual framework highlighted that intermediary organizations might engage in assistance strategies that interrupt status quo practice in central office in ways consistent with the research-based ideas (Tharp and Gallimore 1991; Wenger 1998). Our findings suggested that particular kinds of support from intermediary organizations may be necessary but not sufficient for realizing such results.

To elaborate, in all our study districts, different intermediary organizations intended to support central office staff with using research to inform their own practice, with staff in ILD-type positions as key targets for their work. All the intermediaries engaged in the assistance practices emphasized in our conceptual framework at least to some degree. But in the mid-sized district with little appropriation, one intermediary mainly worked with the school, not central office staff. During interviews, central office staff reported that the intermediary offered some modest suggestions for their work with principals such as the importance of setting norms for meetings and a protocol for conducting classroom observations. However, despite extensive time on site, our team captured the intermediary interacting only with principals and not central office staff. For example, the intermediary ran meetings with principals focused on improving their leadership. In the meetings we observed, central office staff attended those meetings several times but did not participate in the meetings themselves. During interviews these staff reported that they did not have a specific role in those meetings and that they had minimal interactions with the intermediary other than quick phone conversations. The lack of assistance for central office staff in this district may at least partly account for its overall low levels of appropriation of any of the research we examined.

In support of such claims about an association between the lack of intermediary assistance and low levels of appropriation, the one ILD in the other mid-sized district whom we identified as not adopting the research-based ideas at any level of appropriation occasionally came late to or left early from professional development meetings with the intermediary organization focused on helping them use the research-based ideas; this ILD also seldom brought the assignments the intermediary requested that participants complete between the meetings to help them integrate the research into their regular practice.

Beyond these extreme cases, we found that the other intermediary staff consistently demonstrated the assistance practices featured in our conceptual framework and ILDs regularly engaged with their intermediary partners, but appropriation levels were quite mixed, as described above. As an example of staff of an intermediary organization engaged in the teaching practices consistent with our conceptual framework, we observed one facilitator run professional development sessions for ILDs at least once a month focused on helping the ILDs engage specifically with the teaching practices highlighted in the emerging research base on ILDs; during those sessions he/she consistently demonstrated such assistance relationship practices.

During one such session, the facilitator convened the ILDs at a school for an entire day and modeled for the ILDs how to teach principals how to conduct classroom observations as a strategy for helping their teachers improve the quality of their teaching. He/she began this session by engaging the ILDs in an intensive discussion, over more than an hour, about how to use an instructional framework to ground the observations. During this discussion, the facilitator guided the ILDs through a process of prioritizing which aspects of the framework to use on that particular visit, explaining the importance of prioritizing to adult learning. Then, he showed the ILDs how to have an extended conversation with their principals about what they would actually look for to know if they were seeing teaching reflective of the element of the instructional framework they prioritized.

The facilitator began the discussion of the so-called look fors by framing the activity with metacognitive comments that he was going to model how they can help principals generate look fors but that they, as facilitators, should also ask principals challenging questions about how the look fors actually reflect the given standards. He said that too often facilitators simply ask principals to brainstorm what they would look for as evidence of particular teaching standards but leave the suggestions unchecked. As a result, principals sometimes observe classrooms with look fors that are not well aligned with the standards.

During the conversation, the facilitator demonstrated how to have an extended conversation that pressed participants to deepen their understanding of how to observe for high-quality instruction—rather than simply asking principals what they will see in classrooms related to student engagement and charting their comments without checking their rationale for how the "look for" exhibits teachers' instructional quality. For instance, at one point an ILD said teacher's checks for students' understanding by asking students to show thumbs up or thumbs down indicated the teacher's ability to engage students at high levels, the element of the instructional framework on which the ILDs were focusing that session. The facilitator asked the ILD, "How do you relate to that to student engagement?" The ILD responded, "It gives all kids an easy way to say whether they are getting it or getting it but need more time." The facilitator challenged the ILD to "calibrate" the look for more tightly according to how the instructional framework defined student engagement. The ILD then elaborated that checks for understanding would give the teacher information on whether all students were accessing the information or not. If there were no checks for understanding, students who did not understand would become disengaged as the teacher moved forward. The facilitator further probed the ILD to explain whether he/she was emphasizing a teacher's checks for understanding or if students had the ability to tell teachers when they did not understand. This dialogue spurred a discussion among the ILDs on the locus of control in classrooms and generated another look for—the quantity and quality of students' questions.

Our conceptual framework suggests that modeling and other assistance strategies are likely to help central office staff engage with research-based practices at deep levels of appropriation. Given the consistency with which the intermediary featured above as well as the facilitators working with the smaller districts engaged in assistance relationship practices, we might expect to see consistently deeper levels of appropriation in districts with such assistance. Those ILDs who frequently appeared in the few examples of appropriation with conceptual underpinnings credited their intermediary facilitators with helping them improve their practice with their principals. However, we did find substantial variation in levels of appropriation with the districts with such assistance, suggesting that intermediary assistance may be helpful but not necessarily sufficient for deepening central office administrators' engagement in the new challenging work practices. What other conditions might help account for such within district differences?

4.4.2.2 Individual Prior Knowledge and Experiences

Our conceptual framework suggests that practitioners' prior knowledge and experiences likely mediated the effects of the intermediaries' assistance strategies. Specifically, practitioners fit new ideas into their prior knowledge, essentially, long-standing patterns of thinking and acting that they have developed from prior experiences (Kennedy 1982; Levitt and March 1998; March 1994; Weick 1995). In the process, absent disruptions to these patterns or frames, practitioners edit or otherwise simplify the new information so it resembles familiar practice. Such tendencies are particularly prominent in situations in which feedback on performance is unavailable or unclear. In our own applications of such ideas in previous studies, we found that central office staff with extensive experience within traditional school systems tend to aspire to traditional central office roles and careers and to be particularly averse to the risks involved in adopting new central office roles (Honig 2004, 2009). Under such circumstances, limited prior knowledge and/or certain prior experiences likely poses greater challenges for intermediaries in shifting practice.

Consistent with these ideas, we found that those central office staff who appropriated the research at deeper levels had prior knowledge that was consistent with the research and, in some cases, limited experience with traditional central office roles that ran contrary to the research-based ideas about ILDs. Those who appropriated these ideas at the level of surface features or below had prior knowledge not consistent with research and relatively long careers or experience with traditional central office roles.

For instance, one ILD in one of our mid-sized districts who appropriated the research-based ideas with conceptual underpinnings had limited experience as a principal (less than 5 years) and welcomed the contrast between the ILD role and his/her own prior knowledge of the principal supervisor position. In multiple interviews, he/she recalled that when he/she was a principal he/she wished he/she had

ILD-type supports. This ILD often named the research report as a "playbook" for his/her practice as an ILD since his/her previous experiences provided examples only of how a principal supervisor should not work with principals. The other ILD in this district who appropriated ILD practices at a similar level of depth likewise had no experience as a central office administrator or with administrators in a traditional central office structure.

By contrast, one ILD who appropriated the role with surface features had spent at least 5 years working at a central office and approximately 10 years as a principal and explicitly aspired to move up the ladder in the traditional central office structure. One ILD in another district who demonstrated low levels of appropriation commented that he/she was "making it up," meaning the job of being an ILD, as he went, a striking comment given that we observed him/her participate in a half day meeting at which he/she and other members of the district leadership team examined the research on ILDs and that the district invested in coaching for their ILDs from an intermediary (discussed further below). This ILD reported using his/her previous experiences as a principal in the district to help principals "problem solve" and to enable principals to have "more time for the instructional piece" and otherwise serve in general support roles for principals quite like the roles the new ILD positions were intended to replace.

However, in the smaller districts, central office staff consistently had limited to no prior knowledge of the research on ILDs, and all had come up through traditional educational administration pathways. Our observations suggested that our focal respondents generally had consistent access to intermediary staff who engaged in assistance relationship strategies. Yet, we still found mixed levels of appropriation at systems and individual levels. What might account for those differences?

4.4.2.3 System Leadership for Research Use

Our data suggest that internal leadership—specifically, district leaders who themselves led the teaching of the new research-based ideas—may be essential to central office administrators' engagement with those ideas at deep levels of appropriation. We base this claim on both positive and negative examples of this leadership in our study districts which corresponded with the differences in degrees of appropriation between districts.

For instance, in the mid-sized district with little to no appropriation, we found scant evidence that executive-level staff were leading change processes within the central office, including those related to ILDs. The superintendent, for example, did create ILD positions but seemed to engage with those staff only minimally and rarely communicated in the system about the new roles or their importance. In the other mid-sized district, an intermediary facilitator talked extensively with the superintendent about leading the central office change process and doing so from a teaching stance. Our frequent observations in this district confirmed that this superintendent regularly mentioned the ILDs in various communications. However, such mentions were brief and typically involved terminology such as "instructional leadership" that, in interviews with other staff, we learned was ambiguous for most listeners. Even the head of the curriculum and instruction unit expressed significant confusion regarding what the superintendent intended the ILDs to do and how they were to relate to his/her staff which also focused on instructional matters. This superintendent basically turned over the weekly meetings of the ILDs to the intermediaries and on only one occasion facilitated one of those meetings.

By contrast, by the second half of our data collection, we saw the superintendents of the smaller system actively leading the central office change process, particularly around the ILD role. For example, during one meeting, typical of those we observed in the smaller districts during the second half of our data collection, we recorded how one superintendent led his/her executive team through the first of several strategy sessions in which he/she explained the process they would use to engage in significant reform of the central office to dramatically improve how it supports principals to realize improved teaching in every classroom. The superintendent started by explaining that he/she would be using a cycle-of-inquiry protocol to scaffold their central office change process. They elaborated that such a protocol prompted the executive team to pick a focus for their central office change effort and then work from evidence to clarify what problem with central office performance they aimed to address, develop a theory of action for addressing that problem, and continuously assess progress and adjust their plan. He/she said that you start with the question.

> What's the problem of student learning [that is prompting us to engage in central office reform]? And then you say "Okay, what do teachers have to do differently to address that?" And then we say, "What do we as leaders need to do differently to get teachers to do that thing to address it?" We really need to start with what we [in the central office] need to do. We can't start with what teachers need to do. Because that next question is what do we need to do to enable teachers to do different work so students are learning... We have to start with what are we going to do differently that's going to cause teachers to do something different...The next question [is], "What do we have to know to do that? What do we as leaders have to do differently or know that we don't know now to enable teachers to change their practice?"

In this and related meetings, this superintendent demonstrated how he/she was taking the ideas about what central office reform should involve and how to facilitate it (i.e., from a teaching stance) and using them to inform his/her own hands-on leadership of the process. Such examples stood in sharp contrast to those in the larger systems where superintendents seemed to rely on the intermediary organization staff to lead key aspects of the central office change process themselves.

4.5 Summary and Conclusions

This chapter begins to elaborate the outcomes and conditions in six districts that aimed to use research that fundamentally challenged the status quo in their central offices. We argued that ideas from sociocultural learning theory can help researchers and practitioners move beyond relatively simple assessments of school systems as either using or not using research to distinguish different degrees of engagement with such ideas. We show that practitioners who attempt to use research to shift their practice may do so at a surface level or with deep conceptual understanding, or somewhere in between. Intermediary organizations can assist these practitioners in shifting their practice, especially when they engage in particular assistance strategies. However, such strategies may not be sufficient absent prior knowledge and experiences that may make practitioners more or less ready to benefit from the assistance from the intermediaries. Internal leadership, particularly that which proceeds from a teaching stance itself, seems essential to realizing deeper levels of appropriation with challenging research-based ideas.

This study suggests several important directions for future research and practice. First, our research demonstrates the value of studying research use processes as learning processes. We show how specific constructs from various theories of learning can help elaborate what such processes involve. In particular, the definitions of degrees of appropriation enabled us to distinguish key variations in how central office staff engaged with research-based ideas. These definitions move beyond binaries too common in discussions of research use that simply indicated whether or not practitioners used research to specify to what degrees practitioners integrated research-based ideas into their practice. Theories of learning also highlight different conditions that enable research use. As noted above, the extant literature mostly chronicles conditions that impede various forms of evidence use. Learning theory highlights supportive conditions.

Second, we would not have been able to capture different degrees of appropriation or the assistance relationship practices of intermediary organizations had we not conducted extensive, real-time observations as our main data collection strategy. For example, in our study, practitioners in the central office used research-based ideas and practices to describe their work. If we had only conducted interviews or had only conducted one or two observations, we might have concluded they were using research to a greater extent to which they were. But in fact, many had appropriated it at the level of talk, not deep practice changes. Observations in real time allowed us to not only make these distinctions in levels of appropriation but also see and understand the sometimes subtle moves of intermediary organizations reflective of their teaching approach.

Future research might also advance knowledge by exploring what degrees of appropriation practitioners might realize with the help from intermediaries over longer periods of time than our 18-month study. Our findings suggest that more time with research-based ideas, especially in the context of certain kinds of assistance relationships, might lead to greater degrees of appropriation. But does it?

This study also raises questions that practitioners might productively consider to advance their own central office change efforts. Among them, to what extent have we hired into the central office staff with the right prior knowledge and experiences to engage in the kinds of ambitious change the research highlights? How might we select the right intermediaries to assist us with our change process—those who take a teaching stance in their work? How can we ensure we do not turn leadership of the work over to intermediaries but rather make sure we build out capacity to lead the work ourselves?

References

Argyris, C., & Schon, D. (1996). *Organizational learning II: Theory, method, and practice*. Upper Saddle River: Prentice Hall.

Augustine, C. H., Gonzalez, G., Ikemoto, G. S., Russell, J., Zellman, G. L., Constant, L., et al. (2009). *Improving school leadership: The promise of cohesive leadership system*. Monograph (No. 978-0-8330-4891-2). Santa Monica: RAND Corporation.

Brown, J. S., Collins, A., & Duguid, P. (1989). Situated cognition and the culture of learning. *Educational Researcher, 18*(1), 32–42.

Bryk, A. S., Sebring, P. B., Kerbow, D., Rollow, S., & Easton, J. Q. (1998). *Charting Chicago school reform: Democratic localism as a lever for change*. Boulder: Westview Press.

Chubb, J. E., & Moe, T. M. (1990). *Politics, markets, and America's schools*. Washington, DC: The Brookings Institution.

Coburn, C. E., & Stein, M. K. (Eds.). (2010). *Research and practice in education: Building alliances, bridging the divide*. Lanham: Rowman & Littlefield Publishers.

Coburn, C. E., Toure, J., & Yamashita, M. (2009). Evidence, interpretation, and persuasion: Instructional decision making at the district central office. *Teachers College Record, 111*(4), 1115–1161.

Collins, A. M., Brown, J. S., & Holum, A. (2003). *Cognitive apprenticeship: Making thinking visible, the principles of learning: Study tools for educators*. Pittsburgh: University of Pittsburgh.

Corcoran, T., Fuhrman, S. H., & Belcher, C. L. (2001). The district role in instructional improvement. *The Phi Delta Kappan, 83*(1), 78–84.

Cuban, L. (1984). Transforming the frog into a prince: Effective schools research, policy and practice at the district level. *Harvard Educational Review, 54*(2), 129–151.

Elmore, R. (1993). The role of local school districts in instructional improvement. In S. Fuhrman (Ed.), *Designing coherent education policy: Improving the system* (pp. 96–124). San Francisco: Jossey-Bass.

Elmore, R., & Burney, D. (1997). *Investing in teacher learning: Staff development and instructional improvement in Community School District #2*. New York: National Commission on Teaching & America's Future & the Consortium for Policy Research in Education.

Fink, E., & Resnick, L. B. (2001). Developing principals as instructional leaders. *The Phi Delta Kappan, 82*(8), 598–606.

Grossman, P. L., Smagorinsky, P., & Valencia, S. (1999, November). Appropriating tools for teaching English: A theoretical framework for research on learning to teach. *American Journal of Education, 108*, 1–29.

Hannaway, J. (1989). *Managers managing: The workings of an administrative system*. New York: Oxford University Press.

Hightower, A. (2002). *San Diego's big boom: District bureaucracy supports culture of learning*. Seattle: University of Washington Center for the Study of Teaching and Policy.

Honig, M. I. (2004). The new middle management: Intermediary organizations in education policy. *Educational Evaluation and Policy Analysis, 26*(1), 65–87.

Honig, M. I. (2008). District central offices as learning organizations: How sociocultural and organizational learning theories elaborate district central office administrators' participation in teaching and learning improvement efforts. *American Journal of Education, 114*, 627–664.

Honig, M. I. (2009). No small thing: School district central office bureaucracies and the implementation of New small autonomous schools initiatives. *American Educational Research Journal, 46*(2), 387–422.

Honig, M. I. (2012). District central office leadership as teaching: How central office administrators support principals' instructional leadership. *Education Administration Quarterly, 48*(3), 733–774.

Honig, M. I., & Ikemoto, G. (2008). Adaptive assistance for learning improvement efforts: The case of the Institute for Learning. *Peabody Journal of Education, 83*(3), 328–363.

Honig, M., Copland, M. A., Rainey, L., Lorton, J., & Newton, M. (2010). *Central office transformation for district-wide teaching and learning improvement*. Seattle: Center for Teaching and Policy, University of Washington.

Hubbard, L., Mehan, H., & Stein, M. (2006). *Reform as learning: School reform, organizational culture, and community politics in San Diego*. New York: Routledge.

Kennedy, M. M. (1982). Evidence and decision. In M. M. Kennedy (Ed.), *Working knowledge and other essays* (pp. 59–103). Cambridge, MA: Huron Institute.

Lave, J. (1998). *Cognition in practice: Mind, culture, and mathematics in everyday life*. Oxford: Cambridge University Press.

Levitt, B., & March, J. G. (1988). Organizational learning. *American Review of Sociology, 14*, 319–340.

Malen, B., Ogawa, R. T., & Kranz, J. (1990). What do we know about school-based management? A case study of the literature—A call for research. In W. H. Clune & J. F. White (Eds.), *Choice and control in American schools* (pp. 289–342). Philadelphia: Falmer.

March, J. G. (1994). *A primer on decision making*. New York: Free Press.

Marsh, J. A., Kerr, K. A., Ikemoto, G. S., & Darilek, H. (2004). The role of an intermediary organization in district instructional improvement: Early experiences and lessons about the Institute for Learning. In *Paper presented at the annual meeting of the American Educational Research Association*. San Diego: RAND.

Marsh, J. A., Kerr, K. A., Ikemoto, G. S., & Darilek, H. (2006). Developing district intermediary partnerships to promote instructional improvement: Early experiences and lessons about the Institute for Learning. In K. Wong & S. Rutledge (Eds.), *System-wide efforts to improve student achievement*. Greenwich: Information Age Publishing.

No Child Left Behind Act of 2001, Stat. 1425 (2002).

O'Day, J. A. (2002). Complexity, accountability, and school improvement. *Harvard Educational Review, 72*(3), 1–31.

Pea, R. (1987). Socializing the knowledge transfer problem. *International Journal of Educational Research, 11*(6), 639–663.

Ravitch, D., & Viteritti, J. P. (1997). *New schools for a new century: The redesign of urban education*. New Haven: Yale University Press.

Rogoff, B., Baker-Sennett, J., Lacasa, P., & Goldsmith, D. (1995). Development through participation in sociocultural activity. *New Directions for Child Development, 67*, 45.

Spillane, J. P., & Thompson, C. L. (1997). Reconstructing conceptions of local capacity: The local education agency's capacity for ambitious instructional reform. *Educational Evaluation and Policy Analysis, 19*(2), 185–203.

Spillane, J. P., Diamond, J. B., Burch, P., Hallett, T., Jita, L., & Zoltners, J. (2002). Managing in the middle: School leaders and the enactment of accountability policy. *Educational Policy, 16*(5), 731–763.

Tharp, R. G., & Gallimore, R. (1991). *Rousing minds to life: Teaching, learning, and schooling in social context*. New York: Cambridge University Press.

Tyack, D., & Cuban, L. (1995). *Tinkering toward utopia: A century of public school reform*. Cambridge, MA: Harvard University Press.

Weick, K. E. (1995). *Sensemaking in organizations*. Thousand Oaks: Sage.

Wenger, E. (1998). *Communities of practice: Learning, meaning, and identity*. Cambridge: Cambridge University Press.

Chapter 5
The Research on Education, Deliberation, and Decision-Making (REDD) Project

Robert Asen and Deb Gurke

The No Child Left Behind (NCLB) Act has pushed research-based decision-making to the forefront of educational policy and practice (Slavin 2002; Wiseman 2010). Mentioning "research" over 100 times, NCLB situates research evidence as the appropriate basis of decision-making for curriculum and instruction, professional development, and more (NCLB 2002; Smith 2003; Honig and Coburn 2008). A research-based approach to decision-making promises several benefits: first, to the extent to which it may provide a common reference point, research may help participants avoid political controversy and partisan battles (Bogenschneider and Corbett 2010; Wyckoff 2009). Second, research may provide a reliable guide to practice. In this spirit, the U.S. Department of Education's What Works Clearinghouse (2012) identifies its mission as serving as "a central and trusted source of scientific evidence for what works in education." Third, research may provide measures for educators, policymakers, and parents to assess the performances of schools in their communities (DeBray 2006; McDonnell 2004; McGuinn 2006).

Yet increased interest in research-based decision-making also has raised concerns among some education researchers regarding the seemingly narrow definition of research articulated in NCLB, which is signaled by the What Works Clearinghouse's reference to "scientific evidence" (Biesta 2007; Chatterji 2004; Cook and Gorard 2007; Trybus 2007). Hess (2008) characterizes the particular definition of research in NCLB and related Education Department efforts as a "medical model" that draws inspiration from clinical trials (see, e.g., Reyna 2002). Seeking to make space for a wider range of methods and frameworks, Hess counters that the

R. Asen (✉)
Department of Communication Arts, Institute for Research on Poverty,
University of Wisconsin-Madison, Madison, WI, USA
e-mail: rbasen@wisc.edu

D. Gurke
Department of Research and Development, Milwaukee Public Schools, Milwaukee, WI, USA

K.S. Finnigan and A.J. Daly (eds.), *Using Research Evidence in Education: From the Schoolhouse Door to Capitol Hill*, Policy Implications of Research in Education 2,
DOI 10.1007/978-3-319-04690-7_5,

social world of education presents contingencies that researchers do not encounter in a clinical setting. Hess (2008, p. 2) urges education scholars to recognize that "research is not a purely technical endeavor but, rather, must be understood as part of an ecosystem of interpreters, advocates, funders, and policymakers." Although education researchers have critiqued narrow "experimentist" (Howe 2005) approaches to research and policy, Hostetler (2010, p. 401) holds that a vision of education research as scientific only to the extent to which it replicates clinical models "could be the minority view among education researchers today, yet it enjoys the sanction of the US federal government."

Concerns expressed by education researchers about overly narrow definitions direct our attention to the contexts in which decision-makers use research evidence and the human relationships that shape this context. The Research on Education, Deliberation, and Decision-Making (REDD) Project focuses on local contexts of policymaking and the ways in which school district officials use—and do not use—research evidence in their decision-making. Our site of analysis was the school board meeting, and we examined the various positions expressed by board members and administrators on policy decisions. The research users in this project, then, were school board members and district administrators. Conducting fieldwork from fall 2009 to summer 2011, we focused on three medium-sized school districts in Wisconsin that vary in terms of socioeconomic status: Beloit, Elmbrook, and West Bend (Wisconsin Information Network for Successful Schools n.d.). Serving a working-class city along the Wisconsin-Illinois border, Beloit contains the highest levels of minority students and the highest levels of economically disadvantaged households. For the 2010–2011 school year, 73 % of Beloit students were designated as economically disadvantaged, and over half of all students were minorities. By contrast, Elmbrook, which encompasses some of the upper-middle-class suburbs west of Milwaukee, serves a financially stable and comparatively homogeneous population. For the 2010–2011 school year, only 11 % of the students were economically disadvantaged, and 20 % of the students were minorities. An "exburban" community northwest of Milwaukee, West Bend is a district in transition. For the 2010–2011 school year, 32 % of its students were economically disadvantaged, while only 10 % were minorities. Yet both figures represent substantial increases in the last 10 years, as the number of economically disadvantaged students has increased from 12 to 32 % and the number of minority students has increased from 4 to 10 % since the 2000–2001 school year.

We begin this chapter by discussing the deliberative framework that oriented our fieldwork and analysis of school board and committee meetings as well as interviews we conducted with board members and administrators. Next, we explain our method, which entailed a hybrid approach that made use of ethnographic observation of school board meetings and textual analysis of transcripts of board deliberations and interviews. We then turn to our findings, which address key issues of evidence (research based and non-research based), context, and trust. We conclude by discussing the implications of the REDD project, which we approach by noting our different perspectives as an academic-practitioner duo, and our contributions to both research and practice.

5.1 Framework

As the title of our project suggests, our approach foregrounds deliberation as an important aspect of educational policymaking. We define deliberation as a reciprocal process of reason giving and weighing of alternative perspectives and positions articulated around a perceived issue of common concern (Bohman 1996; Burkhalter et al. 2002; Gastil 2008; Gutmann and Thompson 2004). The idea of reason giving intimates that deliberation differs from declaration or assertion in that participants do not simply state a position but offer reasons *why* they hold a position and/or why others should subscribe to their view (Brockriede 1975; O'Keefe 1977; Toulmin 1958). However, reason giving does not necessitate a formal interaction guided by explicit rules and procedures and specified standards of evidence and devoid of emotional appeals and values. Scholars of deliberation have long pointed to the otherworldly character of formal logic and its limited utility in real-world contexts (see Cox and Willard 1982). Rather, we hold that people deliberate in a wide variety of ways: some participants may present a numbered list to state their reasons for supporting a policy, while others may tell stories to make their points (Fisher 1989; Hariman 2007; Palczewski 2002). We agree with Robert Ivie (2002, p. 278) that deliberation may proceed as a passionate, "rowdy" affair, where disagreement does not necessarily signal error but may indicate the expression of competing, reasonable proposals for addressing common problems. Moreover, deliberation proceeds as a context-specific encounter (Tindale 1999), which means that scholars should study deliberation "as issuing from actual people in a time-, place- and institution-bound context" (Keith 2007, p. 169).

As Burkhalter et al. (2002) maintain, "weighing" lies at the heart of most definitions of deliberation, because deliberation encourages participants to evaluate different proposals to arrive at a sound decision (Estlund 1997; Hicks 2002). Christian Kock and Lisa Villadsen (2012, p. 4) explain that weighing "implies holding together all reasons and considerations relevant to the issue—not only those of one's own that speak for a given policy but also others that may speak against it." Weighing invites a practice of considering the views of others and placing one's own position in the context of others' views (Arendt 1961; Asen 2004; Willard 1989). Weighing stands in contrast to simply voting without discussion or rubber-stamping a decision imposed by an authority.

We distinguish our conception of deliberation from some of the overly idealistic frameworks that have oriented research on deliberative democracy. In a seminal essay, Joshua Cohen (1997) discerns in deliberation an alternative to interest-based models of democracy and decision-making that assume that people's preferences cannot change and that differences must be resolved through negotiation. Instead, Cohen (1997, p. 72) envisions democratic decision-making as involving "a commitment to the resolution of problems of collective choice through public reasoning." While we support this move, we maintain that Cohen (1997, p. 75) at times asks too much of citizens, such as when he identifies consensus as the goal of deliberation: "ideal deliberation aims to arrive at a rationally motivated *consensus*—to find reasons that are persuasive to all who are committed to acting on the results of a free and reasoned assessment of alternatives by equals." Some scholars (e.g., Phillips 1996; Willard 1987) have argued that when consensus serves as a goal of deliberation, it may trivialize disagreement or compel holdouts to publicly support a position for the sake of a group. Decision-making amid disagreement better recognizes the diversity of local policy settings in school districts and elsewhere. Similarly, deliberation does not proceed as a disinterested effort to reach a decision apart from the particular interests of participants (see Habermas 1981/1984). On school boards and other decision-making bodies, members recognize that they may participate in a mutual process of both trying to understand other positions and trying to persuade others to accept their positions (Jacobs et al. 2009; Tracy 2010). This dual focus strengthens the deliberative process rather than diminishing it.

Proceeding with a deliberative orientation, we situate evidence as the support that participants offer for their positions. Interlocutors may offer a variety of types of evidence to support their positions, and they may combine evidence types in arguing for a position. In our analysis of school board meetings, we identified six different types of evidence: research, experience, testimony, data, example, and law/policy (Asen et al. 2013). We defined research as empirical findings derived from systematic analysis of information, guided by purposeful research questions and method. Experience referred to firsthand knowledge, skill, or perspective derived from direct observation of or participation in events or activities. Testimony was defined as representing through quotation or paraphrase the perspective of an individual or group. Data was defined as measurable quantitative or qualitative information systematically collected to describe a set of conditions or trends. Example indicated a specific case or incident used to illustrate typical or exceptional characteristics of a topic or issue. Law/policy was defined as rules and regulations that permit or prohibit particular actions, behaviors, or programs. Our definition of research evidence highlights analysis, questions, and method. These characteristics may be stated explicitly or they may be conveyed implicitly in an instance of research evidence. In developing this definition, we wanted to remain flexible enough to include practitioner-generated and district-generated research but also strict enough to distinguish among evidence types and to discount unsupported claims.

Focusing on the connection between evidence and deliberation, our framework contributes to the scholarship on the use of research evidence. First, our framework recognizes the wide variety of evidence employed by participants in deliberation and decision-making. Studies on the use of research evidence show that decision-makers and practitioners sometimes ascribe this variety to research itself (Honig and Coburn 2008; Nutley and Davies 2008). Second, just as deliberation operates as a collective enterprise, so, too, does the use of research evidence by school boards occur in a group setting, which underscores the importance of relationships (Tseng 2012; Finnigan et al. 2013). A single person—whether a board member, administrator, or someone else—may introduce research evidence during a board meeting, but once introduced the research evidence gets used by members of a group. While research may serve a variety of functions (Nutley and Davies 2008; Weiss 1980), these functions reflect the judgments of the group, though this judgment may not comport with the specific views of every member of a group. Third, as deliberation unfolds over time, the evidence used by participants in deliberation acquires meaning and significance. The use of research does not occur instantaneously, with board members and administrators fully understanding research evidence the moment someone introduces it. Rather, as deliberation proceeds, participants may come to appreciate the value of research evidence—or dismiss it. Further, as participants may return to specific research evidence over subsequent deliberative exchanges, the meaning and significance of this research evidence may shift.

5.2 Method

Studying deliberation and decision-making in Beloit, Elmbrook, and West Bend, we employed a hybrid approach that combined ethnographic observation of school board meetings and textual analysis of transcripts of board deliberations and interviews. School board meetings are not typically recorded, so transcripts of their meetings are generally not available. Attending and recording school board meetings allowed us to create texts that we could use to examine how school boards used research evidence in their deliberation and decision-making.

The REDD project encompassed two phases. In the first phase, which occurred during the 2009–2010 school year, members of the REDD team attended 160 school board meetings and committee meetings. While most of the meetings were sparsely attended, several drew large numbers of citizens, particularly in the West Bend district, which experienced a controversy over the budget in fall 2009. REDD members took field notes and made audio recordings of the meetings which were used to create transcripts. Given the large number of hours of recorded meetings, and the proportion of time during these meetings when board members did not engage in deliberation, we decided to review the audio recordings to identify when school board members were engaged in deliberation and transcribe only these sections. Each member of the REDD team read a subset of meeting transcripts and determined which sections of the transcripts constituted deliberation. We used the following criteria to determine which parts of meetings to transcribe: when school boards addressed a policy issue, such as Internet usage in the schools; when they exchanged reasons in support of or opposition to a policy initiative; and when board members considered an issue where they needed to take action. Applying these criteria to the 160 meetings, we determined that portions of 107 meetings warranted transcription. From a total of 260.5 h of recorded meeting time, we identified 109 h for transcription.

As qualitative, interpretive researchers, we approached the analysis of the transcripts from the perspective of critical discourse analysis (Campbell and Huxman 2009; Fairclough 1995; van Dijk 2008). As this approach references a range of analytic methods, we adopted a specific method of close textual analysis (Brummett 2009; Leff and Sachs 1990). Like grounded theory (Corbin and Strauss 2008), close textual analysis comprises an inductive method that instructs investigators to discern emergent concepts and themes in texts. Analysts approach texts with their research questions as a guide: ours concerned uncovering the relationships that constitute school board decision-making as a deliberative process.

The first step in our analysis required us to identify when board members used evidence and to create a list of evidence categories—both research and non-research based. Using a sample of meeting transcripts that were read by all members of the REDD team, we identified six categories of evidence types: experience, examples, testimony, data, research, and law/policy. We coded all of the transcripts for these six evidence types. Each transcript was coded by two people, and the individual results were compared to ensure consistency. When differences in coding arose, we returned to the meeting transcript of the specific meeting and reconciled the different interpretations as a group. Through this process, we identified various evidence types and the frequency of their use by board members, administrators, and others who participated in the meetings. After this initial approach, we returned to the transcripts to see how the various types of evidence fit into the context of the deliberation and to get a better understanding of how participants specifically used research evidence.

In the second phase, which proceeded during the spring and summer of 2011, we conducted 31 interviews with board members, administrators, and one community activist. Lasting between 1 and 2 h, our interviews followed a semi-structured, open-ended format. While modifying some of our questions slightly to account for district-specific issues, our interview protocol addressed three core areas: board dynamics, research, and district culture. With respect to board dynamics, we asked interviewees to describe their individual and their board's decision-making processes, including what they regarded as more and less productive aspects of these processes. We also inquired about interviewees' perceptions of the cohesiveness of their boards, their shared and/or differing senses of their district's mission, and their strategies for conflict resolution. Under research, we asked interviewees to identify the kinds of information they used in their decision-making, including research and other non-research types of evidence, as well as how they acquired this information. We queried about how they evaluated evidence to assess its credibility and reliability. We then asked the interviewees to define research, sharing with them the definition of research in NCLB and asking them to compare this definition with their own understanding. In terms of district culture, we inquired about their views of the proper role of the community in decision-making. We asked how they learned about community perspectives on educational issues and how they handled potential conflicts between their views and community perspectives. We also asked interviewees to indicate their view of the proper role that their personal views on education should play in their decision-making.

5.3 Findings

Our findings present a picture of research use in school board deliberations as a complex interaction of information, contexts, and human relationships. In school board deliberations, research evidence does not express a clear meaning and prescription for action independent of the people who use research evidence and the situations in which they use research evidence. Research evidence does not speak for itself, and even if it could speak, research evidence would not speak with one voice. Our findings may be clustered into themes of evidence, context, and trust. The theme of evidence refers to the ways that board members, administrators, and others use evidence—research and other types—for various purposes. The theme of context addresses the characteristics of speakers and local communities that influence research use. The theme of trust signals that the use of research evidence depends on the quality of the human relationships—with trust being a key indicator—among participants in school board deliberations.

5.3.1 *Evidence*

In our analyses of school board and committee meetings, we found that each of the evidence types used by board members offered opportunities to use evidence effectively. The use of the six evidence types described above revealed none as intrinsically superior or inferior but each as appropriate for use in particular situations. For instance, board members in West Bend engaged in an extensive debate about whether or not to offer 4-year-old kindergarten to children in the district, exchanging competing interpretations of research findings about the ability of 4 K to compensate for differences that children from different socioeconomic backgrounds experienced in their home environments. Board members did not delve extensively into the academic literature directly, but they nevertheless sought to ground their claims in research evidence. In contrast, when school board members in Elmbrook addressed 4 K, they relied more extensively on testimony, since they served a more privileged and homogeneous community, where they perceived the key issue relating to 4 K as whether the community would support the program. One interviewee stated that 4 K had become a key issue for board campaigns: "if you look at the blogging community, they're watching every single board election, every single board member. Will this person be a 4 K advocate or not?" In contrast, interviewees in West Bend did not attribute this level of public attention to 4 K. Participants in both of these debates over 4 K used the evidence they saw as appropriate for the issues they addressed.

Although board members and administrators in all three districts used research evidence, they did not rely on research evidence as extensively as other evidence types. In comparison to the other evidence types, research was used the fifth most frequently, ahead only of law/policy. Examples and experience constituted the most frequently used evidence types. More important than frequency, however, was the way that research was used. We discerned two uses: general and specific references. General references mentioned research only in passing, often providing incomplete and potentially misleading information about studies. General references to research represented inefficient uses, except in cases where all participants were familiar with the particularities of a study cited in passing. Specific references to research provided complete information about the questions, methods, populations, and designs of particular studies, informing the deliberations of board members and administrators. In debating the property tax levy in Beloit, one board member shared a study from the University of Wisconsin-Whitewater: "Researchers found that parents who live in communities with high property values with comparatively low tax rates often send their children to districts that spend more on students and presumably tax more as well." This statement demonstrates that specific references did not require extensive elaboration; in a single sentence, the board member noted the researchers, the study population, the research design, and the findings.

5.3.2 Context

While the use of research evidence overall trailed other evidence types, we found that some participants referred to research evidence more frequently than others. Individuals tended to reference research more frequently when their backgrounds and interests resonated with particular studies. Job experience that required the use of research and educational training that exposed people to research—regardless of the level of one's education—tended to increase references to research. In terms of interests, particular participants repeatedly mentioned some research paradigms during meetings. The Beloit superintendent frequently compared proposed reforms to what he championed as the "Stevenson model," referring to the high-performing Adlai Stevenson High School in Lincolnshire, Illinois, and its use of professional learning communities. For instance, in a discussion of student achievement, the superintendent remarked: "We always talk about Stevenson. Even though it's a high-performing school and all of that, they pretty much structure their whole school towards high achievement for all students and we're going to have to do the same thing." Board members and administrators tended to reference research specifically when addressing more homogeneous rather than heterogeneous audiences, since the former shared background knowledge and operated according to commonly recognized procedures. School board members and administrators looked to apply research to the specific contexts of their districts.

When using research evidence, school board members and administrators preferred more local forms of research evidence to findings from other states and localities. They resisted research evidence that they perceived as applicable elsewhere. This resistance appeared across levels of education, such that even board members and administrators with advanced degrees preferred to use Wisconsin studies to understand the issues in their districts. This finding does not mean that these local decision-makers rejected research conducted elsewhere, but that they wanted to see explicit connections to the contexts and issues faced in their own districts. A few Elmbrook board members expressed skepticism about statements claiming that the "research says," since they believed that studies referenced in debates over curricular reforms did not resonate with what they regarded as the distinctive, high-performing character of the Elmbrook school district. In debates over 4 K, for example, one board member recounted:

> We had one of the administrators stand up and say, well, 4 K has been proven to help your graduation rate, well our graduation rate is 99 %. I don't think adding 4 K is really going to

> affect it a lot. So you, you know, stand up, and you say that, and you have research that shows that 4 K helps your graduation rate, and that's all well and good, but that's not a problem that we have in our district.

This board member expressed a sentiment shared across the districts that board members sought research that they believed addressed district issues directly.

As they used research evidence during their meetings and discussed research during their interviews, board members and administrators operated with a wide understanding of what constituted research, which differed from the narrow definition presented in the No Child Left Behind Act (NCLB). Focusing on "scientifically based research," NCLB highlights objectivity, reliability, and validity in its definition of research, placing the greatest confidence in randomized control trials (Cook and Gorard 2007; Hess 2008; Hostetler 2010). In contrast, school board members and administrators understood research evidence widely, including academic research that fits the NCLB definition but also qualitative research, district-generated research, practitioner reports and studies, widely accepted practices, feasible practices, longstanding practices, and district policies and procedures. While some of these variations may raise legitimate concerns about the rigor of the evidence understood as research—such as casual Google searches that did not assess the credibility of online sources—we found that their broader understanding of research better accounted for complexities of their decision-making, which required these local policymakers to balance technical considerations against the needs, interests, and values of their communities. Even though some Elmbrook board members sometimes expressed skepticism about what the "research says," they nevertheless served on district committees that produced sophisticated analyses of district enrollment trends, tying projections to a range of local factors. Along these lines, the board commissioned an Enrollment Management Study Team (EMST) in 2010 consisting of board members and community residents. The EMST met regularly and produced a detailed technical report evaluating and scoring various proposals to reduce a budget deficit.

5.3.3 Trust

In their interviews, board members and administrators identified trust as a key factor that influenced their use of research-based and non-research-based types of evidence. Trust matters because research often appears in educational decision-making contexts through the statements of particular participants, who may be subjected to the judgments of others (Bryk and Schneider 2002; Daly and Finnigan 2012; Tseng 2012). When a board member and/or administrator presents a viewpoint supported by research evidence, others make judgments about the credibility and trustworthiness not only of the evidence cited but also of the person presenting the evidence. Judgments about the latter may shape understandings and evaluations of the former. Higher levels of trust among decision-makers may encourage the adoption of research presented during deliberations, and low levels of trust may discourage the adoption of research. In West Bend, as elections changed the composition of the school board, tensions between the board and the administration increased during the period of our fieldwork, such that some board members refused to accept anything that the administration—especially the superintendent—said at face value. Justifying this skepticism, one board member complained that the information the board received was "spoon fed for us from the district." This board member held that the administration "wants you to vote in a specific direction . . . The information you're going to get is going to be skewed to that point." Another board member who supported the administration retorted that his colleagues had "trust issues against the administration" that produced a knee-jerk reaction: "It was, 'I don't believe the administration. I don't know why, but I don't.'" A district administrator offered a third perspective. Referring to the entire board, this person observed that "there's so little trust there if, if they're not all in the room together they're automatically going to ask questions."

Rather than understanding trust as a uniform practice, board members and administrators ascribed different qualities of trust to the different relationships they maintained with people in the district. Four relationships of trust emerged from our interviews: administrators and school board members, among board members, decision-makers (administrators and school board members) and researchers, and decision-makers and the community. While articulating some similarities, interviewees also ascribed distinct qualities that fostered trust in each of these four relationships. These qualities comported with what they saw as the different roles and responsibilities of actors in an organization (Lewicki et al. 1998; Pirson and Malhotra 2011). Although only one of the four relationships that emerged through our interviews explicitly references research, all four relationships may influence decision-makers' willingness to use research- and non-research-based evidence. As the above quotes suggest, some board members in West Bend transferred their distrusting relationship with the administration to the researchers that the administration cited; these researchers, some board members believed, also operated with an agenda. One board member held that "I know there's plenty of studies out there that can tell us every possible way to do things, but then for every study we're going to find another study tells us, 'no, you should do it this way.'" Further, interviewees reported that a single person's behavior could positively or negatively influence relations of trust among groups of decision-makers, such that an adept board member or administrator could mediate potential breaches of trust while a disruptive person could weaken wider relationships of trust. In Beloit, board members praised the transparency of the current superintendent, who was hired into the district as we began our fieldwork, in helping to repair previously strained relations with the board and the previous administration. Recalling the previous superintendent, one board member explained:

> There was no trust there, because there was a belief, which was expressed and felt differently by different board members, but there was a belief that became almost universal among the board members that, you know, he was manipulating data and information in order to fool us into thinking that we were doing better than we really were.

The current superintendent interacted with the board openly and directly, which improved relations: "We bring in [the current superintendent] who is Mr. Transparent, Mr. Honest, Mr. Here's-What-It-Is guy, and, you know, that was, again, that was a good transition." In West Bend, a shifting composition of decision-makers weakened relations of trust, while in Beloit a change strengthened relations of trust.

5.4 Implications

As an academic-practitioner duo, we believe that discussing these ideas through our distinct voices may illuminate the implications of our project. We believe that our different approaches to this subject matter have created a productive dynamic in our investigations, presentations, and publications. Our collaboration itself may exemplify a means of furthering the use of appropriate evidence—research and other types—in deliberation and decision-making.

As someone who studies public policy deliberation, Asen sees the methodological implications of the REDD project in its combination of ethnographic observation, interviewing, and textual analysis. Analyzing transcripts of board and committee meetings (the "texts" in this project) enables careful examination of how participants make arguments, how they respond to the arguments of others, how they support—or fail to support—their arguments with evidence, and how they evaluate evidence presented by others. As a complementary method, ethnographic observation and interviews offer insights into people's motives, perceptions of relationships with others, nonverbal means of communication, and unspoken group dynamics that may inform deliberation. Some communication scholars have utilized multiple methods (see, e.g., Hess 2011; Pezzullo 2007; Middleton et al. 2011), but this approach remains underdeveloped.

As someone who has served on and worked with school boards, supporting their efforts to improve their ability to effectively govern their districts, Gurke sees the findings as evidence of the need for school board members to improve their communication with one another and with members of the administrative team. In her work, Gurke has observed school board members participating in many of the same behaviors as those that surfaced in the REDD project and has developed training that enables school board members to improve their deliberation, including incorporating practices of inquiry to break through conflicts when deliberation gets stuck.

Conceptually, our project may help widen the discussion of evidence-based decision-making from the currently prominent emphasis on scientifically based research to other types of evidence used by decision-makers. With this emphasis comes an implicit—and sometimes explicit (Wyckoff 2009)—hierarchy of evidence types that places particular types of research at the top. Yet any such hierarchy appears disconnected from any actual use and fails to recognize the limits of research evidence, such as its inability to adjudicate fundamental value conflicts. Our project also underscores the importance of moving away from linear models of policymaking that restrict the use of research evidence to various stages, to a multidirectional model that recognizes how research evidence may be introduced by different people at different stages in the process to accomplish various purposes (Stone 1997).

Sometimes, policymakers may address a problem and use research evidence to help identify an efficacious solution. At other times, research evidence may be used to justify already accepted solutions (Nutley et al. 2007; Weiss 1977). In any case, these possibilities and others should dampen dreams of a value-free decision-making process. Furthermore, our project points to the pivotal role of meaning making and interpretation in the use of research evidence in policymaking. Instrumentalist approaches often assume that information, which incorporates research evidence, circulates with transparent and common meanings (Fischer 2003). In contrast, our project shows that different participants may interpret the very same piece of research evidence in different ways, which leads them to support different policies.

Further, our project confirms a model of trust in local school districts as relational (Bryk and Schneider 2002). To build trust, practices of inquiry may need to precede deliberation geared toward decision-making. We offer a series of questions that may facilitate participants taking time to engage with the research. Simply referring to "the research" shortchanges the contribution that a more complete consideration of the research could provide. Research rarely speaks with one voice, so looking at the research in more detail can uncover differences. Participants may start with questions that uncover the basic details of the study, as well as the details that matter to specific individuals. These observational questions include the following:

- Who conducted the study?
- What question does the study try to answer?
- When was the study done? Is it timely?
- Are the study's subjects comparable to your situation?
- Are the students similar in terms of age, racial composition, gender, diversity?
- What are some of the study's key points?

Participants also may benefit from spending time understanding the various value positions of the deliberators. School board members can use questions to uncover the value positions of the various members of the school board. Spending the time to understand the various perspectives of board members, rather than working as if values were not part of the discussion, can help everyone understand the various positions around the table and contribute to a richer discussion of the issues. The following questions serve as a basis for engaging in that inquiry:

- What do you most appreciate about the studies and what does that mean to you?
- Why is this important to you? What concerns you most about the studies? What new insights or ideas have you gained?
- What implications does each study bring to the district?
- Do board members agree in some areas, and can you build on those to reach a decision that is acceptable to all?
- How do these studies resonate with our community's values?
- How do these studies help us advance our strategic plan?

District officials also must consider several potential audiences. Administrators should consider the school board as an audience. School board members come from a variety of backgrounds, and they may not be familiar with education jargon, complex policy issues like finance, and dynamics that may play out under various iterations of their decisions. The community may also play the role of an audience, as various stakeholders will engage and disengage as issues come and go. Community members may not be aware of the history of an issue, the limitations statutes can place on potential options, the costs and impact of various issues on the district's budget, and more. Individuals presenting information to various audiences should consider their needs. Here are some questions that may facilitate this reflection:

- What does my audience know about the issue?
- How involved have people been in the issue?
- Have all interests been considered and acknowledged?
- What examples or experience might help explain this research?

Federal policymakers could consider how local approaches to decision-making and uses of evidence may differ. By adopting a strict definition of research evidence in NCLB, federal policymakers lose a valuable opportunity to learn from localities, which often generate crucial insights in "nonscientific" but systematic ways. Policymakers need to work to build trust with each other as well as with people who provide them with information for decision-making. This effectively entails accepting the implications of a relational conception of trust. Doing so would mean that under strained relations of trust, policymakers would not simply give up or hope for an improvement, and under productive relations, policymakers would not take for granted their successes. Local policymakers would benefit from greater interactions with policymakers in other localities to recognize similarities in their situations. This might engender greater receptivity to research evidence generated from other districts and a greater commitment to the scholarly principle of generalizability.

Even as the role of state and federal governments in education policy has expanded, school boards continue to play an important role in policymaking. Researchers could be clearer about this when communicating research to state and federal policymakers. The REDD project has sought to understand how school board members, administrators, and others use research evidence in their deliberation and decision-making. We have operated with the belief that research evidence alone cannot direct policymakers to sound decisions. Instead, researchers and practitioners alike must combine research evidence with a better understanding of policymakers' deliberative practices and a commitment to bolstering trust as well as decision-making, combining research use with an openness to inquiry.

References

Arendt, H. (1961). *Between past and future*. New York: Viking Press.

Asen, R. (2004). A discourse theory of citizenship. *Quarterly Journal of Speech, 90*, 189–211.

Asen, R., Gurke, D., Conners, P., Solomon, R., & Gumm, E. (2013). Research evidence and school board deliberations: Lessons from three Wisconsin school districts. *Educational Policy, 27*, 33–63.

Biesta, G. (2007). Why 'what works' won't work: Evidence-based practice and the democratic deficit in education research. *Education Theory, 57*(1), 1–22.

Bogenschneider, K., & Corbett, T. J. (2010). *Evidence-based policymaking: Insights from policy-minded researchers and research-minded policymakers*. New York: Routledge.

Bohman, J. (1996). *Public deliberation: Pluralism, complexity, and democracy*. Cambridge, MA: Massachusetts Institute of Technology.

Brockriede, W. (1975). Where is argument? *Journal of the American Forensic Association, 11*, 179–182.
Brummett, B. (2009). *Techniques of close reading*. Los Angeles: Sage.
Bryk, A. S., & Schneider, B. (2002). *Trust in schools: A core resource for improvement*. New York: Russell Sage Foundation.
Burkhalter, S., Gastil, J., & Kelshaw, K. (2002). A conceptual definition and theoretical model of public deliberation in small face-to-face groups. *Communication Theory, 12*, 398–422.
Campbell, K. K., & Huxman, S. S. (2009). *The rhetorical act: Thinking, speaking, and writing critically*. Boston: Wadsworth.
Chatterji, M. (2004). Evidence on 'what works': An argument for extended term mixed method (ETMM) evaluation designs. *Educational Researcher, 33*(9), 3–13.
Cohen, J. (1997). Deliberation and democratic legitimacy. In J. Bohman & W. Rehg (Eds.), *Deliberative democracy: Essays on reason and politics* (pp. 67–91). Cambridge, MA: Massachusetts Institute of Technology Press.
Cook, T., & Gorard, S. (2007). What counts and what should count as evidence. In *Evidence in education: Linking research and policy* (pp. 33–49). Paris: Organisation for Economic Co-operation and Development.
Corbin, J., & Strauss, A. (2008). *Basics of qualitative research: Techniques and procedures for developing grounded theory* (3rd ed.). Thousand Oaks: Sage.
Cox, J. R., & Willard, C. A. (1982). *Advances in argumentation theory and research*. Carbondale: Southern Illinois University Press.
Daly, A. J., & Finnigan, K. S. (2012). Exploring the space between: Social networks, trust, and urban school district leaders. *Journal of School Leadership, 22*, 493–530.
DeBray, E. H. (2006). *Politics, ideology, & education: Federal policy during the Clinton and Bush administrations*. New York: Teachers College Press.
Estlund, D. (1997). Beyond fairness and deliberation: The epistemic dimension of democratic authority. In J. Bohman & W. Rehg (Eds.), *Deliberative democracy: Essays on reason and politics* (pp. 173–204). Cambridge, MA: Massachusetts Institute of Technology Press.
Fairclough, N. (1995). *Critical discourse analysis: The critical study of language*. London: Longman.
Finnigan, K. S., Daly, A. J., & Che, J. (2013). Systemwide reform in districts under pressure: The role of social networks in defining, acquiring, using, and diffusing research evidence. *Journal of Educational Administration, 51*, 476–497.
Fischer, F. (2003). *Reframing public policy: Discursive politics and deliberative practices*. New York: Oxford University Press.
Fisher, W. R. (1989). *Human communication as narration: Toward a philosophy of reason, value, and action*. Columbia: University of South Carolina Press.
Gastil, J. (2008). *Political communication and deliberation*. Thousand Oaks: Sage.
Gutmann, A., & Thompson, D. (2004). *Why deliberative democracy?* Princeton: Princeton University Press.
Habermas, J. (1984). *The theory of communicative action, volume one: Reason and the rationalization of society* (T. McCarthy, Trans.). Boston: Beacon Press. (Original work published 1981)
Hariman, R. (2007). Amateur hour: Knowing what to love in ordinary democracy. In K. Tracy, J. P. McDaniel, & B. E. Gronbeck (Eds.), *The prettier doll: Rhetoric, discourse, and ordinary democracy* (pp. 218–249). Tuscaloosa: University of Alabama Press.
Hess, F. M. (2008). When education research matters. *Education Outlook, 1*, 1–6.
Hess, A. (2011). Critical-rhetorical ethnography: Rethinking the place and process of rhetoric. *Communication Studies, 62*, 127–152.
Hicks, D. (2002). The promise(s) of deliberative democracy. *Rhetoric & Public Affairs, 5*, 223–260.
Honig, M. I., & Coburn, C. (2008). Evidence-based decision making in school district central offices. *Educational Policy, 22*, 578–608.
Hostetler, K. (2010). (Mis)understanding human beings: Theory, value, and progress in education research. *Educational Studies, 46*, 400–415.

Howe, K. R. (2005). The question of education science: Experimentism versus experimentalism. *Educational Theory, 55*, 307–321.
Ivie, R. L. (2002). Rhetorical deliberation and democratic politics in the here and now. *Rhetoric & Public Affairs, 5*, 277–285.
Jacobs, L. R., Cook, F. L., & Delli Carpini, M. X. (2009). *Talking together: Public deliberation and political participation in America*. Chicago: University of Chicago Press.
Keith, W. M. (2007). *Democracy as discussion: Civic education and the American forum movement*. Lanham: Rowman & Littlefield.
Kock, C., & Villadsen, L. (2012). Introduction: Citizenship as rhetorical practice. In C. Kock & L. Villadsen (Eds.), *Rhetorical citizenship and public deliberation* (pp. 1–10). University Park: Pennsylvania State University Press.
Leff, M., & Sachs, A. (1990). Words the most like things: Iconicity and the rhetorical text. *Western Journal of Speech Communication, 54*, 252–273.
Lewicki, R. J., McAllister, D. T., & Bies, R. J. (1998). Trust and distrust: New relationships and realities. *Academy of Management Review, 23*, 438–458.
McDonnell, L. M. (2004). *Politics, persuasion, and educational testing*. Cambridge: Harvard University Press.
McGuinn, P. J. (2006). *No Child Left Behind and the transformation of federal education policy, 1965–2005*. Lawrence: University Press of Kansas.
Middleton, M. K., Senda-Cook, S., & Endres, D. (2011). Articulating rhetorical field methods: Challenges and tensions. *Western Journal of Communication, 75*, 386–406.
No Child Left Behind Act of 2001, Pub. L. No. 107–110, § 9101, 115 Stat. 1552, 1645, 1964–1965 (2002).
Nutley, S., & Davies, H. (2008). *Using research to provide stronger services and programs for youth: A discussion paper for the William T Grant Foundation*. Unpublished manuscript.
Nutley, S., Walter, I., & Davies, H. T. O. (2007). *Using evidence: How research can inform public services*. Bristol: Policy Press.
O'Keefe, D. J. (1977). Two concepts of argument. *Journal of the American Forensic Association, 13*, 121–128.
Palczewski, C. H. (2002). Argument in an off key: Playing with the productive limits of argument. In G. T. Goodnight (Ed.), *Arguing communication and culture* (pp. 1–23). Washington, DC: National Communication Association.
Pezzullo, P. (2007). *Toxic tourism: Rhetorics of pollution, travel, and environmental justice*. Tuscaloosa: University of Alabama Press.
Phillips, K. (1996). The spaces of public dissension: Reconsidering the public sphere. *Communication Monographs, 63*, 231–248.
Pirson, M., & Malhotra, D. (2011). Foundations of organizational trust: What matters to different stakeholders? *Organization Science, 22*, 1087–1104.
Reyna, V. (2002, February). *What is scientifically based evidence? What is its logic?* Presentation at the use of scientifically based research in education conference, U.S. Department of Education, Washington, DC.
Slavin, R. E. (2002). Evidence-based education policies: Transforming educational practice and research. *Educational Researcher, 31*(7), 15–21.
Smith, A. (2003). Scientifically based research and evidence-based education: A federal policy context. *Research & Practice for Persons with Severe Disabilities, 28*, 126–132.
Stone, D. (1997). *Policy paradox: The art of political decision making*. New York: Norton.
Tindale, C. W. (1999). *Acts of arguing: A rhetorical model of argument*. Albany: State University of New York Press.
Toulmin, S. E. (1958). *The uses of argument*. Cambridge: Cambridge University Press.
Tracy, K. (2010). *Challenges of ordinary democracy: A case study in deliberation and dissent*. University Park: Pennsylvania State University Press.
Trybus, M. (2007). Understanding scientifically based research: A mandate or decision tool? *Delta Kappa Gamma Bulletin, 73*(4), 5–8.
Tseng, V. (2012). The uses of research in policy and practice. *Social Policy Report, 26*, 3–16.

Van Dijk, T. A. (2008). *Discourse and context: A sociocognitive approach*. Cambridge: Cambridge University Press.
Weiss, C. H. (1977). Research for policy's sake: The enlightenment function of social research. *Policy Analysis, 3*, 531–545.
Weiss, C. H. (1980). Knowledge creep and decision accretion. *Knowledge: Creation, Diffusion, Utilization, 1*(3), 381–404.
What Works Clearinghouse. (2012). *About us*. Retrieved September 12, 2012, from http://ies.ed.gov/ncee/wwc/aboutus.aspx
Willard, C. A. (1987). Valuing dissensus. In F. H. van Eemeren, R. Grootendorst, J. A. Blair, & C. A. Willard (Eds.), *Argumentation: Across the lines of discipline* (pp. 145–157). Dordrecht: Foris.
Willard, C. A. (1989). *A theory of argumentation*. Tuscaloosa: University of Alabama Press.
Wisconsin Information Network for Successful Schools. (n.d.). WINSS successful school guide: Data analysis. Retrieved from http://data.dpi.state.wi.us/data/
Wiseman, A. W. (2010). The uses of evidence for educational policymaking: Global contexts and international trends. *Review of Research in Education, 34*, 1–24.
Wyckoff, P. G. (2009). *Policy and evidence in a partisan age: The great disconnect*. Washington, DC: Urban Institute Press.

Chapter 6
The Intermediary Function in Evidence Production, Promotion, and Utilization: The Case of Educational Incentives

Janelle Scott, Christopher Lubienski, Elizabeth DeBray, and Huriya Jabbar

6.1 Introduction

At least two factors are transforming educational policymaking in the USA. First, the federal government has expanded its role in education over the last decade around particular reform agendas, while foundations and philanthropies have championed some of the same reforms at the state and school district levels by funding pilot programs, expansion efforts, and research in support of these policies. Secondly, philanthropic and public policymakers increasingly demand evidence of the effectiveness of educational interventions. These dynamics have invigorated an already vibrant sector of intermediary organizations (IOs) that seek to package and promote research on educational policies and programs for policymakers, typically around a specific policy agenda.

The policies of concern in our research are those that fall into the incentivist arena: charter schools, vouchers, "parent trigger" laws, merit pay for teachers, and pay-for-performance for students, for example. Because these policies are politically charged, and as such, particularly conducive to advocates using evidence to promote their efficacy and expand their adoption or provide proof of their shortcomings in order to curtail their use, they are an especially fruitful policy area

J. Scott (✉)
Graduate School of Education and African American Studies Department, University of California-Berkeley, Berkeley, CA, USA
e-mail: jtscott@berkeley.edu

C. Lubienski
College of Education, University of Illinois, Champaign, IL, USA

E. DeBray
Department of Lifelong Education, Administration and Policy, College of Education, University of Georgia, Athens, GA, USA

H. Jabbar
Graduate School of Education, University of California-Berkeley, Berkeley, CA, USA

K.S. Finnigan and A.J. Daly (eds.), *Using Research Evidence in Education: From the Schoolhouse Door to Capitol Hill*, Policy Implications of Research in Education 2,
DOI 10.1007/978-3-319-04690-7_6,

in which to build knowledge on the political use of research evidence. In addition, advocates of incentivist reforms have identified the pollination of selected urban districts as the best way to show evidence of the reforms' effectiveness, in the hopes that national, state, and other local district policymakers will be convinced by what they believe to be the success stories of these local policy cases and expand them across the country.

A number of researchers have examined educational IOs and their research/evidence functions across a range of policy tiers. IOs may work in partnership with school districts to facilitate the use of research-based curricular and instructional reforms and help with their implementation (Coburn et al. 2009; Honig 2004), with state governments to enact school improvement strategies (Massell et al. 2012; Goertz et al. 2013), and at the national level to persuade policymakers to enact particular policies or initiatives, such as the Common Core State Standards (McDonnell and Weatherford 2013). This literature has yielded rich and valuable insights about the multiplicity of ways in which sundry individuals and IOs promote, produce, and utilize research evidence to improve or influence educational policy, often through particular social networks within school districts or state governments (Finnigan et al. 2013). This literature has also made clear that IOs operate in incredibly diverse fashion and that a broadening of our gaze on this sector to the political arena can help to shed additional insight into their place in the overall landscape of research utilization. Our research on IOs and incentivist reforms benefits from the findings of sociological investigations of research utilization and extends those insights to an examination of the political terrain.

We conceptualize IOs and their role in incentivist educational policies in a multifaceted way, focusing on the function they serve. Our definition of intermediary organizations is broad *and* targeted in order to capture the range of organizations that are producing, promoting, and utilizing research evidence around incentivist reforms. In our research, we see IOs as brokers, producers, funders, interpreters, and disseminators of research. In terms of their utilization of research evidence, they perform multiple functions and, most importantly for our case, operate in a highly politicized landscape. Yet our research indicates that intermediaries are performing multiple roles in incentivist educational reforms and that these roles are increasingly blurring the lines between research, policymaking, and political advocacy. For example, many IOs are not only providing research evidence on charter schools, but are also funding the incubation of new charter schools, such as New Schools for New Orleans. We include as IOs nonprofit and for-profit nongovernmental groups that work in coalition with one another *and* between districts, school boards, state and federal government, and schools. Intermediaries can provide start-up funding and sundry curricular and administrative support. Some intermediaries have a network of affiliated schools. As we discuss in this chapter, IOs serve different roles around research production, promotion, and consumption, and some engage in different aspects of these activities, where one or more is slightly more prominent depending on the organizational and strategic goals and on the organization's research capacity. Table 6.1 provides a taxonomy of the kinds of IOs included in our research.

Table 6.1 The intermediary sector and research function

IOs by type	Examples of IOs by type	Research function (producer, promoter, consumer)
Think tanks/ research institutes	American Enterprise Institute, Pelican Institute, Brookings Institute, Center on Reinventing Public Education, Research Alliance for New York City	Producer/promoter
Foundations	The Broad Foundation, The Rose Foundation, The Piton Foundation, The Walton Family Foundation	Producer/promoter/ consumer
Advocacy groups	Students First, Democrats for Education Reform, Stand for Children, Parents Across America, Network for Public Education	Producer/promoter/ consumer
Civil rights organizations	NAACP, Parent Revolution, Urban League, La Raza	Producer/promoter/ consumer
Teachers unions/ professional organizations	National Education Association, American Federation of Teachers, American School Boards Association	Producer/promoter/ consumer
News media and social media	Education Week, Education Nation, Twitter, Facebook, Blogs, Documentaries	Producer/consumer
School reform organizations	KIPP, New Schools for New Orleans, New Leaders for New Schools, Teach For America, National Alliance for Public Charter Schools	Producer/promoter/ consumer

6.1.1 Organization of the Chapter

We organize the chapter into three major sections in order to discuss the ways in which many of these IOs are working to produce, promote, or utilize research evidence. First, after providing a more detailed discussion of the current policy context, we offer an enhanced conceptualization of IOs and their multiple functions in the educational policy landscape, drawing from existing research literature. Secondly, drawing from our study of IOs and research utilization, we consider how these IOs function to shape research and its use through their efforts at funding, interpreting, and dissemination around incentivist reforms like charter schools, teacher compensation incentives, and student pay-for-performance. We discuss several findings that demonstrate the ways in which intermediaries are assuming a political role in the research production and promotion process. Finally, we discuss the implications of the intermediary function in the case of incentivist educational reforms for policymakers, researchers, and practitioners.

6.2 Policy Context

Over the last 15 years, the Bush and Obama Administrations have explicitly emphasized the importance of research on educational interventions, demanding evidence of effectiveness in improving schooling. For instance, the landmark *No Child*

Left Behind (NCLB) legislation repeatedly called for "scientifically based research," and shortly after assuming office, the Obama Administration declared that the multibillion-dollar Race to the Top (RttT) funding would be dispersed based on "what works," not on ideological preferences or fads (*Washington Post* 2009). Similarly, venture philanthropists are searching for assurance that their investments in educational reforms will pay off in terms of better outcomes for students, and also are promoting evidence that the reforms they favor are having their desired effects (Scott 2009).

Yet even as policymakers, funders, and reformers endorse an evidence-based standard for the scaling up of particular school reforms, many popular reforms such as charter schools and pay-for-performance for teachers and students have been expanding virally despite the lack of research consensus regarding their effectiveness. Researchers have proposed that some ideas are advanced by repeated citations to a small, select group of studies, thereby creating a self-containing "echo chamber" (Lubienski and Garn 2010). This theory about a research evidence echo chamber in the case of incentivist educational reforms raises questions about what research gets promoted, cited, and utilized and what evidence might be relatively neglected (Goldie et al. 2014). Thus, the push by public and private/philanthropic policymakers to endorse policies based on demonstrated evidence of effectiveness, however laudable, begs the question as to who defines "what works" and also what evidence counts in the politics of research utilization. Indeed, the increasing gulf between the notably bipartisan educational agendas of policymakers regarding some popular reforms and the findings from established research communities suggests that if research evidence is indeed important to policymakers, they are often drawing from sources other than the traditional university- and think tank-based sector. To date, however, it has been unclear from what organizations and individual researchers such evidence is generated.

The rapid spread of several prominent education policy approaches, spurred on by considerable federal and private resources, reflects a new political environment for educational policymaking in which is emerging a broad consensus regarding the usefulness of incentives in education—a policy agenda actively advanced by new IOs that operate in the space between policymaking and traditional modes of knowledge production. Yet there has been virtually no systematic or comprehensive analysis of the evidence such groups use to promote their agendas, nor how their efforts actually impact policymakers.

Furthermore, we believe that it is important to point out that the very idea of "policymaking" now encompasses both public policymakers in the government and policymakers based at private philanthropies and foundations that often span traditional ideological and partisan divides. Foundations and philanthropies are proving to be pivotal in the educational intermediary organization sector. These nongovernmental entities have gained considerable influence in terms of setting agendas and funding pilot projects, research centers, media, and reform strategies. For instance, they can often dictate policy preconditions for granting substantial resources to cash-starved districts—often working with public policymakers as well as with other private groups to promote specific agendas. Thus, the philanthropic sector does not simply provide funding, but establishes and advances policy. In this way, philanthropies are assuming multiple roles: they function as intermediaries themselves, they provide funding to strengthen existing intermediaries, and they invest resources in helping to create new ones (Scott and Jabbar 2014). Intermediaries are actively participating in the educational policy process in ways as yet not well understood by policy researchers. Therefore, public and private policymaking appears to be shaping the institutional landscape in which intermediaries broker research evidence.

6.3 Conceptual Framework: The New Politics of Research Utilization in an Era of Intermediary Influence

Our framework joins literatures from political science, educational reform, and an array of work on research utilization from multiple disciplines, including sociology, economics, and public policy. A new politics of research utilization has emerged in the context of "incentivist" educational reforms—i.e., charter schools, teacher merit pay, vouchers, parent trigger laws, and student rewards premised on the notion that extrinsic rewards are the best approach for improving education. We extend the literature on research utilization to include the interaction between national policymakers, intermediaries, and school districts. In this new policy terrain, we see IOs working on the supply and demand sides for evidence in support and opposition to these highly contested politicized educational policies. And as we have noted, advocates and opponents in national and local policy coalitions understand that the school districts where incentivist reforms are underway are, in many ways, demonstration sites to further expand or curtail the reforms in other districts and across the country.

6.3.1 Supply Side: Examining the IO Networks of Evidence Production

To analyze the emerging role of these new networks of IOs, which channel the production and consumption of research—and in so doing, comprise what we understand to be the "supply side" of research in support of incentivist reforms—we started with the Advocacy Coalition Framework (ACF). However, there are several complementary perspectives that help us to refine our conceptual analysis of what we term "local intermediary organization (IO) networks."

According to the ACF, a policy "subsystem" in a given domain consists of "actors from a variety of public and private organizations who are actively concerned with a public problem or issue" and includes not just the traditional "iron triangle" of interest groups, the executive agencies, and the Congress but also "journalists, researchers, and policy analysts, all of whom play important roles in the generation, dissemination, and evaluation of policy ideas" (Sabatier and Jenkins-Smith 1999, p. 17).

Since its inception in 1993, the ACF has allowed researchers to examine the role of advocacy organizations, researchers, journalists, and policymakers in formulating, advocating for, and adopting policy initiatives in a particular policy subsystem.

In addition to the ACF, there are several other complementary perspectives about education coalitions that characterize the local IO networks, or policy communities, including perspectives that highlight the role that foundations play in setting policy (Ball and Junemann 2012; Scott 2009; Reckhow 2012). Stephen Ball and Carolina Junemann (2012) also highlight the changing nature of government in relation to those outside in the "reform" community: those inside the government are increasingly likely to "contract out" policymaking to those outside. At least in England, they contend, this shift toward network governance has occurred partly because it is viewed as a way to bring more players to bear in a process of problem-solving; and also, policy networks "can provide an environment for consensus building" that can then limit implementation resistance (Ball and Junemann 2012, pp. 5–6). Lubienski (2013) describes this not as policies promoting privatization, but privatization of the policymaking process. Scott and Jabbar (2013) have identified the role philanthropies are playing in the funding and implementation of data gathering, analysis, and communication of research on student performance to media, policymakers, and reform networks.

That is, many IOs seem to be acting in concert around specific issues, with efforts toward research funding, production, and "harvesting" or accumulation; interpretation and packaging research for policymakers; and media penetration and management of public perceptions. Rick Hess, Director of Education Policy at the American Enterprise Institute, summed up this type of integration as it operates around school choice programs: "In Wisconsin, the Bradley Foundation and the Olin Foundation were instrumental in getting the Milwaukee Parental Choice Program passed — the first real voucher model in the country. They were then instrumental in providing political air cover for the program. They found and supported researchers to document it, and they helped promote it nationally. The Walton Family Foundation has done the same thing with charter schools…" (quoted in Barr et al. 2008).

While popular conceptions of policymaking processes may assume that education policymakers carefully weigh research evidence on complex issues, this generally does not appear to be the case. As Nelson et al. (2009) have shown in their study of education policymaking, people responsible for making policy decisions often feel ill equipped to interpret or evaluate complex research reports. Instead, they often rely on intermediary individuals or organizations to gather, summarize, and package research for policymakers—a function that gives such intermediaries a remarkable authority in representing the research evidence. To date, there has not yet been sufficient scrutiny of the role of intermediaries in research acquisition, interpretation, and implementation, particularly in terms of their role in shaping educational policies.[1] There does exist a rich and helpful body of research on the use of research evidence in education that has focused on the school and classroom level

[1] The Campbell Collection is an attempt to follow educational research use in policymaking and is an exception to this overall trend.

and within and across school districts from which our study benefits (see, e.g., Gurke et al. 2011; Daly and Finnigan 2009; Finnigan et al. 2013; Coburn and Talbert 2006).

As a result, there is a good conceptual and empirical foundation for understanding research use in schools, classrooms, and school districts and the role intermediaries play in shaping that research utilization, particularly framed with insights from organizational sociology (Coburn 2005). Much of this work demonstrates a complex context for the use of research evidence in decision-making and policy adoption and implementation. While some policy actors are receptive and desirous of research evidence to inform their thinking, they vary greatly on how they use such evidence and what other sources of information they employ to make informed decisions. Moreover, researchers have discovered that much of the evidence utilized is anecdotal, subject to multiple interpretations, and utilized conceptually or symbolically. Our goal is to extend this broader literature on research utilization to include the political interaction between intermediary organization representatives, policymakers, and school district officials. This intermediary sector includes think tanks and policy centers but also encompasses networks of single-issue advocacy outfits, coalitions of groups with common areas of interest, philanthropic organizations, and nonprofit associations—often with substantial resources as well as policy and media acumen for shaping policymaking as well as research agendas.

For instance, reformers advocating for school choice have successfully garnered bipartisan support in Washington, but have also set up national- and state-level organizations, and have cultivated diverse forms of grassroot support in many different communities, arming them with information on the effectiveness of policies. Newly formed philanthropies provide significant financial support for these advocacy efforts, helping to strengthen what had been somewhat disparate policy networks (Scott 2009). Jeff Henig (2008) notes that such private sources account for three times what the federal government has provided for research on charter schools and vouchers. Indeed, philanthropies such as the Gates Foundation and the Broad Foundation have emerged as de facto policymakers in several areas by driving educational reform in key urban school districts (Riley 2009).

We also examine both the public and private, "behind-the-scenes" dimensions of the work of these IOs (McGuinn 2012). However, these groups do not form a monolithic "coalition" that works in close concert to achieve its goals. Instead, as McGuinn (2012) argues, "While many ERAOs share goals and move on parallel paths, and coordinate where it makes sense, no one group dominates or is in charge" (p. 27). The reason for this, he argues, is the variation in the policy and political landscapes, which "necessitates that reform coalitions and agendas be built state by state" (p. 27). Therefore, our analysis examines how intermediaries, including those that are not education specific, partner in light of the particular policy contexts of the state and county.

Yet another vital recent theoretical perspective is political scientist Jeff Henig's characterization of the "end of educational exceptionalism" (2013). Henig explains the shift less in terms of coalitions than of the entrance of non-educators (notably members of the business community, mayors, governors, and philanthropists) into the education policy arena, rendering formerly tight networks far less politically powerful. The local level is a particularly important venue for observing these changes because of how new governance arrangements, whether mayoral control or state intervention, have brought in new actors, including "non-traditional education service providers—who are looking for new markets—along with an array of national political entrepreneurs, advocacy organizations, and funders who are eager to turn the pioneering districts into laboratories for new ideas" (Henig 2013, pp. 148–49). These are all changing elements on the "supply side" of IOs; yet there have also been shifts in policymakers' demand for research and information, to which we turn next.

6.3.2 Demand Side: Goods and Information

While the advocacy coalition framework helps us to examine the actions of actors producing and promoting research, we also want to better understand how policymakers sort through the multiple and competing efforts to persuade them to adopt specific policy agendas and how that may shape advocacy. Indeed, even as policymakers and philanthropists demand "scientifically based research," evidence of "what works," and "data-driven decision-making," there are in fact many perspectives and interests offering very different, and often conflicting, answers as to what evidence should count for demonstrating evidentiary support for policy alternatives and which alternatives should be discarded. In some areas where research is highly technical and specialized and assumes quite a different rhetoric than policy discussions, groups are essentially divided by a language barrier reflecting differences not just in objectives but also in assumptions and analytical traditions (e.g., Amara et al. 2004). Thus, policymakers may look for ways of evaluating the level of trust they should place on different forms of evidence that are claimed to support or undercut policy proposals.

In this regard, we may conceive of research production and use in simple economic terms, as a form of transaction between producers and consumers, mediated by intermediary brokers who essentially try to "sell" policymakers on a particular set of research findings. Yet different contextual factors affect the ways that such simple economic transactions occur, and informational asymmetries may exist. For instance, in the case of education research, producers may have informational advantages over consumers, who may be poorly positioned to evaluate the "goods" or the productive processes that went into creating them. In such instances, where consumers have difficulty witnessing or evaluating the quality of such goods, they may look to other forms of surrogate information to assess the quality of their options.

In view of the old adage of "caveat emptor," the informational advantages that research producers may have over research users, especially in a field with sophisticated and arcane analytical techniques, policymakers have to decide how to sift through multiple and often contradictory research claims. This may give intermediary actors the opportunity and incentive to shape policymakers' perceptions of the credibility of research evidence that supports (or challenges) the agenda with which an IO is associated.

6.3.3 The Political Dynamics of Intermediaries and Advocacy Coalitions

In considering the supply and demand sides for research evidence, we conceptualize intermediaries as organizations performing as producers, promoters, and consumers of advocacy, policy, and evidence. We see intermediaries purposefully positioned between research production and consumption in order to gather and then distribute evidence to support policymaking agendas, both nationally and locally. Although their primary purpose typically does not center on creating new research, some of these organizations may be blurring the traditional boundaries between research production and dissemination (Rich 2004), and their role in promoting and funding research likely influences research production. In recent years, intermediaries have become influential actors in the educational policy-planning network, and this more diffuse role has led to a variety of terminologies in the research literature (Fowler 2008; Burris 2008). Where some have identified intermediaries as "education reform advocacy organizations (ERAOs)" and others have focused on specific types of organizations in policy networks, we see these groups as connected sufficiently through coalitional efforts to advance incentivist reforms that distilling between them does not appear to be conceptually or empirically justified.

The extant research on the use of research evidence in education has focused on the school and classroom level and, more recently, across school districts (Coburn 2005; Coburn and Talbert 2006; Daly and Finnigan 2009), but we know much less about the role intermediaries play in shaping that research utilization at the level of public policy.

Advancing from our past work on advocacy coalitions, we are especially interested in exploring institutional landscapes that serve as fertile grounds for IOs (DeBray-Pelot et al. 2007). The national and local arenas contain a subset of organizations that invoke or utilize research independently of policy actors in the other areas. Within the education policy arena, these coalitions have become central brokers of knowledge, ideas, and influence beyond the federal level; and their capacity as well as range of ideological diversity has increased since the advent of the *NCLB* era (DeBray and McGuinn 2009).

A final consideration for our theoretical framework emerges from the political science insight about "new policies creating new politics" (Schattschneider 1935, p. 288). This "new politics" is most apparent at the federal level. President Obama has demonstrated that he will buck the teachers unions by supporting "what works" with regard to incentivist policies. In that regard, we argue that Secretary Duncan's strong financial inducement around charters and merit pay via RttT can help to explain the galvanizing of the think tank and interest group sectors to endorse the ideas in order to gain either resources or legitimacy in the form of access to the legislative process, notably, the reauthorization of the Elementary and Secondary Education Act (ESEA)/NCLB. As Carol Weiss's (1979) "political model" of research utilization would predict, some university-based researchers favorable to that agenda may enjoy access to the policy process in defining what works, while others may be excluded as the administration attempts to make a public case for those measures (see, e.g., US Department of Education 2010). The exclusion of research contrary to an administration's agenda becomes more likely if the existing empirical basis used to justify the diffusion of these educational policies is relatively thin—what Davies and Nutley (2008) refer to as "tactical" use or misuse.

In fact, we see evidence of this type of tactical research utilization around incentivist policies. Lubienski and Garn (2010) have posited the emergence of an "echo chamber" in research use for educational policymaking, where a relatively small and selective set of studies are repeatedly cited by other researchers and advocacy organizations within an advocacy coalition in support of a policy agenda. The findings of these studies are then simplified as they reverberate through policymaking discussions as proven truths, reinforced by repetition without the nuance and complexity that they deserve. These studies are then cited in the press and in blogs, often by sophisticated policy advocates, to advance that agenda or to counter perceived threats (e.g., Thomas 2006; Watkins 2006).

In summary, the recent shifts in educational policymaking have created a new politics of education characterized by an increasingly assertive federal agenda (and thus diminished standing of state policymaking) and the rise of quasi-public policymaking by private philanthropies, both at the national and local levels. In this climate, IOs appear to be "brokering" research evidence through policy coalitions encompassing think tanks, foundations, and advocacy groups. These organizations work in tight and loose coalitions across governmental levels around core beliefs. This brokering takes place in an increasingly diverse advocacy terrain—traditional lobbying, conferences, web-streamed media events, social media such as Facebook and Twitter, the publishing of op-eds in key news markets, the production and promotion of research to key constituencies and the news media, bypassing peer review, and testifying before legislative bodies.

6.4 Description of the Study

Our goal with this chapter is to conceptualize the emerging role of IOs in brokering knowledge for policymakers and to build theoretical understandings of how that emergent force may impact not only the "consumption" of knowledge by policymakers but also the production of knowledge, as research from various institutions must then increasingly be "marketed" to have an impact. Our primary data are empirical and theoretical research literature, policy reports, organizational websites, blogs, news media reports, interviews, and research produced by IOs.

Our 3-year (2011–2014), mixed-methodological approach involves an extensive review of the research literature on research use and educational policymaking. We also employ analytic strategies for making sense of this literature through the prism of theoretical and conceptual understandings of the role of intermediaries in the policymaking process. A third aspect of our methodological approach includes our mapping of existing IOs through tracking organizational websites, intermediary leadership and board membership, bibliometric analysis of research advanced by

Table 6.2 Interviews by city

City	Number of interviews
New Orleans	52
Denver	42
Washington, DC	30
New York	23
Additional interviews (journalists, bloggers, university researchers)	15
Total	**162**

intermediaries in media reports, and research promoted by IOs. We are also conducting in-depth interviews with informants in cities where incentivist reforms are taking hold. This includes Denver, New Orleans, New York, and Washington, DC. To date, we have conducted a total of 162 interviews.

Table 6.2 displays the number of interviews conducted across each city between 2011 and 2013. Across all of our data, we have utilized a purposive sampling technique, aimed at garnering the insights, activities, and perspectives of the IOs, individuals, and school districts in which incentivist reforms are being seeded and developed.

Respondents include policymakers, journalists, legislative aides, teachers' union officials, foundation leaders and program officers, researchers, community advocates, school reform consortia staff, school district officials, and representatives from think tanks. All interviews were recorded and transcribed.[2] We read over the interviews several times, coding them for emerging themes and categories. We also read and collected reports and articles cited in these interviews. Finally, we kept track of the frequency and kinds of IOs and individual researchers mentioned across the data. From this initial analysis, several key themes emerged, to which we turn in the next section.

6.5 Findings: New Functions, Existing and Emerging Advocacy Coalitions

Our overarching finding is that there remains a sense of uncertainty about the overall effectiveness of incentivist reforms by many policymakers, but that this uncertainty has not impeded IOs' advocacy efforts to expand those reforms using research evidence as the rationale. In fact, in all the school districts where our work is grounded, policymakers are expanding some types of incentivist reforms. IOs are playing an important role here by generating research aimed at swaying policymakers or public opinion, promoting research that aligns with their stances, and using their networks to disseminate research.

[2] A few respondents requested to not be recorded, and in that case, we took copious notes of the interviews.

Our data show that specific IOs are also performing a *political function* that includes advocacy, evidence creation and promotion, and some effort to engage in policymaking. Some of which seem to inhabit only the space between knowledge producers and consumers,[3] while others span multiple functions along that continuum. This key finding is significant as there is a gap in the literature that charts the organizational landscape of education policy from funding agencies, idea brokers, and policy entrepreneurs to end users from a political advocacy standpoint. In this section, we highlight three central findings related to this issue of how intermediaries are functioning within advocacy coalitions to promote, produce, or consume and interpret research evidence.

6.5.1 The Limited Appeal of University-Based and Traditional Academic Research

Our first finding concerns the relative importance and utility of research produced by researchers in traditional academic departments at universities. Our data indicate that for many intermediaries and legislative staff, traditional, university-based research has limited appeal and impact in their work. They regard the work as inaccessible, too expensive to produce, not timely, and narrow in its appeal. This critique of university-based research helps to explain why IOs' research production and promotion might be filling a vacuum for policymakers (Lubienski et al. 2011). According to one Washington DC staffer, for example, "I will say I don't think the university research filters down very much."

At times the most influential research was not necessarily seen as reliable because of its source. And other times, respondents were more likely to cite the source of evidence as being influential or reliable, rather than the evidence itself. In other words, if the evidence came from a particular person or IO that the respondents tended to align with politically, they often referred generally to those sources in lieu of a particular study produced by them. When asked to indicate whom or what research they regard as influential and/or reliable, our respondents tended to identify reports or people who worked outside traditional academic departments. For example, we heard names such as Diane Ravitch, a research professor at New York University, whose critiques of market-based reforms and testing have attracted national attention; Rick Hess from the conservative American Enterprise Institute; or references to research organizations within universities, but independent of academic departments, such as the Center for Research on Education Outcomes (CREDO) at Stanford University, or contract research organizations such as Mathematica or RAND.

While there are important exceptions to finding about the declining significance of university-based research and the tendency to privilege trusted sources, we think it is significant that much of the research utilized and promoted in the intermediary

[3] Consumers can include policymakers as well as the public, since many advocacy groups seek to sway public opinion. However, in this chapter we are focusing only on the former.

sector has a diverse review or vetting process. Moreover, a great deal of the research tends to reflect the stance of the researcher or organization, and, not surprisingly, the reports frequently contradict one another. And university-based researchers are not well positioned under current promotion and tenure systems—which require publication in relatively obscure, peer-reviewed publications that are not accessible to the general public—to enter into the debates in a timely fashion.

Groups like the National Research Council (NRC) engage in even more rigorous peer review than individual university researchers, and the reports it generates are oftentimes the result of years of deliberation and collaboration of researchers from multiple disciplines. The aim is to reach consensus among a given set of researchers through careful meta-analyses, such as the 2011 report the NRC produced on educational incentives. Explained a staff member:

> We also have this pretty rigorous internal review process that's set up to be, basically its scientific peer review, the way you would do it for a journal. But instead of 3 or 4 reviewers for an article, we'll have about the same number as the committee. So it's 12 to 15 reviewers for a report. For the framework we actually have 21 reviewers, and the idea is-it's like a shadow committee, almost the idea if you pulled together a different committee. Would they buy this? And the idea is, the report's supposed to lay bare the logic, the evidence on which the sort of logical argument is based, and then the conclusions that the committee drew. And then if there are recommendations, that's even another step and we are actually being asked that the organizational level to pull back on the recommendations step, and just lay out the conclusions predominately and not-so recommendations…so a conclusion is going to say "Based on the evidence, this is what the landscape looks like." The recommendation would say, well, given this landscape, this is what you, you, and you should do.

This kind of traditional academic work, subject to the time it takes to do careful peer review, tends to appear long after the policy debates have cooled or policy cycles have moved on. And as a result, the work is largely ignored in the emerging intermediary sector that champions incentivist approaches to educational reforms.

Teachers' union officials, often those working in the research arms of the organization, were an exception to this general trend. Those respondents reported consuming university research and used it in their communications to their memberships. In addition, they utilized such research in their own internal research reports. And university researchers, along with researchers working in traditional, nonpartisan research organizations such as the National Research Council or National Academy of Education, are active consumers of research produced by other academics. For example, a union researcher asserted, "I do believe in following the university-based research. I do believe that that is where most of the good research comes from. I know it doesn't come from think tanks. It comes from university researchers, and a handful of 'think-tankish' places like Mathematica—that's my opinion." Andrew Rich (2004) has posited that those on the political left are more likely to trust university-based researchers than those from other political orientations, but we have not fully explored this ideological aspect around research utilization as yet in our research.

There was a general sense across many respondents that the organizational source often determined the research findings, and when individuals who identified as more objective needed to weigh the relative merits of research findings, we did find evidence that university research had more credibility, even as it lacked visibility and accessibility. For example, according to a Democratic legislative staffer, "…I often view that as much more of an unbiased, because it's more academic study. And that can be really helpful-university research, as can federal government, or any government's research. When an organization does it, you definitely have to sniff through the bias there." Yet we also found that for all of its status, university and more traditional researchers did not engage in the kind of active promotion and aggressive dissemination of their findings as reformist IOs, a trend we discuss in our second finding. This presents a conundrum for university researchers, while their work appears to be considered more trustworthy by some policymakers, they find it difficult to see their work being utilized in policymaking. Our data indicate that one explanation for this seeming mismatch is the strategic differences in research promotion between traditional academics and IOs.

6.5.2 Strategic Differences in Research Utilization and Promotion by Organizations

Our second finding concerns strategies for promoting and utilizing research evidence on incentivist reforms. We find that IOs engage in heavy promotion and dissemination of research and data, whereas researchers tend to be more conservative with their promotion, preferring to "throw it over the wall," and trust that interested stakeholders will read the findings and take them up in policy.

Here, our data show that university and traditional researchers for the most part rely on tried and true dissemination strategies: publishing research results in academic journals and posting reports on organizational websites, sometimes with a press release aimed at attracting the attention of news media or policymakers and/or their staff. While there are certainly exceptions to this strategy—the National Research Council holds events to brief federal policymakers on their research in advance of the public release—academic research tends to be released fairly quietly. According to an NRC staff member, "Yeah, this is an area that the [National Academies] knows it needs to work on. So it's very archaic—I would call it the "throw it over the wall and they will find it" kind of strategy, like the, you know, we'll throw the book over and they'll see the wisdom, and they'll pick it up, and they'll transform their lives, which is not how it works."

In contrast, IOs and advocates engaged in much more targeted promotion and packaging of research. Social media venues such as Twitter, Facebook, and blogs were key in their promotion. Through social media, organizations are able to disseminate research and advocacy in a timely and relatively inexpensive way. One blogger for a teacher's union-affiliated organization observed that his writing reached a wide audience:

> But I know that a lot of journalists read it, and they're very important. Obviously I know that a lot of teachers read it, I know a lot of think-tanky people read it, I know a lot of academics read it, and I like to think it gets sent around to legislators and their staff. But I don't know, I mean we get hits from Congress and the White House…

While this blogger was aware that he had a broad audience, he also admitted that he did not actively promote his work, explaining, "…you know, I don't really, I mean, I put it out there, and whatever happens, happens. I don't send it around. I probably should." In contrast, Teach For America, whose alumni are often leaders of the reforms in question, has organized to help shape the public understanding of the research produced on its efficacy. One TFA leader explained this coordinated approach, saying, "We are looking to pull out the good news, frankly." She went on to explain:

> We have a team that's managing media when a study comes out that's a good story. What that team needs to do is to understand accurately what the findings say, and to find pros and cons of that study and findings…We do two things: we create a summary document that we try to make it as objective and as informative as possible, and then the communication teams generate a set of talking points that we then check for accuracy.

This pattern mapped on to what we found to be a broader trend in our analyses of social media, where ideologically based differences often manifested themselves. With blogs by conservatives and rightist organizations, we see significant efforts geared at promoting their political agenda and citing their own research or research by their allies. Comparatively, liberal and left-leaning blogs tended to focus on what the right is saying and why it was, from their perspective, flawed. This tendency on the left could possibly be attributed to the sense that it was outnumbered and overpowered by more conservative or neoliberal organizations whose research quality was questionable. The sum total of the debates and rhetoric emanating from social media, research reports, and media spin is that there appears to be a sense from our respondents that it is increasingly difficult to rely on research when considering educational policy, a finding we turn to next.

6.5.3 Disagreement About What Counts as Quality Research

A third and final finding concerns the prevailing perceptions of research and what counts as reliable evidence. Almost all of our respondents, when asked to identify research that had informed or changed their perspective on the school reforms in question, were unable to identify specific research findings or reports and instead pointed to the importance of seeing "what works" or following the trends of the business or political leaders in their particular setting. This finding aligns with findings from Coburn (2005), Amara et al. (2004), and Weiss (1977), who have discovered that people who profess to use research tend to do so conceptually. That is, while they might often forget the specifics of the study—they incorporate those findings into their preexisting knowledge or it helps them to see the issue in a new way.

We argue that this tendency to use research primarily at the conceptual or confirmatory level leads to a policy terrain in which—despite the nominal focus on policies that "work"—there is a discernable relaxing of what counts as quality research. This trend is especially prominent with respondents who held a clear reform or ideological agenda. In these cases, as other researchers of school voucher policies have been observed, ideology can often trump research evidence

(Belfield and Levin 2005). IOs, and their advocacy of particular incentivist polices, appear to be critical in this, shifting the importance of research. For example, an aide to a legislator in Illinois explained his support of charter schools as stemming from personal experience with particular charters—confirming his beliefs about the schools as effective:

> For him, I don't think it was as much research as seeing it hands on and also then the outcomes. Maybe that is research. But in Chicago, the high schools with the highest ACT scores are charter schools, the top 10 ACT non-select high schools in Chicago, 8 of them or 9 of them are charter schools. That speaks for itself. And probably other civic and business leaders in Chicago who have spent more time on education issues than he has in the city, and them talking about and highlighting charter schools. And it's not just the big networks, he's been to see and I've been to see and our Chicago staff has been to see the kind of mom-and-pop charter schools that just start in one community and serve one community and have been successful. So there's research that goes into how those schools are successful, I think [the legislator] probably hasn't dove into what that research is but he's seen the outcome and that's what matters.

Another charter school reform organization leader echoed this sentiment, arguing that the research focus should be on charter schools that had managed to survive and sustain themselves, comparing the charter school sector to the range of failed Internet start-ups:

> By no means does that mean that the dot-coms and the Internet and the web-based businesses are a failure. The ones that have done well, that have taken advantage of the opportunity have done well by their business, by their customers, have run their businesses well and have the right formula: those guys are thriving. That's called eBay and Facebook and everything else that we know out there. And I feel that it's kind of the same thing in the charter sector. What we need to be looking at is, "can we say the model works, not based on the aggregate, but based on the survivors, the eBays?"

Key in influencing perceptions of quality and effectiveness is the lobbying done by intermediaries themselves. We have learned that some charter school management organizations, such as KIPP, employ external relations staff to appeal to federal lawmakers to pass favorable legislation—such as the bill allowing CMOs to apply directly to the Department of Education for funding. In this case, we saw evidence of a connection between local advocacy and that taking place at the national level around the importance of scaling up what were considered successful charter school models, which are typically operated by CMOs—and the evidentiary basis for that success was an amalgamation of student test score data, legitimacy conferred on the organizations by policy elites, and heavy lobbying. An aide to a Colorado legislator explained the panoply of advocacy:

> Sometimes it's the national, national charter school associations. Sometimes it's alternative teacher preparation programs. Like in that case, it could be the school districts organizations, whether that's the superintendents, principals, school boards…Sometimes the teachers unions may have a certain position they'll want us to consider. Sometimes it's some of the education reform groups. And [the legislator] has-is interested and I would say broadly, generally supportive a lot of the goals that the general education reform groups. I would say those kind of groups may include groups like Education Trust, Democrats for Education Reform, Center for American Progress, some others too-National Center for Teacher Quality, Stand for Children, groups like that.

Frequently, the credibility or quality of the research was established not just by who sent it, but after someone in the organization gave it the mark of quality. Advocacy organizations and think tanks often have a few methodologically trained staffers who are able to weigh in on research matters, and respondents shared that they frequently turned to those internal experts when discerning research quality. For example, a director at a Denver school reform organization observed about their research expert, "If you walk into his office, he's got like shelves of books and I have none here. Which doesn't mean I don't read, but like I'm out raising money and building partnerships. And it's also different like personality and orientation."

Yet a trend that stood out in this tendency to question what counted as quality research was the notion that there was no prevailing consensus in the research community about a particular issue for a variety of reasons. These included the reforms being too new to evaluate meaningfully; the problem with having only small, pilot programs and nothing implemented on a broader basis to be able to generalize; and also the fact that research findings often contradicted each other or were problematic methodologically. For example, a leader at a school reform organization in Denver explained:

> Well, I mean we're constantly fighting this battle of: are charter schools better than or worse than public schools? And it's kind of a silly argument, right? There are good schools that are district-run; there are bad schools that are district-run. There's always some report coming out trying to say that charter schools aren't serving kids effectively, the data looks… lumps data together so broadly that it isn't really meaningful, these studies that say charter schools aren't doing any better than traditional district schools.

We found this sentiment repeated across our interviews that the research on charter schools, for example, did not mean much in the aggregate or that although teacher evaluation data systems might not be as sophisticated in measuring value-added as we hope, that policy needed to move ahead. Undergirding much of these arguments was a prevailing sense that educational policy had to date failed too many poor and disadvantaged students and that reformers felt an urgency to act—even if those actions were not grounded firmly in research evidence, as university researchers have traditionally understood it. Intermediary organizations are playing pivotal and, often, central roles in advancing these arguments. We see this happening within local contexts, across local contexts in terms of shared networks, and between the national level and localities, and our current analyses are documenting these connections.

6.6 Discussion and Implications

This chapter advances our understanding of the political use of research evidence by examining how IOs broker research evidence as participants in policy coalitions in education. Our research is rooted in three local school districts as well as at the national level around the long-stalled reauthorization of the Elementary and Secondary Education Act, and these local sites and the efforts afoot at the national level demonstrate important local-national advocacy coalitions at work to establish evidence of the effectiveness or lack of effectiveness of incentivist reforms. The new coalitions and new politics created by these new policies stand to have implications for the extent to which the reforms are taken up in other school districts within states and across the country. IOs are working to produce, promote, and ensure that evidence is consumed or utilized by policymakers who are not necessarily situated to be discriminating consumers of sophisticated research, but who might nonetheless influence the growth or restriction of incentivist reforms. And our data indicate that they are drawing on a range of evidences to build their case.

Our findings make it clear that institutions not traditionally associated with research or policy processes are also playing an important, even essential, intermediary role, confirming Henig's argument that the current era is one in which traditional elites in educational policy have lost influence over policymakers. For instance, new media such as independent bloggers as well as podcasts from established institutions appear to be critical in promoting ideas directly to policymakers as well as indirectly by shaping the popular "climate of opinion" that informs possible policy agendas (Cohen and Garet 1975; Kingdon 2003). An illustrative example of this would be the recent films that have been released in 2010 evidently in support of charter schools, including *The Lottery* and, more famously, *Waiting for Superman*. Such documentaries make reference to research while promoting an incentivist agenda and are supported not only by their own marketing campaigns but also by financial and publicity backing from blogs, think tanks, philanthropies, and advocacy organizations—including special screenings attended by policy elites (Turque 2010). Moreover, the new politics brought by the new policies indicates that philanthropies and foundations are playing roles typically associated with public policymaking, and are active in determining which reforms and organizations receive private and public investments and get scaled up within and across districts. In determining organizational worth, these private actors are also producing, promoting, and consuming research evidence. Moreover, they are helping to establish and solidify coalitional networks within and across school districts.

Our review of the literature and examination of political dynamics reveals that connections between these intermediary organizations are helping them to play different roles in the institutional arena. Certainly, some larger organizations combine multiple roles within their organizational structure. An example would be the Gates Foundation, which commissions, funds, produces, and promotes research, in addition to playing a (private) policymaking function by establishing policy agendas that many local policymakers follow. But while such organizations may be vertically integrated on their own, we also allow for the possibility that networks of independent organizations may essentially replicate those functions that are integrated in larger entities. That is, a given funding agency may focus resources on a particular set of researchers at specific organizations that tend to produce evidence in support of or opposition to an incentivist agenda, which is then promoted primarily by certain intermediaries, possibly to a defined set of policymakers.

Although researchers in many disciplines lament policymakers' lack of reference to research, the failure of research to inform policymakers is more evident in some fields than others (National Research Council 2012). Education policy and practice have traditionally operated rather independently of research on education interventions. Recent requirements for research evidence on interventions raise—but do not answer—the question of who decides what constitutes research evidence. With multiple and often conflicting agendas in this field, evidence on education effectiveness is particularly open to selection, interpretation, and marketing processes that can be used to promote certain types of evidence at the expense of others. In the case of incentivist reforms, our data show that traditional university researchers are still trusted by many legislative staffers and policymakers, but that their research is often not reaching them in the ways that other research evidence is.

However, while the increasing role of the intermediary sector is apparent, there remains much to learn about how these private IOs produce, package, and share ideas and information. This chapter builds on the still emergent theoretical and empirical work on how policy ideas and information travel through networks of IOs and how they move between federal/national and local arenas in the era since *No Child Left Behind* was implemented. We also see much room for investigating how policymakers assign value to, and consume research from, IOs.

As the intermediary sector becomes more synergistic and also complex and fractured, we plan to determine how "research" is defined, interpreted, and then used (or neglected) in the agenda-setting and policymaking process. As Tseng (2012) has noted, "Relationships are vital conduits for acquiring research. When confronted with questions about a program or reform, agencies and legislators often turn to trusted peers and intermediaries. Translation is also key. Because research does not speak for itself, policymakers and practitioners must always interpret its meaning and implications for their particular problems and circumstances" (p. 1). We are witnessing the ways in which intermediary organizations, through their coalitions, are providing this relational, yet political function to a host of policy actors and the public writ large. As our research moves forward, we plan to attend to the ways these coalitions continue to strengthen or perhaps begin to split as more evidence is employed on various incentivist reforms. We are witnessing some of these coalitional cracks in Louisiana, for instance, where the passage of a statewide voucher program has charter school advocates arguing that charters are more effective and worthy of investment and growth.

Knowledge of these issues is crucial for assessing the potential of the intermediary sector for moving educational policymaking toward a more empirical basis while shifting the institutional models for knowledge production away from university-based research toward more private (and perhaps more efficient) modes of funding and accountability. In addressing this issue, the research helps to produce a clearer conception of how networks of advocacy groups may be redefining the political economy of knowledge production in educational policymaking, and points to promising empirical and theoretical directions for future research around the political use of research evidence for educational policymaking.

References

Amara, N., Ouimet, M., & Landry, R. (2004). New evidence on instrumental, conceptual, and symbolic utilization of university research in government agencies. *Science Communication, 26*(1), 75–106. doi:10.1177/1075547004267491.

Ball, S., & Junemann, C. (2012). *Networks, new governance, and education*. Chicago: The Policy Press.

Barr, S., Hess, F., Kirsch, V., Klein, J., & Tough, P. (2008). *How many billionaires does it take to fix a school system?* Retrieved November 2, 2013, from http://www.nytimes.com/2008/03/09/magazine/09roundtable-t.html?pagewanted=all&_r=0

Belfield, C., & Levin, H. (2005). Vouchers and public policy: When ideology trumps evidence. *American Journal of Education, 111*(4), 548–567.

Burris, V. (2008). The interlock structure of the policy-planning network and the right turn in U.S. state policy. *Research in Political Sociology, 17*.

Coburn, C. (2005). The role of nonsystem actors in the relationship between policy and practice: The case of reading instruction in California. *Educational Evaluation and Policy Analysis, 27*(1), 23–52.

Coburn, C., & Talbert, J. (2006). Conceptions of evidence use in districts: Mapping the terrain. *American Journal of Education, 112*(4), 469–495.

Coburn, C. E., Toure, J., & Yamashita, M. (2009). Evidence, interpretation, and persuasion: Instructional decision making at the district central office. *Teachers College Record, 111*(4), 1115–1161.

Cohen, D. K., & Garet, M. S. (1975). Reforming educational policy with applied social research. *Harvard Educational Review, 45*(1), 17–43.

Daly, A., & Finnigan, K. (2009). A bridge between worlds: Understanding network structure to understand change strategy. *The Journal of Educational Change*. Available online at: http://www.springerlink.com/1040n7231740m232/. Accessed 22 Jan 2009.

Davies, H. T. O., & Nutley, S. M. (2008). *Learning more about how research-based knowledge gets used: Guidance in the development of new empirical research*. New York: William T. Grant Foundation.

DeBray-Pelot, E., Lubienski, C., & Scott, J. (2007). The institutional landscape of interest groups and school choice. *Peabody Journal of Education, 82*(2–3), 204–230.

DeBray-Pelot, E., & McGuinn, P. (2009). The new politics of education: Analyzing the federal education policy landscape in the post-NCLB era. *Educational Policy, 23*(1), 15–42.

Finnigan, K., Daly, A., & Che, J. (2013). Systemwide reform in districts under pressure: The role of social networks in defining, acquiring, and diffusing research evidence. *Journal of Educational Administration, 51*(4), 476–497.

Fowler, F. (2008). *Policy studies for educational leaders: An introduction*. Saddle River: Prentice Hall.

Goertz, M., Barnes, C., Massell, D., Fink, R., & Francis, A. (2013). *State education agencies' acquisition and use of research knowledge in school improvement strategies*. Philadelphia: Consortium for Policy Research in Education.

Goldie, D., Linick, M., Jabbar, H., & Lubienski, C. (2014). Using bibliometric and social media analyses to explore the "Echo Chamber" hypothesis. *Educational Policy*. http://epx.sagepub.com/content/early/2014/01/31/0895904813515330.abstract

Gurke, D., Asen, R., Conners, P., Solomon, R., & Gumm, E. (2011). The right call: How and when should you use research to influence and enhance your decisions? *American School Board Journal, 198*(3), 29–31.

Henig, J. R. (2008). *Spin cycle: How research is used in policy debates: The case of charter schools*. New York: The Russell Sage Foundation.

Henig, J. (2013). *The end of exceptionalism in American education: The changing politics of school reform*. Cambridge, MA: Harvard Education Press.

Honig, M. (2004). The new middle management: Intermediary organizations in education policy implementation. *Educational Evaluation and Policy Analysis, 26*(1), 65–87.

Kingdon, J. (2003). *Agendas, alternatives, and public policies* (3rd ed.). New York: HarperCollins.
Lubienski, C. (2013). Privatizing form or function? Equity, outcomes and influence in American Charter Schools. *Oxford Review of Education, 39*(4), 498–513.
Lubienski, C., & Garn, G. (2010). Evidence and ideology on consumer choices in education markets: An alternative analytical framework. *Current Issues in Education, 13*(3), 1–31.
Lubienski, C., Scott, J., & DeBray, E. (2011). The rise of IOs in knowledge production, advocacy, and educational policy. *Teachers College Record Online* (Commentary).
Massell, D., Goertz, M. E., & Barnes, C. (2012). State education agencies acquisition and use of research knowledge for school improvement. *Peabody Journal of Education, 87*(5), 609–626.
McDonnell, L., & Weatherford, M. S. (2013). Evidence use and the common core standards movement: From problem definition to policy adoption. *American Journal of Education, 120*, 1–26.
McGuinn, P. (2012, Summer). Fight club: Are advocacy organizations changing the politics of education? *Education Next, 12*(3). Retrieved from http://educationnext.org/fight-club/
National Research Council. (2012). *Using science as evidence in public policy*. Washington, DC: The National Academies Press.
Nelson, S. R., Leffler, J. C., & Hansen, B. A. (2009). *Toward a research agenda for understanding and improving the use of research evidence*. Portland: Northwest Regional Educational Laboratory. Retrieved November 10, 2013, from http://educationnorthwest.org/webfm_send/311
Reckhow, S. (2012). *Follow the money*. Oxford, UK: Oxford University Press.
Rich, A. (2004). *Think tanks, public policy, and the politics of expertise*. Cambridge: Cambridge University Press.
Riley, N. (2009). We're in the venture philanthropy business. *The Wall Street Journal*. Retrieved from http://online.wsj.com/news/articles/SB10001424052970204251404574342693329347698
Sabatier, P., & Jenkins-Smith, H. (1999). The advocacy coalition framework: An assessment. In P. Sabatier (Ed.), *Theories of the policy process* (pp. 117–166). Boulder: Westview.
Schattschneider, E. E. (1935). *Politics, pressures, and the tariff*. New York: Prentice Hall.
Scott, J. (2009). The politics of venture philanthropy in school choice policy and advocacy. *Educational Policy, 23*(1), 106–136.
Scott, J., & Jabbar, H. (2013). Money and measures: Foundations as knowledge brokers. In D. Anagnostopoulos, S. Rutledge, & R. Jacobsen (Eds.), *The infrastructure of accountability: Mapping data use and its consequences across the American education system*. Cambridge: Harvard Education Press.
Scott, J., & Jabbar, H. (2014). The hub and the spokes: Foundations, intermediary organizations, incentivist reforms, and the politics of research evidence. *Educational Policy*. Available at: http://epx.sagepub.com/content/early/2014/01/28/0895904813515327
Thomas, C. (2006, November 22). Friedman's Greatest Legacy: School Choice? *Real Clear Politics*. Retrieved November 10, 2013, from http://www.realclearpolitics.com/articles/2006/11/the_other_milton_friedman.html
Tseng, V. (2012). The uses of research in policy and practice. *Social Policy Report, 26*(2), 1–16.
Turque, B. (2010, September 16). Rhee: Election result 'devastating' for D.C. schoolchildren. *Voices: Washington Post*. Retrieved from http://voices.washingtonpost.com/dcschools/2010/09/rhee_election_result_devastati.html#more
U.S. Department of Education. (2010). *Research behind the Obama administration's proposal for reauthorizing the Elementary and Secondary Education Act (ESEA)*. Washington, DC: U.S. Department of Education.
Weiss, C. H. (1977). Research for policy's sake: The enlightenment function of social research. *Policy Analysis, 3*, 531–545.
Weiss, C. (1979). The many meanings of research utilization. *Public Administration Review, 39*(5), 426–431.
Washington Post. (2009, July 30). Dollars for Schools. *Washington Post*, editorial.
Watkins, S. (2006, September 1). *Are public or private schools doing better? How the NCES study is being misinterpreted* (pp. 1–4). Washington, DC: Heritage Foundation Backgrounder.

Part II
Using Research Evidence at the State and Federal Level

Chapter 7
Research Use in the Policy Process: New Information to Help Meet the Demand

Elliot H. Weinbaum

The chapters in this section can be viewed as intensive investigations of research use for different purposes, by different actors, at different stages of education policy making. As Milbrey McLaughlin points out, a nuanced understanding of policy "gives prominence to the diverse information needs of various actors in the process over time" (1987, p. 176). With that statement in mind, this section contributes to our increasingly nuanced understanding of policy and the role of research and evidence within the policymaking process. In addition, this section builds on the previous one in this volume by moving "further" from the schoolhouse door. Borrowing McLaughlin's terms, the distance covered in this section takes us from the "micro-level" of state education agency support activities to the "macro-level" of federal policy setting. Through examinations of research use in state education agencies, regional and national support organizations, and national movements and policies, the authors in this section further our thinking about what research and evidence gets used by whom. Overall, we gain a better understanding of how research and policymaking sometimes intersect. Because the authors also identify occasions in which research and policymaking do not intersect, this section and this introductory chapter illuminate opportunities for shaping research to be more influential in the policy process.

Barnes, Goertz, and Massell focus their research on the use of evidence within three state education agencies (SEAs). Barnes and colleagues explore the work of the SEAs as agency staffs design and implement policies, support mechanisms, and instruments that will help schools and districts to improve. The authors categorize evidence in three ways, two of them quite traditional – formal research studies and local analyses of data – and add to our larger conversation about evidence by including "models, protocols, or other tools that embed research…in somewhat specified guides to action" (p. 4). Barnes, Goertz, and Massell also dig deeply into

E.H. Weinbaum (✉)
Senior Program Officer, William Penn Foundation,
Philadelphia, PA, USA
e-mail: eweinbaum@williampennfoundation.org

K.S. Finnigan and A.J. Daly (eds.), *Using Research Evidence in Education: From the Schoolhouse Door to Capitol Hill*, Policy Implications of Research in Education 2,
DOI 10.1007/978-3-319-04690-7_7,

the networks that facilitate exchange of evidence. They focus primarily within the SEAs while noting considerable outreach by SEA staff to external parties. The high levels of communication about research within and outside of the SEAs suggest a desire by SEA leaders for useful research to guide policy development and implementation.

McDonnell and Weatherford share many similar themes with Barnes, Massell, and Goertz but expand the discussion of evidence and actors, discussing at least six types of evidence and the use of these types of evidence by state education agency leaders, policy entrepreneurs, and national organizations as they pursued the design and adoption of the Common Core State Standards. McDonnell and Weatherford help us to see the broad range of evidence that is used at various stages of the policymaking process and how different types of evidence are used to inform politics and policy. They highlight the importance of building networks of communication to transmit evidence and facilitate its entry into policy conversations. In doing so, the authors illustrate the need for a "big tent" to include as many stakeholders as possible in a process that puts a priority on large, carefully constructed, and well-maintained communication networks.

Haskins and Margolis focus entirely on the federal government and its efforts to support research and policy that are based on evidence from impact evaluations. They describe how leaders in the executive branch sought to shift government from investments focused on formulaic inputs to investments guided by a particular type of evidence. Though it seems apparent that policymakers hoped to rely most heavily on evidence generated through randomized controlled trials (RCTs), the available research base tempered the exclusive commitment to RCTs and allowed for inclusion of other types of evidence. In fact, only half of the federal initiatives described ended up with a requirement that applicants provide a particular type of evidence. Even in those programs that did have such a requirement, the majority of applications and funded evaluations did not adhere to the "gold standard" that had been set as the goal. In this chapter, we see that even with a relatively limited set of actors, negotiating political concerns and confronting the realities of what evidence is available are inescapable. While the types of evidence are more circumscribed in this chapter (in comparison with the others in this section), like the others it shows a strong demand for evidence that is highly aligned with policy goals.

In combination, these three chapters point to the necessity for multiple types of evidence to be available, mechanisms through which to share and discuss that evidence, and systems to access "the right evidence at the right time." In her discussion of the challenges of measuring implementation, McLaughlin (1987) talks about "macro-level analyses" and "micro-level analyses." She argues, and these chapters support her contention, that the kinds of evidence and analyses that are most germane to one level may not be the most germane to another. To use examples from this section, an RCT about a particular intervention may be helpful for the federal level, but will not necessarily provide the SEA level with the information it needs about how to provide training or support to ensure that schools can implement that intervention.

The federal government (the macro-level) puts an emphasis on RCTs because it has little responsibility for how programs are actually implemented in states, districts, or schools. Instead, it is focused on setting the broad parameters for best practice – identifying programs that "work" and those that do not. Policy entrepreneurs, state organizations, and others described in McDonnell and Weatherford's chapter – which could be considered a "meso-level" not identified by McLaughlin – focus on formal research as well as professional judgment, state and federal policies, and personal stories because they are involved in policy promotion and design. Because actors at this meso-level are rarely concerned with the details of implementation, McDonnell and Weatherford note that "the enabling resources necessary for the CCSS…were not stressed as the idea of Common Core standards was promoted and developed" (p. 10).

These "enabling resources" are one of the biggest areas of focus for the "micro-level" of SEA staff, analyzed by Barnes, Goertz, and Massell. However, SEAs are also concerned with the types of evidence that are used by policymakers at other levels. Because of the range of roles that SEAs fill – they develop policy, promote its adoption, and assist with its implementation – SEAs can be considered macro-, meso-, and micro-level actors. To some extent, SEAs are situated between federal policymakers and the schools and districts that they oversee. In order to succeed in this position, they seek input from, and credibility with, those above and below. As a result, it appears that the SEAs rely on the widest range of types of evidence to support their work. In addition, because they are often on the leading edge of change, promoting innovation, they must rely on a diversity of types of evidence, as there is not sufficient evidence from a single type of study or analysis. The combination of needing to meet a variety of demands and working in areas for which there is no single applicable evidence base creates a need for continuously evolving evidence searches. In addition to challenges this may pose, it also makes SEAs a rich context for further study of frequently used types of evidence.

Not only do the types of evidence used vary across these three chapters, the *use* of that evidence also varies according to the stage of the policy process, the "level" of the actor, and the availability of research. Though the authors in this section do not describe it in this way, we can see examples of a range of research uses described elsewhere as imposed, political, conceptual, and instrumental (Nutley et al. 2007; Weiss 1977; Weiss et al. 2005). These uses can be viewed as a continuum, from research use that is done for political purposes and has little direct impact on policy to use of research that is applied directly to policy development.

Haskins and Margolis are most focused on the imposed use of research (though perhaps it would be more appropriately called the "incentivized" use of research in this case, given that no one was required to apply for funding through the programs described in their chapter). Grantees seeking funding had to justify their request by citing previous research suggesting that their programs were likely to have impacts and had to provide a plan for developing the research base further. McDonnell and Weatherford provide many examples of political use of research as advocates for the Common Core developed products integrating research such as a "messaging toolkit" (p. 8) to convince the public and legislators that the Common Core would represent improvement. McDonnell and Weatherford also describe conceptual uses of research that helped to frame the problem and inform development of the standards. Barnes, Goertz, and Massell provide the most compelling examples of instrumental use of research. The authors describe cases in which SEA staff sought out "research-based guidance for very specific concrete steps or tools that they could use in their work" (p. 15).

Reading across these three chapters, one could begin to create a matrix that identifies the position of the research user within the education system and the stage of the policy process. In the cells of that matrix, one could identify the types of research and evidence that are likely to get used and the types of use one could expect. For example, evidence from these chapters would suggest that a technical advisor to an SEA developing policy is likely to use syntheses, summaries, or reviews of evidence in a conceptual fashion to inform policy design. A policy entrepreneur seeking commitment from elected officials to support an innovative or untested policy is likely to use statements of expert opinion.

Such a matrix could be helpful for a number of audiences. It could help researchers to understand the types of research that are needed by policymakers and the ways in which research should be presented or disseminated in order to influence decisions by different actors at different points along the policy process. Funders of research could also use such a matrix to support research projects and products that are most likely to be used by policymakers and practitioners. Finally, policymakers could use this matrix to reflect on the diversity of their own research and evidence base as they design and implement policy. Though additional research would be needed to flesh out such a matrix, the chapters here provide a solid foundation on which to build.

In addition to helping us identify the types of research use that are prevalent at a number of "levels" of the education policy system, the evidence presented in these chapters also suggests that policymakers and practitioners at multiple levels of the system have assimilated the idea that research and evidence should be used to inform, and justify, their policy choices. Furthermore, it appears that SEA staff, national organizations, advocates, and federal policymakers search extensively for research and evidence that will be of use to them. Thus, what has sometimes been called the "demand" side for research appears to be active and energized. The question now is whether the "supply" side has developed research and evidence – understood in the broadest terms as presented in these chapters – in the right form and on the right topics to meet that demand. In all of the chapters in this section, we see that policymakers used the "best available" research, though it did not always meet their specific needs or goals.

It is likely that the research and evidence that will match most closely with policymaker needs will only be successfully created through lasting partnerships between researchers and policymakers/practitioners. Because the needs for research and evidence are likely to evolve as more evidence becomes available, as topical concerns arise and subside, and as knowledge and skill sets change, ongoing partnerships provide our best hope of developing research that will be used. As McLaughlin (1987) described more than 25 years ago, the challenge "lies in integrating these two communities of discourse in models that accommodate these multi-level, multi-actor complexities" (p. 177). In the 25 years since McLaughlin articulated this challenge, a number of such models to integrate the researcher and policymaker communities have developed. Recent work by Coburn et al. (2013) describes elements, and examples, of partnerships between researchers and school district leaders. The U.S. Department of Education, through the Regional Educational Laboratories and the Comprehensive Centers, is supporting partnerships between researchers and policymakers at the state and local levels. The research produced by such state and local partnerships, and the immediate relevance of this work for policymakers and practitioners, has helped to build the demand for research as described in the chapters in this section. This partnership approach to research must now be further developed to successfully meet the demand. Expanding and enhancing such partnerships will depend on sustained support, attention to carefully cultivated communication networks, and potential modification of professional incentive structures to encourage collaboration. This section makes clear the need and appetite for the kind of research that such partnerships could provide; it is now up to us to make sure that they are developed.

References

Coburn, C. E., Penuel, W. R., & Geil, K. E. (2013, January). *Research-practice partnerships: A strategy for leveraging research for educational improvement in school districts.* New York: William T. Grant Foundation.

McLaughlin, M. W. (1987). Learning from experience: Lessons from policy implementation. *Educational Evaluation and Policy Analysis, 9*(2), 171–178.

Nutley, S., Walter, I., & Davies, H. (2007). *Using evidence: How research can inform public services.* Bristol: Policy Press.

Weiss, C. H. (1977). Research for policy's sake: The enlightenment function of social research. *Policy Analysis, 3*(4), 531–545.

Weiss, C. H., Murphy-Graham, E., & Birkeland, S. (2005). An alternate route to policy influence: How evaluations affect D.A.R.E. *American Journal of Evaluation, 26*(1), 12–30.

Chapter 8
How State Education Agencies Acquire and Use Research Knowledge for School Improvement

Carol A. Barnes, Margaret E. Goertz, and Diane Massell

8.1 Context

Improving achievement in high-poverty schools has long been an intractable social problem in America with strong implications for equitable opportunities among our nation's youth. Over the last two decades, state and federal laws and grant programs, such as state accountability policies, the No Child Left Behind (NCLB) Act, Race to the Top, and Title I School Improvement Grants, have given state education agencies (SEAs) considerably more responsibilities for directing and guiding the improvement of low-performing schools. This charge is far different than SEA's more traditional compliance tasks. At the same time, these policies have pressed SEA professionals whose work involves school improvement to incorporate research-based school improvement policies and practices in their statewide systems of support for low-performing schools, technical assistance for districts, professional development for teachers, and school improvement programs. Policymakers have urged SEAs to engage with organizations external to their own agencies to extend their strained capacity to provide improvement supports for schools and districts and to help them collect and use research or other evidence (see, e.g., Rennie Center 2004).

Yet no studies existed of whether and how SEA staff sought, acquired, and used research or other forms of evidence in their work generally, or in school improvement work specifically, and the most recent in-depth study of SEAs was conducted nearly 20 years ago (Lusi 1997). The exploratory study on which this chapter is based was designed to fill this gap by examining which SEA staff search for research,

C.A. Barnes (✉) • D. Massell
Consortium for Policy Research in Education (CPRE),
University of Michigan's School of Education, Ann Arbor, MI, USA
e-mail: barnescl@umich.edu

M.E. Goertz
Consortium for Policy Research in Education, University of Pennsylvania's
Graduate School of Education, Philadelphia, PA, USA

K.S. Finnigan and A.J. Daly (eds.), *Using Research Evidence in Education: From the Schoolhouse Door to Capitol Hill*, Policy Implications of Research in Education 2,
DOI 10.1007/978-3-319-04690-7_8,

evidence-based and practitioner knowledge related to school improvement and how they conduct those searches; whether and how SEA staff use research and these other types of knowledge to design, implement, and refine school improvement policies, programs, and practices; and how SEAs are organized to manage and use such knowledge (Goertz et al. 2013).

8.2 Framework

The framework underlying our study is drawn from several lines of research and theory that we have linked conceptually to focus, in this chapter, on the organizing structures and processes by which research or other knowledge is spread and by which SEAs acquire and use it (see Fig. 8.1).

8.2.1 The Organization of Knowledge Diffusion, Search, and Use

The literatures on organizations, social networks, and knowledge utilization all argue that individuals are embedded in relational systems that can promote or block the spread and use of resources or new knowledge. In their study of schools, for example, Frank et al. (2004) defined social capital as actors exchanging resources, such as knowledge or expertise, through interactions that are not mandated by a formal structure. In her research comparing two SEAs, Lusi (1997) argued that nonhierarchical, less segmented management structures could help build internal

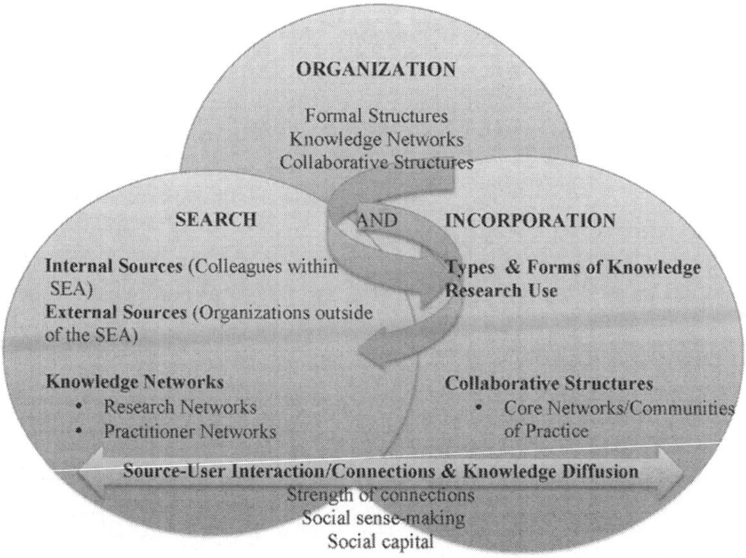

Fig. 8.1 Sea organizing structures and knowledge use processes

and external connections to produce the kind of flexible organization that was more effective for complex school reform, a relatively new task assigned to SEAs. Flatter, more integrative organizational structures, she argued, were more conducive for the flow of new ideas about school improvement. More recent studies in other organizations confirm that professional connections across traditional organizational boundaries improve problem solving by using varied but relevant expertise (Dutton and Heaphy 2003; Weick and Sutcliffe 2001). But many still perceive SEAs as largely "siloed" organizations (Unger et al. 2008).

Sociologists have long studied these kinds of internal and external connections, known as "social networks," to understand the diffusion of knowledge and innovation within and across organizations, including more recent studies of schools and districts (Daly 2010; Finnigan et al. 2013). A few researchers have used social network theory and methods to study state education policy networks, most notably Miskel and his colleagues (Miskel and Song 2004; Song and Miskel 2005) who employed these methods to identify the most central, influential, or "prestigious" actors in state reading policy networks. We know of no studies using these lenses to explore the flow of knowledge in SEAs and from whom, how, even if, they search for and use research or other evidence.

8.2.2 *Search and Incorporation Process: The How, Who, and What of Research Use*

These lines of research and theory comport well with newer more constructivist models of knowledge diffusion that cast research use not as a one-way transmission of research to the users but instead as an interactive "social process" (Hood 2002) involving collective sense-making of varied types of knowledge. From these perspectives the potential users of research (in our study, SEA professional staff) search for or receive information and expertise about how to improve both internally from colleagues and externally through intermediary organizations. They incorporate different forms of research, practitioners' advice, and other types of evidence into their policies or practices through a social sense-making process taking place over time, across locations, and with varied expertise (Honig and Coburn 2008; Spillane et al. 2002). This social search-incorporation process helps individuals and organizations identify and integrate often decontextualized research findings into their strategies (Argyris and Schön 1996) and within some collaborative forms of networks such as "communities of practice" (Wenger et al. 2002) even construct new forms of "useable" knowledge for guiding action (Brown and Duguid 1991; Barnes et al. 2010).

8.2.2.1 Sources of Knowledge

Social network studies have shown that members of organizations often connect with colleagues closest or most similar to them for advice and information (see, e.g., Supovitz and Weinbaum 2008; Coburn et al. 2009), a pattern that can sometimes limit information flow and access to new ideas. But studies have also identified boundary spanners who connect to those less similar, including external intermediaries who can be key conduits for providing and helping educators translate research-based knowledge into local practices (Honig 2004). A variety of external organizations focused on the business of school improvement have grown considerably over the past several decades (Rowan 2002). For example, the federal government has targeted resources on helping SEAs acquire research to develop a system of supports through the reauthorized ESEA comprehensive assistance centers (CAC) and other sponsored centers.

8.2.2.2 Types and Forms of Knowledge

To clarify the nature of evidence that SEAs sought and used in our study, we distinguished three types of knowledge: research-based knowledge, other evidence-based knowledge, and practitioner knowledge. We defined research as findings that have been to varying degrees "collated, summarized, and synthesized," then presented in ways that provide empirical or theoretical insights or make them otherwise informative (Davies and Nutley 2008). We included in this category published original research, research syntheses, summaries or meta-analyses, and evaluation reports. We expanded our conception of research to include forms of research that are designed for use in practice as implementation studies suggest research with more specificity and scaffolding is more likely to be used and with less variation (Rowan et al. 2009), that is, models, protocols, or other tools that embed research or research-based practices in somewhat specified guides to action. Because contextual knowledge is critical to developing "useable" knowledge (Lindblom and Cohen 1979; Weiss et al. 2008), we also examined SEA's use of practitioner knowledge, which we defined as the information, beliefs, and understanding of context that practitioners acquire through experience, and other evidence-based knowledge, such as local data.

We apply social network, organizing, and knowledge utilization lenses to study not only the extent to which SEAs search for and incorporate research or other knowledge into school improvement policies but also how they are organized for such work, the interactive process they use, who searches from whom, and what kind of information they seek out and use.

8.3 Methods

We studied three SEAs located in different regions of the country and varying in size (from 250 to 500 staff). Data for the study were collected between 2010 and 2012. We conducted in-depth interviews with high-level SEA staff involved directly in school improvement and in related programs (e.g., curriculum and instruction, accountability, special programs, teacher policy) and with leaders in external organizations that were central to these SEAs' research use.

Table 8.1 Number of surveys and interviews by state

	State A	State B	State C	External to SEA	Total
# of surveys administered	171	245	194	0	610
# of completed surveys	111	177	162		450
Overall response rate	64.9 %	72.2 %	83.5 %		73.8 %
# of respondents self-identifying as involved in school improvement work	97	127	81		305
# of interviews	20	23	17	5	65

We also sent a web-based survey to all professional staff in the two smaller SEAs and to all staff working in school improvement and related departments and a representative sample of other professional staff in the third SEA. The overall survey response rate was 73.8 % but ranged from 64.9 % in State A to 83.5 % in State C. All survey respondents were asked whether their work related "in any way to improving low-performing schools and school districts" in their state. We used results from those respondents who answered "yes" to this question, that is, staff who self identified as being involved in school improvement work regardless of the SEA office in which they worked, in our analyses.

8.3.1 *Data and Analysis*

Our analyses are based on a total of 65 interviews and 305 surveys in the three SEAs, as well as documents describing SEA school improvement policies and tools (Table 8.1). We examined broad search or user-source interaction patterns. The survey, among other questions, asked respondents to identify the offices, organizations, and individuals they turned to both within and outside their SEA for work or when seeking research, data, and practitioner advice on programs targeted at improving low-performing schools and school districts.[1] To analyze these data for this chapter, we employed UCINET (Borgatti et al. 2002), a network analysis software program, and descriptive statistics to investigate how the research and practitioner networks were configured compared to SEA's more formal authority structures (e.g., we examined cross-department, within-department, and external communication patterns). We considered network size (the extent to which SEAs and particular individuals search for or interact around research) and relational properties such as

[1] For this chapter we focus primarily on research and practitioner networks, using examples of work and data networks as context or to elaborate points. We were unable to collect the names of individuals from whom the respondents sought research or other types of advice and information in State A and use office or department names instead.

the strength[2] of network ties. We broadly identified and categorized the sources of research as well as the types and forms of practitioner knowledge or research that were sought after.

8.3.1.1 Sociograms

The socio-matrices in UCINET served as the base for visualizing the network configurations and actors' positions in them through sociograms or maps of each network created by NetDraw. We relied on sociograms and rank ordering of SEA staff mentions of external sources to identify influential externals (as we did not survey externals). The nodes in the sociogram, Fig. 8.2, are coded by shape and shade to show SEA actors' department or office assignment. Black shapes represent the types of external intermediaries involved in the networks. Arrows represent the direction of connections. We triangulated accounts of search and use of research across respondents, tools, and documents to improve validity.

8.3.1.2 Centrality

We also analyzed the relative importance or centrality of individual actors or offices within the networks to identify broad patterns of influence, but also to explore in much more depth the "ego networks" for these focal individuals at the level of direct, interpersonal, connections. Cognitive interview prompts asked respondents to elaborate on their interactions over time with key internal or external sources of research or other knowledge they found most useful. This allowed us to understand the search and incorporation processes in more depth.

To identify these individuals, offices, or organizations, we used a rank order of standardized centrality measures, along with our sociograms. More specifically we used Freeman's degree centrality. In these networks, an individual or office can be the originator of a tie (the seeker of research information) or recipient of ties (the named source of research or practitioner information). The former is considered an "out-tie" while the latter is considered an "in-tie." Because the direction of the ties or connections among SEA staff and internal or external actors is important, we used "in-degree" as well as "out-degree," that is, a node's actual ties as a proportion of all those possible if an actor (or office) were directly connected to every other in the network (see, e.g., Scott 2013).

---

[2] The strength of network connections was measured through a combination of the frequency of communication about research or other kinds of information, and the influence respondents perceived the resulting information to have on their work (a range from highly influential/daily contact (200) to not influential/a few times per year contact (0.5)).

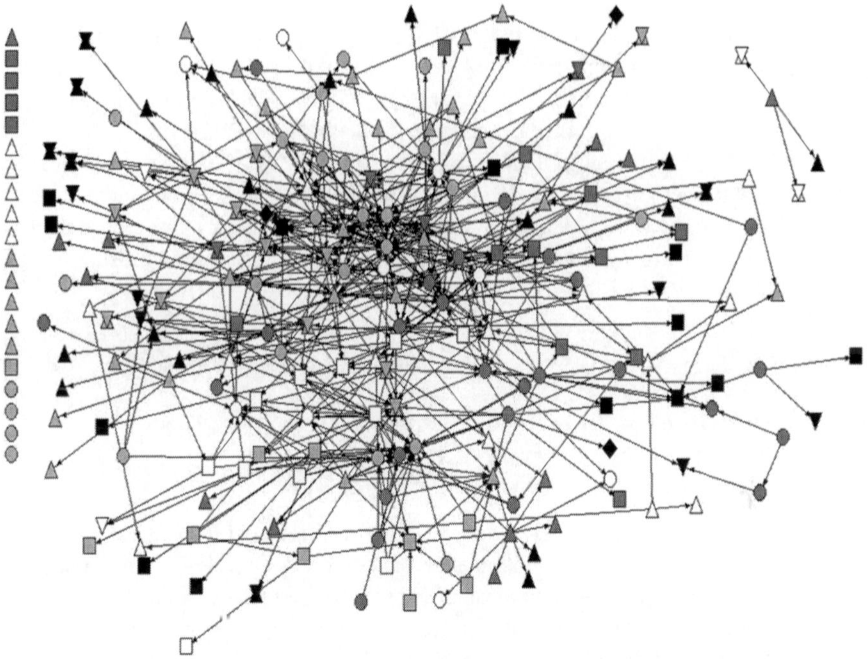

Circle (light gray) = School Improvement	Hour glass (light gray) = Curric. & Instr.
Circle (dark gray) = Fed. Prog. Monitoring	Hour glass (dark gray) = Research
Circle (white) = Commissioners Office	Hour glass (white) = Other SEA Office
Triangle (light gray) = Assessment & Account.	Square (light gray) = Career & Tech Ed.
Triangle (dark gray) = Administration	Square (dark gray)= Early Childhood
Triangle (white) = Special Ed.	Square (white) = Licensure & Prof. Ed.

Fig. 8.2 State B research network

8.4 Findings

SEA staff searched extensively for research and other kinds of information from internal and external sources and incorporated this knowledge into their improvement strategies. Lateral, informal connections within the SEA showed more cross-agency communication than the conventional image of siloed SEAs would suggest and allowed the flow of research or new ideas across departments. However, formal structures also influenced the flow of information: within office connections were stronger, and staff's location in the hierarchy influenced their position in the networks. SEAs turned to a broad array of external intermediaries, particularly government sector agencies and professional membership associations (PMA) for research and practitioner advice. A few of these external organizations were highly influential in helping states translate research into new or revised school improvement strategies.

Several important factors related to the search-incorporation process (including the kind of knowledge and expertise staff valued) led a few of the most influential SEA staff to draw from across different networks and form flexible, more informal working groups or "core networks" with a few external organizations to make sense of and adapt research findings to local contexts. Thus, informal flexible networks—weak and strong—allowed for a more fluid search and incorporation process and, in the case of core networks, often led to the joint development of concrete solutions to specific state needs. SEA staff coupled research, particularly research that was synthesized or packaged in a form they found usable, with practitioner knowledge and data during this decision-making process.

8.4.1 Information Flow in SEA Knowledge Networks: Search and the Sources of Research

We found that SEA staff actively searched for and were receptive to research ideas or related information from both within and outside their agencies, with a majority searching from one or more internal and/or external sources. Respondents reported using research knowledge more than any other type of evidence, though most turned to colleagues in their own or other offices within their agency for it. Specifically, about 75 % of the staff in each agency asked their SEA colleagues for research. A little less than one-third turned to external organizations or individuals for similar information. The majority of staff turned to their colleagues for practitioner and data advice as well. The preponderance of internal search suggests a pattern seen in network studies of districts and schools where district offices and site leaders tend to favor closed, reciprocated relationships within their own group—district or site (Stein and Coburn 2007; Finnigan and Daly 2010). But we found not only reasonably extensive search patterns but also a more varied configuration of weak to strong, within-group and cross-group, professional connections in our three SEA organizations.

8.4.1.1 The Organization of Internal Search and Information Flow

Contrary to the usual image of SEAs as "siloed" organizations, our survey network analyses showed considerably more cross-office work and research-related connections than we anticipated given the literature on SEA structures. The webbed nature of the State B research network in Fig. 8.2 illustrates these cross-department connections between staff, especially those that were central in school improvement work. These include school improvement (light gray circles), curriculum and instruction (light gray hour glass), assessment and accountability (light gray triangle), federal program monitoring (dark gray circle), the commissioner's office (white circle), and few members of the research office (dark gray hourglass). We found a similar configuration of departments and cross-department staff connections in the State C networks although in this state the special education department was also more central. These offices in State A were situated in interactive hubs of activity, with multiple connections between them, but the research and accountability offices were more central there.

Most respondents reported the lateral connections for knowledge exchange and work were relatively new in their organizations and attributable to multiple factors: state and federal accountability demands, competition for federal grants, reduced SEA staffing, and SEA leaders committed to collaboration. For example, the Race to the Top grants stimulated the formation of ad hoc cross-office teams and the flow of research or other knowledge in States B and C. A respondent in State B reported: "When we decided to go for Race to the Top, the demands of what they wanted in that application required that the department work collectively.... Teams were created for each of the core reform areas.... That was the first time I've ever seen the whole department kind of come together to craft a strategy." In State C, special education staff perceived that NCLB subgroup accountability requirements had brought them into the school improvement meetings in an unprecedented way. State A established cross-departmental task forces to design its system of tiered intervention. Leadership in all three SEAs created cross-agency teams to share information, including research or other knowledge or to coordinate tasks.

But these cross-department connections were weaker than within-department connections, suggesting that colleagues within the same department engaged in more frequent research-related discussions and had more influence on one another's work than did the cross-department connections. In the State A research network, for example, 114 within-department ties have an average strength of 71.04, while the 305 cross-department ties have an average strength of 28.07. This pattern is similar in States B and C.

Nevertheless, broad, more informal, and weaker cross-department and external connections facilitated the flow of research, ideas, or expertise in the SEAs. Some directors, for example, searched for research from many departments, were well informed, but maintained only weak ties with most of these sources. Moreover, as the earlier examples show, we found multiple instances where individuals with diverse expertise interacted through less frequent, cross-department task groups or through "boundary spanning" staff liaisons providing intermittent expertise to groups in departments other than their own. In creating its tiered intervention task force on instruction, State A brought together different perspectives and ideas: "We never had brought together academic tiered instruction with social-emotional tiered instruction. So we wanted to bring those together to make a very strong statement to our districts that this is a regular ed responsibility." State C's special education staff took new information, research, and ideas into school improvement meetings through intermittent planning sessions. These findings align with social network studies that have shown that weak ties between individuals whose work is less similar and who are more likely to work in different networks or seek information from different sources support a more varied flow of knowledge and expertise (see, e.g., Scott 2013). Weak ties allow an actor to have broader connections to many more people as the time and effort invested are limited, while stronger, more frequent interaction requires a greater time commitment but allows for more complex, collaborative, and interdependent work.

While staff interaction around research was broad, some SEA staff or offices in the networks had many more direct connections (in-ties and out-ties) to colleagues than others and thus are more likely to have access to a wider variety of knowledge resources. These staff will also have more influence over research in the network, because they are frequently important sources of knowledge and expertise. Influential participants are those who were highly sought after for research information (many in-ties). We conceptualized the most central "well-connected" internal network actors or offices, those who both sought research ideas and information from a range of sources (many out-ties) and, at the same time, provided information to multiple colleagues (many in-ties) as "knowledge brokers." The two sets of individuals/offices overlapped considerably as the two measures can be highly correlated (see, e.g., Song and Miskel 2005; Burt and Minor 1983). These influential or well-connected individuals and offices tended to be clustered more centrally in the core of the network maps (e.g., Fig. 8.2).

Formal organizational structures also influenced lines of communication and the makeup of networks. Formal hierarchy stratified many of the internal ties in State B and C.[3] In these states, influence and knowledge brokering tended to be concentrated in formally designated higher-level or coordinating roles. The directors of school improvement, for example, were the most influential and well-connected SEA staff in these states. Note the many arrows directed into and out from the light gray circles representing the school improvement director and several of his managers in Fig. 8.2. In State B, the director's standardized in-degree (in-tie) and out-degree (out-tie) centralities were both about 4 SDs above the mean. In State C, the director's in-degree centrality was almost 6 SDs above the mean with out-ties to others about 3.5 SDs above the mean. Importantly, 12 of the 19 most influential staff[4] in the State B research network, from across the departments we described earlier, were directors or middle managers, and all three of the key research brokers[5] were directors. Similarly, in State C, 8 out of 11 of the most influential staff were directors or middle managers[6] as were the two key knowledge brokers from school improvement and special education. From the social network perspective, the concentration of information brokering in a few higher-level positions could constrain the timely distribution of knowledge if brokers are overloaded or make SEAs more vulnerable to the loss of critical staff who hold a great deal of knowledge resources (Daly 2010). From another view, a few brokers who have access to multiple kinds of expertise are more likely to coordinate and otherwise productively integrate a range of knowledge into key decisions and policies (Wenger et al. 2002). We found that the turnover of key staff was a challenge in at least two of the states, and productive collaborative work by brokers existed in all three states.

---

[3] We do not include State A here as the unit of analysis; there was office, not individuals.

[4] They were at least one SD above the mean on standardized in-tie scores.

[5] They were at least one SD above the mean on both standardized in-tie and out-tie centrality scores.

[6] Four were at least one SD above the mean, and seven more were above the mean, but less than one standard deviation above the mean.

8.4.1.2 The Organization of External Search and Sources of Research

While SEAs turned to fewer external than internal sources, some of these intermediaries nevertheless played a key role in providing or collaborating on school improvement research, strategies, and tools. Influential knowledge brokers—the office or department directors located at the core of the networks—engaged directly with them (direct ties). In States B and C, the few external intermediaries who were in "the thick of network relationships" (Burt and Minor 1983) were typically either partners with the state in the delivery of school improvement supports or part of the federal comprehensive assistance center (CAC) system designed to help states implement No Child Left Behind. These intermediaries were involved in the improvement work on an ongoing basis. In State B, for example, Fig. 8.2 shows three external organizations—a statewide professional membership association (black triangle), the state's regional CAC (black square), and a state university (black diamond)—were more centrally located than other externals and had more or stronger connections to the key school improvement staff. In addition, the Center on Innovation and Improvement (CII), a federal content CAC (a black square in the right, upper quadrant of the sociogram), and a national professional membership association (black triangle in the right upper quadrant) were also quite influential sources of research or expertise. State C was similarly configured, with similar influential externals, while the situation was quite different in State A, where named external sources were not engaged in a sustained way in the delivery or design of school improvement supports.

While many influential knowledge brokers in these SEAs were mid- to upper-level staff, those who conducted external searches came from all ranks of the SEA hierarchy. Most had fewer and weaker in- or out-ties[7] and in fact were not directly connected to the most influential SEA brokers. Thus, many of the external organizations were located on the periphery of the core networks (see Fig. 8.2).[8] So while the states had access to a wide array of external sources—between 37 different in State A and 42 in State B—a significant share of that external knowledge may not have made its way into the core conversations with influential staff. Some of that information may not be the kind of knowledge needed in the core working groups; for example, research on regulations specific to the responsibilities of lower-level staff may not be necessary there. But the predominance of external resources on the periphery could also indicate weaknesses in the flow of important external information. Other studies suggest that information in social networks is more likely to be distorted from its original form as it passes through multiple colleagues or contacts rather than through a direct link (Bidwell et al. 1997).

[7] Furthermore, a sizable share of the external organizations were named by just one SEA staff member on the survey, suggesting that many sources tended to be very particular to individuals. In State A, two-thirds of the distinct outside organizations or groups were named by just one SEA staff member; in States B and C, about half of the external sources were also identified by only one person.

[8] Another reason is that we did not survey externals and thus do not have out-ties from them.

The external organizations that these states brought into their work shared some similarities but also some points of difference. SEAs relied heavily on intermediaries in the federal government sector and the professional membership association (PMA) sector. Federal government organizations represented 32–42 % of the external research mentions in each state. Most often, these were central federal agencies, particularly the U.S. Department of Education and its divisions, such as the Institute for Education Sciences, and numerous technical assistance and research and development centers dispersed throughout the country, including 22 ESEA CACs, regional education labs (RELs), and more. The CACs are of particular note in this context, because the Congress redesigned them to assist SEAs in adopting research-based practices in domains essential to NCLB, including school improvement.

PMAs comprised the second largest sector for research. PMAs include specific subject matter associations or those focused on teaching and learning more generally, such as ASCD. PMAs represented about one-third of the external mentions in States B and C, compared to only one-tenth of the mentions in State A. In the former two states, one to two PMAs were more integral to the design and delivery of coaching and other supports. That was not the situation in State A.

Whether SEA staff sought outside assistance, and from whom, depended upon a confluence of factors related to perceived policy and organizational needs, past relationships, and source credibility. These factors also shaped how SEAs engaged with external organizations around research. SEAs and state or federal lawmakers made decisions about the problems of extant school improvement efforts. Stakeholders in State A were generally satisfied with the broad direction of their district-focused improvement work. In contrast, States B and C were struggling. They had a legacy of directing their supports at the school level, and, as more and more K-12 schools became the target of federal or state accountability and funding tightened, they determined that these strategies needed major overhaul. They also recognized that they did not have requisite knowledge or capacity. For example, both had little to no staff with curricular expertise at the high school level. For them, federal CAC organizations became key sources of research and long-term assistance. This was not the case in State A, which was more likely to draw upon various RELs for specific, short-term work.

In addition to specific expertise, SEAs sought external organizations to provide an outside perspective on whether their own efforts were within the bounds of good practice—an important metric for SEAs engaged in the often uncertain work of school improvement. State A asked a REL to identify any new research related to its school improvement standards, "so that people understand they're being held accountable to things the research tells us are important." Organizations with state membership or representation were especially valued: "because they are doing it with schools, and state agencies that we are familiar with, we get to talk to the people who are actually involved in it. So I think that increases, in your mind, the validity… [It's] a trust thing…there is a lot of stuff out there." State C sought the advice of a particular university staff member who had been a respected former superintendent, recognizing that his support would lend credibility to the state's initiatives.

8.4.2 *The Search and Incorporation Process*

While broad but relatively weaker, cross-department, and external research networks facilitated the search process and the flow of diverse ideas in the SEAs, a set of the most influential SEA knowledge networks brought research and other kinds of information from these different sources into stronger, but flexible, working groups, we conceptualized as "core networks." SEA brokers and even a few influential externals acting as brokers[9] played pivotal roles in forming these groups that, unlike more formal structures, could draw from diverse sources, readily substitute members and otherwise adapt to collectively address particular problems of school improvement. Core networks generally included influential leaders and staff in school improvement offices, a few external organizations, and occasionally colleagues from other departments.

The core networks emerged or were organized in part, because SEAs sought research in forms that were practical and provided some specified guidance for action. Influential SEA staff often sought research that would address quite specific problems or needs. At the same time practitioner advice or expertise was highly prized, and thus, stronger ties developed with a few external organizations that could provide or assist states in creating or adapting this mix of relevant information to state contexts.[10] We found that SEA staff incorporated research into their school improvement strategies through a distinctly social process in which network members sought out, grappled with, challenged, and otherwise made sense of research over time, in light of other kinds of information (Honig and Coburn 2008; Spillane et al. 2002). One influential office director said of the sense-making process: "We digest it [research] together. And people challenge each other." She continued with an example of a similar process: "We solve problems.... And people bring in research...then we'll challenge the research." Another said, "There is no one individual that holds all the information, which is why we have a group." During the search and incorporation process that could also include problem identification, feedback, and revision, the core network members used local practitioners' feedback, state professionals' experience, and external partners' knowledge of relevant research to contextualize various research findings based on their states' school improvement needs.

Across all three states, school improvement brokers formed strong core network connections with a few key external and internal sources that could assist them in matching or adapting reliable research and other evidence to specific school improvement problems. Unlike models of research dissemination in which generalized, primarily decontextualized findings are transmitted to users, in these core

[9] We identified influential external organizations on sociograms and if or what brokering role they assumed using qualitative evidence.

[10] This is not meant to imply staff outside of the core networks did not want these same forms of research.

networks, users and a few influential providers worked collectively to adapt research, and in some cases co-construct new useable knowledge concrete enough to guide action. This interactive, social process took place over multiple meetings in light of practical challenges and other kinds of evidence that either SEA or external brokers would bring to bear. For example, one very influential member of an SEA broker's core network in State C, a CAC director, described the development process. "It was very joint…We first created it [district guidance tool] to solve a problem…[The school improvement director] said, 'our school improvement planning process is not working.' And then with them we devised the solution and developed it….So, it has been very co-developed." Here as in other settings, communities of practice formed or emerged as "people address recurring sets of problems together" (Wenger et al. 2002, p. 26).

Influential SEA staff also formed strong ties with external sources who not only provided research but also helped school improvement teams make sense of that research with practical, how to advice, through improvement models and work with colleagues in other states. One such staff member in State B explained his strong ties to the CAC system this way: "A [regional CAC], the CII…those folks. That's where you go [for research]." He continued: "And then *for strategies, for how to do it*, first place I go is to… see if they've [other states] figured out how to get it done. What's nice about [the CAC] is that they pull the states together on a regular basis so you can learn what the states are doing." Key school improvement staff in States B and C who had developed strong ties to liaisons in the federal CAC system were able to learn about promising practices or research and how to apply it from developers of school improvement models and with states who were puzzling over similar problems. Not only could the SEA staff in these states access research relevant to particular school improvement policy needs they faced, but they could then see how it might be put into action from early implementers in other SEAs.

In contrast, the school improvement director and a few staff in State A formed weaker ties with multiple external providers, including the CAC system, as they addressed different components of their school improvement delivery system. The State A school improvement department developed stronger ties to the agency's own research and accountability offices. Both compiled local data on specific components of state school improvement strategies that could be used to address emerging problems. One influential explained: "Our key partner in getting information about districts and using that data… comes from [the research department]…. We've been spending a lot of time pouring through [data]—trying to figure out, grapple with how we can best intervene in districts. Looking at our past practices, what worked and hasn't worked according to the data." This core group emerged, in part, as influential school improvement staff, and others collectively made sense of local research evidence or data that would allow them to figure out what works best in specific contexts.

SEA brokers' core networks in all three states also included strong ties to networks of practitioners "on the ground" and in professional associations, as well as to the research networks. Practitioner networks provided advice and feedback on how research-based improvement strategies were working in the field, what needed clarifying, or what could be changed. A State C staff member said of a group of field-based practitioners with strong ties in his network: "They're the ones that see it in action and they know where our course correction should be. They're the ones that can say, 'This is working great, this is not working.'" School improvement staff in State A described the evolution of collective problem identification in their search-incorporation process: "What's the process for identifying challenges? It's a mix of what we bring and what [district superintendents] see." Another member reported: "You'll see research embedded in these pieces... but those toolkits helped us only to a point." Districts would say, "Why don't you come to key meetings and when things bubble up, that's how we'll all know [what we need]." Therefore: "I think we've grown to a place where it's real time need, really fluid work. And that's the best of our work." These kinds of network connections allowed for a social sense-making process that kept SEAs more flexible and state school improvement strategies responsive to changing contexts or emerging problems, as opposed to top-down and static.

As the examples of incorporation suggest, SEA staff often coupled research with practitioner knowledge or in other ways adapted it to their own context. More broadly, SEA staff gravitated to research that they perceived as relevant to their context, such as studies conducted in similar settings (e.g., small states, states with diverse student populations) or studies that addressed a current problem. They preferred research that was actionable and feasible for them to do under current staffing or other conditions. They wanted research-based guidance for very specific and concrete steps or tools that they could use in their work, sometimes called "research designed for use." State C worked with the CII and their regional CAC to develop "change maps," a process for the SEA to use to tailor their assistance to the different needs of sites. It built on research from Banathy (1996), among others. Similarly, SEAs wanted research or evidence with rich, descriptive details of practice to pass on to educators or support providers. State B staff, for example, read and encouraged their school improvement providers to use *Instructional Rounds in Education* (City et al. 2009), a book that offers research-based guidance on a method of observing and supporting teacher improvement tied to student learning and academic content. State A sought research on how to create and maintain effective professional learning communities and adapted it into guidance with the help of local educators and the National Institute for School Leadership.

8.5 Conclusion and Implications

SEA staff in our three study states were receptive to research and actively sought it from multiple external sources as well as through internal lateral connections to design and elaborate their school improvement strategies. Federal and state incentives played a role in creating states' demand for the advice and products of external intermediaries and, importantly, in forming relatively new knowledge networks that crossed external and internal department boundaries. Not only did network connections in these cases bring different perspectives into the search, incorporation, and implementation process, but they created what Lusi (1997) and other researchers suggest are much more flexible structures for generating or managing knowledge such that it can be responsive to pressing school improvement problems. All of this may be a surprise to critics who view SEAs as more siloed, compliance-oriented bureaucrats uninterested in research or innovation. Nevertheless, both formal organizational structures and more informal flexible networks affected how research was diffused or constrained and how SEAs sought, acquired, and used it with other evidence.

While external organizations were key in providing access to a diverse array of research, a few of them, primarily federal agencies and PMAs, became influential in the core networks of key SEA actors and thus in the development of states' school improvement strategies. This was so in part, because they offered synthesized, packaged research and "research designed for use" that provided concrete guidance for program development. Importantly, they also assisted states in generating or adapting this mix of relevant information to particular state problems through a collective sense-making process.

Contrary to a unidimensional model of knowledge utilization, where research users are viewed as passive recipients of published research, search-incorporation was a multidimensional, social process that allows for the joint creation of workable, research-based, state strategies. A few influential intermediaries and SEA brokers, primarily higher-level staff, formed core networks that drew from and engaged with diverse kinds of expertise over time, thus helping them manage two classic problems frequently limiting research use: matching research to specific contextual needs and translating research knowledge into less abstract, more concrete forms for guiding program development and implementation (Weiss et al. 2008; Argyris and Schön 1974).

Although the findings reported here come from an exploratory study of only three SEAs in one policy area, they shed light on ways to strengthen research use in these organizations. Policy incentives should expand methods that move beyond simply transmitting research or disseminating best practices to SEAs or other state agencies. Instead these incentives and provider networks should assist in cultivating more of the varied groups of expertise we found, including SEA brokers, key research sources, and practitioners, to adapt generalized findings into more useable information, thus managing prominent obstacles to research use. SEAs can help external intermediaries become more effective knowledge partners if they identify and connect them not only to the influential internal brokers but also to staff who may be essential to the task but are currently more peripheral to the core working groups. This would make SEAs less vulnerable to turnover or staff overload. Finally, policymakers should encourage and support SEA evaluations of their own school improvement programs. These can provide critical feedback to agency staff, but SEAs often lack the human resources to design these studies and the fiscal resources to conduct them.

This study also has several implications for further research. First, because this was an exploratory study of knowledge use in school improvement policy by a small, purposive sample of SEAs, researchers should study SEAs or other state agencies to see if our findings generalize to other settings. Second, future research should track how the integrity of research is maintained during the interactive social processes that appear to be productive in fostering research use, to understand the trade-offs between fidelity to research principles and adaptation to contextual contingencies. Third, there is a need to assess the quality of research acquired by SEA staff and underlying "research designed for use" products. While many of these products were written by or cited national experts, sometimes research was added in a fairly superficial manner, and some of the underlying studies were weak. The implications of our study for improving the quality of school improvement policies are also indirect. Our findings are not derived from an analysis of the effects of these policies on schools. Thus, further research should investigate the interaction effects of state and local networks and research-based policies on schools and districts.

References

Argyris, M., & Schön, D. (1974). *Theory in practice. Increasing professional effectiveness*. San Francisco: Jossey-Bass.

Argyris, C., & Schon, D. (1996). *Organizational learning II: Theory, method, and practice*. Reading, MA: Addison-Wesley.

Barnes, C., Camburn, E., Sanders, B., & Sebastian, J. (2010). Developing instructional leaders: Using mixed methods to explore the black box of planned change in principals' professional practice. *Educational Administration Quarterly, 46*(2), 241–279.

Banathy, B. H. (1996). *Designing social systems in a changing world*. New York: Plenum Press.

Bidwell, C. E., Frank, K. D., & Quiroz, P. A. (1997). Teacher types, workplace controls, and the organization of schools. *Sociology of Education, 70*, 256–284.

Borgatti, S. P., Everett, M. G., & Freeman, L. C. (2002). *Ucinet 6 for windows*. Harvard: Analytic Technologies.

Brown, J. S., & Duguid, P. (1991). Organizational learning and communities-of-practice: Toward a unified view of working, learning, and innovation. *Organization Science, 2*(1), 40–57.

Burt, R. S., & Minor, M. J. (Eds.). (1983). *Applied network analysis*. Beverly Hill/London/New Delhi: Sage Publications.

City, E. A., Elmore, R. F., Fiarman, S. E., & Teitel, L. (2009). *Instructional rounds in education: A network approach to improving teaching and learning*. Cambridge, MA: Harvard Education Press.

Coburn, C. E., Honig, M. I., & Stein, M. K. (2009). What's the evidence on district's use of evidence? In J. Bransford, D. J. Stipek, N. J. Vye, L. Gomez, & D. Lam (Eds.), *Educational improvement: What makes it happen and why?* (pp. 67–86). Cambridge: Harvard Education Press.

Daly, A. J. (Ed.). (2010). *Social network theory and educational change*. Cambridge, MA: Harvard Education Press.

Davies, H. T. O., & Nutley, S. M. (2008, September). *Learning more about how research-based knowledge gets used: Guidance in the development of new empirical research*. New York: William T. Grant Foundation.

Dutton, J., & Heaphy, E. (2003). Coming to life: The power of high quality connections at work. In K. Cameron, J. Dutton, & R. Quinn (Eds.), *Positive organizational scholarship*. Williston: Berrett-Koehler.

Finnigan, K. S., & Daly, A. J. (2010). Learning at a system level: Ties between principals of low performing schools and central office leaders. In A. J. Daly (Ed.), *Social network theory and educational change* (pp. 179–195). Cambridge, MA: Harvard Education Press.

Finnigan, K., Daly, A., & Che, J. (2013). Systemwide reform in districts under pressure: The role of social networks in defining, acquiring, using, and diffusing research evidence. *Journal of Educational Administration, 51*(4), 476–497

Frank, K. A., Zhao, Y., & Borman, G. (2004). Social capital and the diffusion of innovations within organizations: Application to the implementation of computer technology in schools. *Sociology of Education, 77*, 148–171.

Goertz, M. E., Barnes, C., Massell, D., Fink, R., & Francis, A. (2013). *How state education agencies acquire and use research knowledge for school improvement.* RR-76. Philadelphia: Consortium for Policy Research in Education.

Honig, M. I. (2004). The new middle management: Intermediary organizations in education policy implementation. *Educational Evaluation and Policy Analysis, 26*(1), 65–87.

Honig, M., & Coburn, C. (2008). Evidence-based decision-making in school district central offices: Toward a policy and research agenda. *Educational Policy, 22*(4), 578–608.

Hood, P. (2002). *Perspectives on knowledge utilization in education*. San Francisco: WestEd.

Lindblom, C. E., & Cohen, D. K. (1979). *Usable knowledge*. New Haven: Yale University Press.

Lusi, S. F. (1997). *The role of state departments of education in complex school reform*. New York: Teachers College Press.

Miskel, C. G., & Song, M. (2004). Passing reading first: Prominence and processes in an elite policy network. *Educational Evaluation and Policy Analysis, 26*(2), 89–109.

Rennie Center for Education Research & Policy. (2004). *Examining state intervention capacity: How can the state better support low performing schools & districts?* Boston: The Rennie Center for Education Research & Policy.

Rowan, B. (2002). The ecology of school improvement: Notes on the school improvement industry in the United States. *Journal of Educational Change, 3*(3–4), 283–314.

Rowan, B., Correnti, R., Miller, R., & Camburn, E. (2009). School improvement by designs: Lessons from a study of comprehensive school reform programs. In B. Schneider & G. Sykes (Eds.), *Handbook of education policy research* (pp. 637–651). Washington, DC: American Educational Research Association.

Scott, J. (2013). *Social network analysis* (3rd ed.). Los Angeles/London/New Delhi: Sage Publications.

Song, M., & Miskel, C. G. (2005). Who are the influentials? A cross-state social network analysis of the reading policy domain. *Educational Administration Quarterly, 41*(1), 7–44.

Spillane, J., Reiser, B. J., & Reimer, T. (2002). Policy implementation and cognition: Reframing and refocusing implementation research. *Review of Educational Research, 72*(3), 387–431.

Stein, M. K., & Coburn, C. (2007). *Architectures for learning: A Comparative analysis of two urban school districts*. Seattle: University of Washington, Center for the Study of Teaching and Policy.

Supovitz, J. A., & Weinbaum, E. H. (Eds.). (2008). *The implementation gap: Understanding reform in high schools*. New York: Teachers College Press.

Unger, C., Lane, B., Cutler, E., Lee, S., Whitney, J., Arruda, E., & Silva, M. (2008). *How can state education agencies support district improvement? A conversation amongst educational leaders, researchers, and policy actors*. Providence: The Education Alliance at Brown University.

Weick, K. E., & Sutcliffe, K. M. (2001). *Managing the unexpected: Assuring high performance in an age of complexity*. San Francisco: Jossey-Bass.

Weiss, C. H., Murphy-Graham, E., Petrosino, A., & Gandhi, A. G. (2008). The fairy godmother and her warts: Making the dream of evidence-based policy come true. *American Journal of Evaluation, 29*(1), 29–47.

Wenger, E., McDermott, R., & Snyder, W. M. (2002). *Cultivating communities of practice: A guide to managing knowledge*. Boston: Harvard Business School Press.

Chapter 9
Research Evidence and the Common Core State Standards

Lorraine M. McDonnell and M. Stephen Weatherford

9.1 The Context

One of the most striking characteristics of US public education, a trait that sets it apart from other countries, has been the absence of national academic standards. Each state has had its own standards specifying the content and skills students are expected to master. However, this element of American exceptionalism began to disappear in 2010, as 45 states adopted common standards in mathematics and English language arts (ELA), setting in motion a fundamental policy change. The process by which these Common Core State Standards (CCSS) were promoted, developed, adopted, and are now being implemented is also notable. CCSS advocates and developers promised that the standards would be "research and evidence based." With that assurance, a group of policy entrepreneurs, standards writers, policymakers, and educators were expected to use education research as they crafted the CCSS. By highlighting research as the basis for the standards, CCSS proponents were distinguishing the basis of the Common Core from that of traditional state standards. In testimony before the House Committee on Education and Labor, the executive director of the Council of Chief State School Officers (CCSSO) noted that the CCSS

> …is being driven by evidence and research. In the past, standards were largely based on personal judgment to determine what concepts are in or out of standards, the process often becomes a negotiation, rather than a reflection on what the evidence and research tells [sic] us about the connection between K-12 experiences and success in higher education and promising careers. (Wilhoit 2009)

However, the reference to research and evidence suggested that the CCSS would be based on more than just findings from formal research studies. Several decades of policy analysis have documented that validated research is not the sole, or often

---

L.M. McDonnell (✉) • M.S. Weatherford
Department of Political Science, University of California – Santa Barbara, Santa Barbara, CA, USA
e-mail: mcdonnell@polsci.ucsb.edu

K.S. Finnigan and A.J. Daly (eds.), *Using Research Evidence in Education: From the Schoolhouse Door to Capitol Hill*, Policy Implications of Research in Education 2,
DOI 10.1007/978-3-319-04690-7_9,

even the most important, basis for policy choices (Stone 2012; Majone 1989). Therefore, in examining the CCSS, we have sought to think broadly about the process of policymaking. A key contribution of our research is to elaborate a typology of different kinds of evidence, ranging from the results of formal research studies to statistical data, judgments based on professional expertise, the personal experience of practitioners, existing policies and practice, and appeals to values articulated through stories and symbols.

The CCSS represent "an idea in motion," moving over the short span of 5 years from its initial conception to the policy agenda and on through the design, adoption, and now implementation process. This process has allowed us to trace the use of research in this major policy initiative in real time, where previous studies of research use have typically relied on the recollections of participants whose views of the process are often shaded by knowing the outcome. Its potential for addressing widely agreed shortfalls in US public education, moreover, meant that the Common Core has engaged a diverse array of actors and drawn on research to inform a variety of tasks. More than 25 organizations have been actively involved in the Common Core: most are interest groups representing specific constituencies, although some are advocates for particular policy agendas. Prominent among them are the National Governors Association (NGA) and the CCSSO that represent elected officials; these organizations acted as policy entrepreneurs in developing the CCSS. Other groups include teacher unions, civil rights organizations, foundations, private providers, and parent groups. Additionally, among the users of research and evidence are the professionals who drafted and reviewed the standards as well as the hundreds of thousands of educators who must now translate the Common Core into classroom instruction.

Over the course of this process, and especially at the stage when the new standards were developed and articulated with current state standards, new communication channels were opened and old ones reinvigorated. The resulting networks linked researchers with curriculum and testing experts in states and school districts, with teachers and teacher organizations, and with public and private entities that supply textbooks, tests, and teacher professional development.

9.2 Frameworks

Because the CCSS initiative is essentially an education reform policy, our conceptual lens is grounded in the policy analytic and political science research literature. Three strands are especially relevant. The first focuses on the policy process and specifies how research and other evidence use vary over phases of the policy cycle. For example, because the solutions or policy options that are considered typically depend on how a policy problem is defined, research-based evidence may be interwoven with normative arguments that appeal to elected officials' and their constituents' core values. In this phase, evidence use typically consists of research and statistics that define the nature, distribution, and likely causes of a problem combined with the strategic use of a variety of evidences linking a problem definition to a particular policy option (Stone 2012; Kingdon 1995). In contrast, once policy options reach the agendas of decision-making institutions, evidence use again combines research and other information, but the focus is on informing the details of policy design – e.g., the effects of different funding mechanisms and administrative arrangements – while also maintaining support and minimizing opposition to the proposed policy. Similarly, other phases, such as policy enactment and implementation, evoke the use of evidence in different combinations.

A second strand of our conceptual framework focuses on explaining a defining characteristic of the CCSS and also exploring a more general dimension of evidence use in policymaking. The question specific to the CCSS is: why was this initiative successful after previous attempts to move the United States toward national standards had failed? One likely reason is that Common Core proponents had learned from earlier efforts to draft voluntary national standards that had become enmeshed in controversies over curricular values and fears of federal encroachment (Rothman 2011). Political and policy conditions had changed over the ensuring decades, but CCSS advocates had to discern what those changes were and their implications for the design and advancement of a new approach to national standards. The broader issue is how policy entrepreneurs use evidence – including research knowledge – about past policy successes and failures in shaping their substantive and strategic agendas.

Organizational learning requires that institutional actors identify and understand the factors contributing to past successes and failures. In doing so, they need to draw inferences from their experience and that of others and then use those inferences to shape and guide future behavior (Levitt and March 1988). That process requires collecting and analyzing information to identify problems and their causes, searching for solutions, and applying them to improve performance (Mahler 2009). In a policy context, organizational learning may take two different forms: political learning that results in more sophisticated advocacy of a policy and policy learning that leads to changes in a policy's scope or its implementation plan. May (1992) notes that the evidence for political learning often involves a shift in advocates' tactics, while policy learning is typically associated with more fundamental changes, including redefined objectives. Although policy learning may lead to altered goals, it can also result in a reaffirmation of the proposed policy's original goals, but with a shift in its scope or targets.

Because of our interest in evidence use, we elaborated our focus on learning by drawing on theories of information processing. Jones and Baumgartner (2005) define information processing as "collecting and assembling, interpreting, and prioritizing signals from the environment" (p. 7). These signals are characterized by uncertainty and ambiguity because it is often not clear if the external environment has actually changed or in what way, thus complicating learning by policy entrepreneurs. Nevertheless, to the extent that they can collect, distill, and validly interpret information about the external environment, they gain a valuable resource not only to aid in their own learning, but also one that can be used as part of their advocacy strategies.

We utilize a third and final body of theory to analyze the interplay between researchers and policymakers. We interpret the process through which research (and other types of systematic evidence) is integrated into policy or practice as analogous with attitude change and persuasion and uses the theoretical approach pioneered in cognitive psychology (Petty and Cacioppo 1986; Bohner et al. 2008). As with the process of coming to a new opinion about an issue, the use of research in an ongoing activity involves more than simply learning new information; the recipient must see the new information as relevant and credible and also understand how its use could improve the ongoing activity (Bohner and Dickel 2011; Holyoak and Chang 2011; cf. Spillane et al. 2002). Thus, this perspective distinguishes two stages in the process of taking up new information: the communication of new ideas and their supporting evidence, and the comprehension and integration of that new information in the context of previously established behaviors and organizational routines (cf. Kennedy 1983; Davies and Nutley 2008).

9.3 Methods

This analysis draws on three data sources.[1] The first is interviews with leaders of the Common Core movement, interest groups supporting the CCSS, members of the work groups and committees charged with writing and validating the CCSS, national and state education policymakers, groups critical of the CCSS, and private providers of curricular and professional development materials. Between May 2011 and June 2013, 116 interviews were conducted at the national level and in California, Indiana, Massachusetts, and Tennessee.[2] These structured interviews focused on the politics and process of Common Core promotion, development, and adoption; why participants chose to use certain types of evidence and what other types were either unavailable or not used; and what they see as major implementation challenges and the types of information and evidence that would be most useful in addressing them. These interviews are the primary basis for the findings presented in this chapter.[3]

[1] The study on which this chapter is based was supported by a grant from the W. T. Grant Foundation as part of its Uses of Research Evidence Program. We were assisted in our data collection by Lisa Argyle, Alex Cortez, Marika Fain, Cecilia Farfan-Mendez, Jeanette Yih Harvie, Natalie Miller, Arlene Perez, Mabel Perez, Kristoffer Smemo, Chelsy Thompson, and Kimberly Zilles at UC Santa Barbara and by Stephanie E. Dean, Ashley Clark Perry, and Lindsay Shouldis at the Hunt Institute.

[2] These four states were selected to provide regional variation and to include representation from states receiving Race to the Top funding and ones not receiving it. Half the interviews were conducted with national-level actors; the balance was divided among respondents in the four states. National-level respondents ranged from congressional staff to executive directors of national organizations (including teachers, school boards, and civil rights groups as well as groups focused on general education policy advocacy), in addition to participants in the CCSS process (including the drafters and members of work groups and validating committees). State-level respondents included state education agency leadership, legislators, university researchers, teachers, and representatives of education policy advocacy groups.

[3] About 10 % of the interviews were conducted over the telephone, the remainder in person. The average duration of the interviews was between 45 and 60 min. Interviewees were assured that their responses would be confidential and not attributed to them or their organization, so only their role positions are noted in citing interview data.

A second data source are research reports, policy briefs, speeches, blog posts, press releases, media accounts, and Congressional testimony related to the CCSS that were produced between 2006 and the end of 2011. Approximately 1,500 artifacts were archived and a sample of 30 %, stratified by stage of the policy process and type of organization producing the artifact, were coded.[4] The coding captures the type of evidence cited, the intended audience, the policy issues discussed, how they have been framed in the CCSS process, and their links to other artifacts and organizations.

The final data source is participant observer notes from weekly conference calls between September 2010 and January 2011 among groups engaged in implementing the CCSS. Initiated and moderated by the Hunt Institute, the confidential calls typically involved 7–14 "advocacy partners," including organizations representing elected officials, teachers and administrators, higher education, parents, and non-profit private providers, most linked by common sources of funding for their work on the CCSS. The participants discuss their individual and shared activities, political developments that advance or threaten the Common Core, and their upcoming information needs. The notes chronicle the continuing role of organizations that serve as research and information intermediaries for various policymaker, professional, and public audiences.

9.4 Findings

The story of the CCSS – its implementation, effects, and the role of research in shaping it – will not be fully known for a decade or more. Yet its early history suggests three major conclusions about the use of research and other types of evidence in promoting the fundamental policy shift that the Common Core represents. The first is that, consistent with the literature on policy analysis, research use differed over stages of the Common Core's development and that variation served both substantive and strategic purposes. Second, advocates learned from the experience of prior standards-based reform attempts, and this political and policy learning enriched the CCSS process in several ways, including fostering a more discerning assessment of the political conditions for change; a more robust appreciation for the federal structure of American education governance, resulting in a state-led (rather than a federal) initiative; and a sharpened sensitivity to the danger that ideology and partisan competition could derail reform if the initiative did not maintain a clear problem focus. Third, throughout the process policy advocates, researchers, and

[4] In addition to those produced by organizations active in the Common Core movement, news articles, op-eds, editorials, and blog posts on the CCSS which have been published by *Education Week*, the *New York Times*, and the *Washington Post* are among the artifacts that have been archived and coded. Similar artifacts were also archived from the largest circulation newspapers in each of the four states (*Los Angeles Times, Indianapolis Star Tribune, Boston Globe*, and the *Memphis Commercial Appeal*).

policymakers combined formal, peer-reviewed research findings with other types of evidence – particularly statistical data, expert judgment, and practitioner knowledge – in a process of collaborative problem-solving that successfully spanned the oft-lamented gap between the "cultures" of research and practice.

9.4.1 Research Use over the Stages of the Policy Development Process

In promoting the idea of standards common across multiple states, advocates used research-based evidence in making two arguments in support of the policy. Drawing on data from the Programme for International Student Assessment (PISA) and the Trends in International Mathematics and Science Study (TIMSS), they argued that the achievement of US students is low as compared with the nation's economic competitors and that unlike the United States, countries with high-achieving students have focused, rigorous, and coherent national standards. For groups with an equity agenda, even more compelling were arguments based on data showing persistent patterns of differential achievement among students depending on their race/ethnicity, social class, and place of residence; students' lack of preparation for postsecondary education or employment; and significant variation among states in the rigor of their standards.[5]

These arguments were substantive in their reliance on international data documenting variations in student performance and suggesting a relationship between test scores and differential learning opportunities. Decades of research highlighted the shortcomings of the United States' fragmented approach to specifying what students should know as compared with other countries' more coherent and focused approach to academic standards. At the same time, research was used strategically in defining the problem of US students' low and variable achievement as one that could be addressed by adopting national standards. Although the achievement of US students as compared with peers in other countries and the generally low quality of state standards were generally accepted, there was less agreement about the relationship between standards and achievement or the causes of the differing levels of achievement by US students. Diagnosing the reason for the relationship, in short, required interpretation, and CCSS proponents identified the cause of US students' low achievement as due to states' low and variable quality standards. That strategic framing pointed to common standards as the primary solution (National Governors Association 2008). In contrast, and as we might expect from the literature on strategic framing (Stone 2012; Majone 1989), some researchers drew a different conclusion and emphasized the lack of system capacity, especially supports for teachers and students (Cohen and Moffitt 2009).

---

[5] We discuss the use of evidence during this early phase of the CCSS in McDonnell and Weatherford (2013).

This same combination of substantive and strategic purposes extended into the development and adoption of the standards. At one level, the CCSS development process was a technical task characterized by the systematic use of research and other types of evidence.[6] Consistent with its promised reliance on research-based evidence, a variety of sources were used, including peer-reviewed journal articles, research syntheses prepared by expert panels convened by federal agencies and professional associations, surveys of postsecondary faculty, and reviews of international test data and the standards of high-performing countries. So, for example, among the works consulted in drafting the mathematics standards were scholarly studies related to teaching mathematics to young children, the final report of the National Mathematics Advisory Panel, National Research Council reports synthesizing research on how people learn, analyses of PISA and TIMSS, the NAEP mathematics frameworks, and standards from about a dozen countries and five US states that had what were considered rigorous mathematics standards (Common Core State Standards Initiative 2010).

However, in addition to producing the mathematics and ELA standards, CCSSO, NGA, and their allies had to concentrate on several other tasks. They needed to ensure that those who would be responsible for adopting and implementing the CCSS, especially state officials and classroom teachers, were invested in the endeavor. Consequently, groups representing those constituencies were regularly consulted, given draft standards to review, and their input seriously considered. In obtaining input from state officials through continued consultation with state departments of education and from interactions with teachers convened by the two national teacher unions, the standards writers were acting strategically. They were also using a different kind of evidence than the results of formal research, viz., the judgments of expert state administrators and experienced classroom teachers about the content of the standards and about how to smooth the process of implementing them. The process of collecting that evidence was strategic in that it helped build trust and acceptance of the standards among key constituencies.

However, the evidence itself played a critical substantive role because it was based on the expert judgments of practitioners familiar with how standards operate once they are translated into classroom instruction. Although past research could provide some information about the school and classroom implementation of standards, input from practitioners not only lent greater credibility to the development process, but it also provided the writers with more finely grained information about the linkages between standards and classroom practice. Classroom teachers were especially attentive to the instructional logic inherent in the order of standards across grade levels and to the language used in communicating the intent of each standard. Members of the American Federation of Teachers (AFT) who were among the teacher reviewers talked about focusing on the Common Core's utility in the classroom and its ability

---

[6] For more details on the different types of research and other evidence used in the standards development process, see Weatherford and McDonnell (2013).

to guide instruction. So, for example, mathematics teachers wanted to see a balance between an emphasis on deep conceptual understanding of mathematical concepts and students' mastery of mathematical procedures (Personal interviews, AFT 2010). During the adoption process, research and other evidence were used strategically to convince state boards of education to substitute the CCSS for their current state-specific standards. The same research findings that had been used to build the initial case for moving toward common standards were repeated in state venues through vehicles such as presentations to the state board of education and in media outlets through letters to the editor and op-ed articles. To assist state-level CCSS supporters, CCSSO and NGA provided a "messaging toolkit" with talking points and sample content for letters to the editor and op-ed articles. In California, for example, then-president of the State Board of Education (SBE), Ted Mitchell, published an op-ed article just prior to the SBE's vote on the CCSS. He echoed points outlined in national discussions and the toolkit: that the Common Core "has been informed by the best available evidence," that it reflects "the realities of the classroom" and "includes rigorous content and skills," and that "the standards are benchmarked to those of other top-performing countries" (Mitchell 2010). At the same time, he raised a controversial issue specific to California about teaching algebra in the eighth grade and argued that the mathematics CCSS better prepare students for algebra and provide another option for students not ready for algebra in the eighth grade.

These generic sources were augmented with analyses comparing the CCSS in detail with current state standards as a basis for demonstrating that the Common Core is at least as rigorous in the topics and skills covered as the state standards and in most cases more coherent and focused. One of the states where such an analysis was critical to support for adoption of the CCSS was Massachusetts because it had both high standards and relatively high student achievement as compared with other US states. With funding from the Gates Foundation, the Massachusetts Business Alliance for Education (MBAE) commissioned WestEd to analyze the extent to which the revised Massachusetts state standards corresponded with the CCSS. In a 500-page report, WestEd presented a crosswalk analysis of the two sets of standards and assessed their degree of alignment on content skills and knowledge, depth of knowledge, and the clarity and measurability of each standard by grade and content area. Because WestEd concluded that both the Massachusetts standards and the CCSS overlapped in content coverage and were comparable in clarity and measurability, the MBAE board decided that Massachusetts "couldn't go wrong either way" in adopting either its own recently revised standards or the CCSS. However, it supported adoption of the CCSS and urged the SBE to incorporate where appropriate Massachusetts standards not reflected in the Common Core (Personal interviews, MBAE 2010; WestEd 2010).[7]

[7] In collaboration with the Massachusetts Department of Education, Achieve also conducted a comparative content analysis of the revised Massachusetts standards and the CCSS and found a 90 % alignment overall. However, MBAE commissioned the WestEd analysis because it perceived Achieve as biased, stemming from its support of the Common Core. The Massachusetts SBE unanimously adopted the CCSS on July 21, 2010. At the same time, one of the major groups

9.4.2 Research Use and Political and Policy Learning

The explanation for the combined use of research for substantive and strategic purposes lies in a second finding about research as a resource in political and policy learning. Because of the highly visible and divisive failure of earlier attempts to promote national standards, the success of the Common Core depended on both political learning, yielding more sophisticated advocacy of the idea, and policy learning, leading to reshaping the institutional arrangements by which standards were developed and would operate. The first challenge for those promoting national standards was to discern, given signals from the policy environment, whether conditions had changed so that national standards were now more politically feasible. Based on several different indicators, the Common Core leaders decided that conditions were now more favorable than in the 1990s. These signals included the participation of 16 states in the American Diploma Project with its common college- and career-ready high school graduation requirements; public opinion polls indicating support for national standards; and state policymakers beginning to see the potential cost advantages of common standards, especially given the requirements of No Child Left Behind (Rothman 2011; Personal interviews). One of the leaders of the CCSS initiative explained how he and his colleagues interpreted these indicators and used them in their advocacy with state policymakers:

> …we had very disparate standards across the country. That was particularly revealed with No Child Left Behind because it required states to define "proficiency" based on their standards, and then to define cut scores. So you had states demonstrating widely different ideas of what they expected kids to know to be ready for the 21st century. That just seemed to me to drive us toward a common core that more truly reflected where we wanted to go…
>
> …to legislators, I would often use a cost-effective argument: Do you really want to be in this business 50 times and try to come up with the best standards, or do you want to pool your efforts at the state-level – not the federal – to collaborate. And I would point to some early examples of collaboration – New England [NECAP], Achieve was already underway with their Algebra II standards. It was important to have some examples of where this was already happening and producing good results.

However, even with greater support than in the past, the resulting policy proposal had to avoid two pitfalls of past attempts: it could not appear to be a federal or even a national incursion into state authority, and it could not become entangled in ideological disputes over curricular values. The first obstacle was avoided when CCSSO and NGA took the lead in organizing the development of the initiative. Constituency organizations representing state officials, CCSSO and NGA outlined an adoption process that would proceed on a state-by-state basis, according to the policy enactment rules of each state. In corresponding fashion, the organizers' insistence that the development process be research and evidence based helped to avoid the second pitfall. Policy learning helps explain much about how this effort was organized.

---

opposing the CCSS, the Pioneer Institute, is located in Boston and continues to argue that the state's adoption of the Common Core is weakening the quality of academic content in the state's classrooms (personal interviews).

Lessons were drawn from the failure of the G. H. W. Bush and Clinton administrations' proposals for national standards and from the "curriculum wars" of the 1990s that had threatened standards policies in some states.

Relying on research and evidence as a primary foundation for the CCSS had the substantive benefit of grounding them in available knowledge about developmental processes, teaching and learning, the structure and logic of disciplines such as mathematics, and the skills needed for students to be prepared for college or for entry-level careers. At the same time, this approach was also strategic. CCSS leaders acknowledged that their commitment to ground the effort in research and evidence was a strategy to avoid past ideological debates that had plagued standards and assessment policies in a number of states during the 1990s (Personal interviews; McDonnell and Weatherford 2013).

The success of the CCSS will ultimately depend on how much policy learning has occurred about the necessary conditions for successful classroom implementation of top-down policies. Although the enabling resources necessary for the CCSS to produce their intended effects – such as instructional materials and provisions for professional development to prepare teachers to work with the new content – were not stressed as the idea of Common Core standards was promoted and developed, its advocates understood that its promise depends on effective implementation. Some 20 years of standards-based reform had taught that lesson.

We do not yet know the extent to which research will be used during the CCSS implementation process. Our interviews with those responsible for implementation in four states and with a number of private providers suggest that use is likely to vary across states and local districts depending on the resources available to support educators, including the strength and quality of existing professional development networks, and whether states and districts have additional funding from sources such as foundations and the federal Race to the Top program. The ambitious aims of the Common Core State Standards, along with the fact that state education budgets have been cut all across the country, mean that implementing the Common Core will also depend much more than with past curriculum reforms on the resources available from hundreds of nonprofit and for-profit providers of instructional materials and professional development. These materials, widely advertised as aligned with the CCSS, will doubtless vary in their effectiveness, because no central body is assessing the quality of the materials being produced by an increasingly dense network of private providers, or the degree of their alignment with the CCSS. Even if the quality of materials and their alignment with the Common Core can be assessed by state agencies and local districts, using tools such as the publishers' criteria for mathematics and ELA developed by the standards writers (Coleman and Pimentel 2012; National Governors Association et al. 2012, 2013), there is still the challenge of how new materials can be incorporated into ongoing instruction. As a researcher working closely with districts in California noted:

> I do think that there is currently a dearth of really strong aligned materials, so availability right now is an issue, but what I see is going to be a bigger issue is there's going to be a ton of stuff out there…The issue is knowing how to use it, knowing how to incorporate materials into your instructional program, into your curriculum, how do you actually build curriculum that reflects the Common Core?

Private providers are playing a critical role in that process and in doing so, they are drawing on a range of evidences. Some market their materials as designed "by teachers for teachers" and draw on surveys of teachers and the developers' experience in working with teachers. Other providers are relying on the former teachers and teacher educators who prepare the instructional materials and professional development programs they sell to revise and adapt existing products for the CCSS. In contrast, some major providers, with funding from sources such as the Gates Foundation, draw directly on research to create templates that teachers can then adapt to their local contexts. One example is the Mathematics Design Collaborative (MDC) whose work on formative assessments is based on research conducted by the Shell Centre at the University of Nottingham and at UC Berkeley. In these cases, research-based evidence is used in such a way that it can be integrated with "the wisdom of practice" (Personal interviews, Phillips and Wong 2012).

9.4.3 *Combining Research with Other Types of Evidence*

That approach leads to our third and final finding: throughout the CCSS process, research has been resourcefully combined with other types of evidence. The political nature of the adoption phase made it appropriate to invoke the sort of strategic reasoning that called on evidence such as teachers' and state officials' judgments, public opinion data, and past policies. However, the integration of research with other types of evidence was an equally prominent part of the process when the purposes were more substantive and technical, as during the formulation and writing of the standards. Certainly the experience of educators, working with different types of students in different institutional contexts, can augment research knowledge. However, there are also aspects of the standards where the relevant research is incomplete or its findings mixed. In those instances, CCSS proponents had to draw on multiple sources of evidence if standards development was to be completed in a timely manner.

For example, research on learning trajectories in mathematics is quite robust at the K-2 level, but not at higher grade levels.[8] Trajectories are better developed in the early grades because developmental psychologists have compiled a rich research base about children's early learning and because concepts and skills at the early childhood level are simpler than the more complex topics and sequencing in advanced mathematics (Clements 2011, p. 20). But the notion of learning progressions was a crucial idea in organizing the standards beyond the research-rich early grades, to ensure that the sequence of topics taught in successive grades would be

[8] Learning trajectories or progressions are defined as "empirically supported hypotheses about the levels or waypoints of thinking, knowledge, skill in using knowledge, that students are likely to go through as they learn mathematics and one hopes, reach or exceed the common goals set for learning. Trajectories involve hypotheses both about the order and nature of the steps toward the goals of school mathematics" (Daro et al. 2011, p. 12). Researchers acknowledge the probabilistic nature of learning progressions and that existing ones require additional examination (Sztajin et al. 2012).

logical and avoid redundancy. Consequently, the standards writers had to look to expert judgments as a substitute for knowledge gained from research studies. They asked multiple researchers, including mathematicians who drew on their knowledge of the logic of mathematics as a discipline and the foundations for higher-level study to offer their best judgment of the appropriate progression of standards, and scholars who study math education, who drew on the research literature on how students learn to assemble their best judgment about what trajectories might look like in higher grades. They then used those inferences in placing topic and skill standards at appropriate grade levels (Personal interviews).

9.5 Conclusion and Implications

The Common Core State Standards initiative involved innovation in both politics and policy. The politics of formulating the CCSS, as much as the process of persuading 45 states to adopt the standards, has been distinguished by an appreciation of the operation of the US federal system at a moment of unusual partisan polarization. Although the idea of strengthening content standards in K-12 education and making standards more uniform across the country was widely seen to comprise an attractive response to the poor showing US students' achievement in international comparisons, previous attempts to move forward with the most obvious version of this reform – national standards disseminated from Washington, D.C. – had generated intense opposition. It took the entrepreneurial insights, and the confidence born of experience in elected office, of a few state-level leaders and organizations to imagine how two risky gambles could cut through the stalemate. Could the states collaborate, where the tradition had been distinctiveness? The leaders of NGA and CCSSO succeeded in organizing a reform process led from the states and yet capable of producing standards that were clearer, higher, and more coherent than what most states had produced alone. But the process would have foundered, if it had become mired in the polarized politics that typify Washington and many state capitals. Could the conventional competition among organized stakeholders over educational standards be set aside in the interests of formulating and adopting better, common standards? The firm admonition that the reform would be "research and evidence based" was intended to transform the historical pattern of standard-setting in the states, but it was unclear at the time whether relying on the stature and legitimacy of scholarly research could succeed in parrying interest groups' drive to capture the process. In the end – although neither the process nor the product is perfect and the implementation of CCSS remains a fragile work in progress – seasoned observers from across the spectrum agree that the accomplishment is quite remarkable. This historic process is clearly one from which useful lessons can be drawn.

Our research, including close observation of the process, document analysis, and interviews with key participants, allows us to contribute to knowledge about the use of research in policy in three ways. First, the challenge of tracing the evolution of a policy initiative in real time forced us to develop techniques that previous scholars, typically observing research use well after the fact, could not utilize. We were able to collect an unprecedented range of documentary information, including formal reports but also press releases, blogs, and advocacy publications – many of which are naturally ephemeral, living out their short life-spans in service to one stage of the policy process. In addition, our interviews with advocates, standards writers, researchers involved in reviewing draft standards, state and district administrators, and teachers took place while they were participating in the process, thus ensuring that their knowledge of events was fresh rather than recollected after a long interlude and often allowing us to check their interpretations and reflections against subsequent public statements and actions.

Second, tracing the process through which the standards documents were produced, and the more overtly political process that brought the standards forward for adoption by the states, pushed us to develop a more thoroughly elaborated concept of "evidence." The CCSS process was distinguished by a rich set of exchanges involving researchers, practitioners, and policymakers, and the currency for these exchanges was "research and evidence" relevant to improving educational standards. One of the strengths of the process, of course, was to invite active engagement by participants from a range of vocational communities and knowledge cultures, but their collaboration hinged on the willingness and capability to move out of their disciplinary niches to appreciate the different ways the evidence helped push the search for solutions forward. The willingness to consult evidence other than peer-reviewed research was especially important in areas where the cumulation of formal research has not yet obtained closure on some question of educational practice or policy, but where progress on formulating standards required setting out a provisional statement. Observing this process led us to reconceptualize the notion of "evidence," developing a typology anchored by the paradigm of peer-reviewed research but also including statistical data, the expert judgments of professionals, the experience-based reflections of practitioners, and even values-based advocacy in some situations. In this conception, the properties of formal research set a standard for validity, but other forms of evidence can carry warrants that are not qualitatively disjoint but differ along a common continuum.

Third, the empirical results of our research encourage us to underline the importance of two aspects of the process of research use in the Common Core State Standards movement: policy learning and networks of communication and information exchange. Neither of these concepts is new, but when we trace the development of CCSS, it is possible to map out their role with a degree of detail and concreteness unavailable in most studies of research use. Specifically, we have been able to observe each of the stages of policy learning, as we traced the way different participants engaged in collecting information about recent events, processing the information and interpreting it in light of previous political and policy choices, reflecting on their experience and drawing inferences, and then considering and deciding to change strategy or to continue on the same course. It is a truism that networks of communication are important for the transmission of new information, such as the results of recent research. But the CCSS process revealed changes – some serendipitous, some intentional – in the crucial network variables of size, density, and age.

The magnitude of the proposed reform created an incentive for actors to join the debate from various corners of the system, from organizations representing occupational groupings such as teachers, to corporations that supply textbooks and tests, to civil rights groups, to representatives of political units such as school districts and state governments. The potential was high for combat among interest groups to dominate the process. Some organizers, however, sought to structure communication to foster cooperation and deflect competition, and they were able to secure foundation funding to deepen ties among established organizations and in a few cases to create new networks of groups advocating standards-based reform. By increasing the density of network ties – creating new links among groups who may share interests in CCSS but had not previously worked together and strengthening existing ties by multiplying the topics on which networked groups communicate – entrepreneurial organizers and funders were able to craft the architecture for cooperative advocacy.

Finally, it is worth noting three implications that we believe our research holds for policy and practice. First, the organizers were successful early on in framing the way people thought about the problem and in shaping the message. The process was centered on a concrete, relatively delimited problem (rather than a large, ideological goal or the ill-fitting summation of the separate demands of coalition partners), and the norm was established that the process would be research and evidence based. This was essential, not only to focusing the work and giving it a clear trajectory but also to circumscribing the role of narrow interests and side-payments that would have undermined the push for strengthening standards and dissipated their coherence. Second, the attention to communication, particularly by creating new networks and revivifying established ties, served two critical functions. As communication channels, the networks kept major players in touch with the progress of the writing group, as well as creating a culture of accountability by transmitting feedback from stakeholders to those working directly on the standards. And as foci for cooperative advocacy work, the networks made it possible to craft well-planned communications when campaigning for the standards with state officials and the public, and to respond to critics with an informed, univocal message. Third, the inclusive nature of the process, undergirded by the implicit acceptance of an image of legitimate evidence that honored different types and sources of evidence but held all claims to comparable standards, made it possible to build and maintain an exceptionally broad-based coalition, spanning not only a wide range of intellectual disciplines but also engaging players whose political views would usually have put them at odds.

References

American Federation of Teachers. (2010, April 15). *Teachers make their mark on Common Core State Standards*. AFT News. http://www.aft.org/newspubs/news/2010/04150standards.cfn

Bohner, G., & Dickel, N. (2011). Attitudes and attitude change. *Annual Review of Psychology, 62*, 391–417.

Bohner, H. E., Erb, H.-P., & Siebler, F. (2008). Information processing approaches to persuasion: Integrating assumptions from dual- and single-processing perspectives. In W. D. Crano & R. Prislin (Eds.), *Attitudes and attitude change* (pp. 161–188). New York: Psychology Press.

Clements, D. (2011, October 27). What do we know about content and curriculum? In *Research in mathematics education: Where do we go from here?* Proceedings. Institute for Research on Mathematics and Science Education, Michigan State University, Washington, DC.

Cohen, D. K., & Moffitt, S. L. (2009). *The ordeal of equality: Did federal regulation fix the schools?* Cambridge, MA: Harvard University Press.

Coleman, D., & Pimentel, S. (2012). *Revised publishers' criteria for the Common Core State Standards in English language arts and literacy, grades 3–12*. www.corestandards.org/assets/publishers_criteria_for_3-12.pdf

Common Core State Standards Initiative. (2010). *Common Core State Standards for mathematics*. www.corestandards.org/Math

Daro, P., Mosher, F. A., & Corcoran, T. (2011). *Learning trajectories in mathematics: A foundation for standards, curriculum, assessment, and instruction* (Research Report #R-68). New York: Consortium for Policy Research in Education.

Davies, H. T. O., & Nutley, S. M. (2008). *Learning more about how research-based knowledge gets used: Guidance in the development of new empirical research*. New York: W.T. Grant Foundation.

Holyoak, K. J., & Chang, P. W. (2011). Causal learning and inference as rational process: The new synthesis. *Annual Review of Psychology, 62*, 135–163.

Jones, B. D., & Baumgartner, F. R. (2005). *The politics of attention*. Chicago: University of Chicago Press.

Kennedy, M. M. (1983). Working knowledge. *Knowledge: Creation, Diffusion, Utilization, 5*, 193–211.

Kingdon, J. W. (1995). *Agenda, alternatives, and public policies* (2nd ed.). New York: Harper Collins.

Levitt, B., & March, J. G. (1988). Organizational learning. *Annual Review of Sociology, 14*, 319–340.

Mahler, J. G. (2009). *Organizational learning at NASA*. Washington, DC: Georgetown University Press.

Majone, G. (1989). *Evidence, argument, and persuasion in the policy process*. New Haven: Yale University Press.

Massachusetts Business Alliance for Education. (2010, July 21). *Statement to the Massachusetts Board of Elementary and Secondary Education in favor of adoption of the Common Core State Standards*. Boston: Author.

May, P. J. (1992). Policy learning and failure. *Journal of Public Policy, 12*(4), 331–354.

McDonnell, L. M., & Weatherford, M. S. (2013). Evidence use and the Common Core State Standards movement: From problem definition to policy adoption. *American Journal of Education, 120*(1), 1–25.

Mitchell, T. (2010, July 30). Common educational standards for common good. *San Francisco Chronicle*, p. A-14.

National Governors Association, Council of Chief State School Officers, & Achieve. (2008). *Benchmarking for success: Ensuring U.S. students receive a world-class education*. Washington, DC: Author.

National Governors Association, Council of Chief State School Officers, Achieve, Council of Great City Schools, & National Association of State Boards of Education. (2012). *K-8 publishers' criteria for the Common Core State Standards for mathematics*. www.corestandards.org/assets/math_publishers_criteria_k-8_summer2012_final.pdf

National Governors Association, Council of Chief State School Officers, Achieve, Council of Great City Schools, & National Association of State Boards of Education. (2013). *High school publishers' criteria for the Common Core State Standards for mathematics*. www.corestandards.org/assets/math_publishers_criteria_hs

Petty, R. E., & Cacioppo, J. T. (1986). *Communication and persuasion: Central and peripheral routes to attitude change*. New York: Springer.

Phillips, V., & Wong, C. (2012). Teaching to the Common Core by design not accident. *Phi Delta Kappa, 93*(7), 31–37.

Rothman, R. (2011). *Something in common*. Cambridge, MA: Harvard Education Press.

Spillane, J. P., Reiser, B. J., & Reimer, T. (2002). Policy implementation and cognition: Reframing and refocusing implementation research. *Review of Educational Research, 72*, 387–431.

Stone, D. (2012). *Policy paradox*. New York: W.W. Norton.

Sztajin, P., Confrey, J., Wilson, P. H., & Edgington, C. (2012). Learning trajectory-based instruction: Toward a theory of teaching. *Educational Researcher, 41*(5), 147–156.

Weatherford, M. S., & McDonnell, L. M. (2013). *Evidence use in education policy: A new perspective on an old problem*. Santa Barbara: University of California.

WestEd. (2010). *Analysis of the Commonwealth of Massachusetts state standards and the Common Core Standards for English language arts and mathematics*. San Francisco: Author.

Wilhoit, G. (2009, December 4). *Improving our competitiveness: Common core education standards*. Prepared testimony before the Committee on Education and Labor, U.S. House of Representatives.

Chapter 10
Obama's Promise: Using Evidence to Fight the Nation's Social Problems

Ron Haskins and Greg Margolis

In his first inaugural address on January 20, 2009, President Obama said that he was not concerned with whether government is too big or too small, "but whether it works … Where the answer is yes, we intend to move forward. Where the answer is no, programs will end."

Rhetoric like this is standard fare for inaugural addresses. As it turned out, however, Obama was serious about his intent to find out if programs work and to expand them if they do. Within the first year of the administration, the Obama team in the White House, at the Office of Management and Budget (OMB), and in several executive agencies had initiated work on six social policy initiatives in which funding was to be based on evidence of success. After a brief review of these six initiatives, we examine one of them in detail, explaining how the administration developed the initiative; how it obtained congressional approval and funding for the initiative; how the money was offered on a competitive basis to states, local government agencies, or private organizations; and how applicants for the grant funds had to use evidence to win the money and to generate additional evidence of performance as the program was being implemented.

The emphasis on evidence of program success from rigorous studies and the requirement to produce evidence of program performance during implementation may have the potential to increase the effectiveness of federal grant programs. The purposes of this chapter are both to document how the initiatives were created and implemented and to analyze issues that arose as the administration tried to bring evidence to the center of policymaking in the nation's capital. Most of the analysis in this chapter is dedicated to the Investing in Innovation (i3) initiative, which was designed to improve education policy and programs through the use of evidence.

R. Haskins (✉) • G. Margolis
Center on Children and Families in the Economic Studies Department
at the Brookings Institution, Washington, DC, USA
e-mail: rhaskins@brookings.edu

K.S. Finnigan and A.J. Daly (eds.), *Using Research Evidence in Education: From the Schoolhouse Door to Capitol Hill*, Policy Implications of Research in Education 2,
DOI 10.1007/978-3-319-04690-7_10, © Springer International Publishing Switzerland 2014

Why would anyone try to document and analyze a policy initiative that has not yet demonstrated its value? We admit that we are optimistic that the Obama strategy of spending federal funds on social intervention programs that have been shown to produce impacts and then carefully evaluating the programs as they are implemented is a better strategy than the current practice of giving states and other organizations money on a formula basis and allowing them great flexibility in spending the federal dollars. We are not arguing that all federal funds should be distributed only to programs with strong evidence of impacts. The total cost of the six evidence-based Obama initiatives is around $5 billion. For this investment, the federal government is getting scores of intervention programs, most with a strong record of having impacts in reducing social problems, as well as scores of evaluations, many of them based on gold standard designs. But even more important, the field of policy analysis will have the opportunity to assess the overall strategy of awarding funds based on evidence of success and employing quality evaluations to measure the degree of impact of the various programs. In the event that this strategy produces some notable successes, our goal is to have explained in detail how the strategy was implemented and how subsequent programs that follow the Obama path of creating evidence-based policy could replicate the Obama evidence-based programs should subsequent administrations or Congresses elect to do so. Our approach in this chapter is to provide some general information about all six initiatives and then to provide a more detailed and nuanced portrait of the Obama administration's i3 initiative.

10.1 Context

As background for the analysis that follows, Table 10.1 provides an overview of the major characteristics of the six Obama evidence-based initiatives. The six initiatives were Teen Pregnancy Prevention (TPP), Home Visiting, Investing in Innovation (i3), the Social Innovation Fund (SIF), the Workforce Innovation Fund (WIF), and the Trade Adjustment Assistance Community College and Career Training Grant Program (Community College). All the initiatives involved collaborative work between an executive branch agency and the Office of Management and Budget (OMB), with some involvement by the White House. The executive branch agencies involved were the Departments of Health and Human Services (for the TPP and Home Visiting initiatives), Education (i3), and Labor (WIF and Community College). The Corporation for National and Community Service, an independent government agency that is nonetheless under the administrative oversight of OMB, was responsible for the SIF initiative.

OMB announced both publicly (Orszag 2009) and within the administration, as only OMB can do, that a major goal of the Obama presidency was to put evidence at the center of its decisions on funding both new and existing grant programs. OMB was the quarterback for all the initiatives, working directly with senior officials in the executive agencies to develop the initiatives and with staff and

Table 10.1 Summary of six evidence-based initiatives

Evidence-based initiative	Initial funding source and amount	Administering agency	Evidence requirement	Date of first awards	Total amount awarded
Teen Pregnancy Prevention	$110 million in Consolidated Appropriations Act of 2010	Department of Health and Human Services	List of programs identified by HHS as evidence based (tier I), 75 % of funds for tier I programs	September 2010	$526 million, one cohort of grants, 102 total awards
Home Visiting	$1.5 billion in Patient Protection and Affordable Care Act of 2010	Department of Health and Human Services	List of programs identified by HHS as evidence based, 75 % of funds for approved programs	July 2010	$1.5 billion to be allocated through FY 2014
Investing in Innovation	$650 million in the American Recovery and Reinvestment Act of 2009	Department of Education	Three tiers of grants, each tied to a higher level of required evidence	August 2010	$1.1 billion, four rounds of grants, 117 total awards
Social Innovation Fund	$50 million in the Consolidated Appropriations Act of 2010	Corporation for National and Community Service	Evidence incorporated into selection criteria; applicants must meet certain level by end of grant	July 2010	$177.6 million, three rounds of grants
Trade Adjustment Assistance Community College and Career Training	$2 billion in the Health Care and Education Reconciliation Act of 2010	Department of Labor and Department of Education	Points given for evidence in selection process	September 2011	$2 billion for FY 2011–FY 2014, three rounds of grants awarded
Workforce Innovation Fund	$125 million in the Department of Defense and Full-Year Continuing Appropriations Act, 2011	Department of Labor	Three tiers of grants reflecting different levels of evidence, more money for higher levels of evidence	June 2012	$147 million, one round of grants, 26 total awards

Members of Congress to formulate the legislation necessary to authorize and fund the six initiatives. As the legislation was being drafted, OMB worked with the agencies to develop the funding notices by which the administration would tell potential applicants (states, local governments, universities, research firms, community-based organizations, and others) what they had to do to qualify for funding. Between the statutory language, which had to be worked out with the committees of jurisdiction in the House and Senate and therefore was not under direct control of the Obama administration, and the funding notices, which the administration could and did control, what it means to be "evidence based" was embodied in both statutory language and the language of the funding notices.

The six Obama initiatives are unique in many respects, not least in the way they bring evidence to the center of the policymaking process. Consider the standards of using research to influence policy proposed by Knott and Wildavsky (1980). This classic set of standards proposes a sequential set of seven stages of research impact, extending from transmitting the research results to potential users such as policymakers and their staffs; understanding of the research by policymakers or their staffs; influencing the way policymakers think about a problem or its solution; using the research to shape a policy or program; adopting the implications of the research by enacting a new policy that was shaped, at least in part, by the research; implementing the research by translating the new policy into practice; and having impact if the new policy or program delivers some benefit to citizens.

Notwithstanding the fact that most research does not even make it to the second stage of the Knott/Wildavsky model, a key point in understanding the uniqueness of the Obama initiatives is that they have already achieved the first six stages of the model. Research is built into the DNA of the initiatives because each of them requires states, school systems, community-based organizations, and others who implement programs to use model programs that have been shown by research of varying degrees of rigor to have significant impacts on social problems. There is something like an assumption chain that explains why the administration expended so much energy, political capital, and money on its evidence-based initiatives:

- Random-assignment program evaluations can accurately identify social intervention programs that work and those that don't (Orr 1998).
- A substantial number of social programs have already been developed that significantly reduce social problems.
- If federal grant funds are spent primarily to expand (or in administration parlance, to "scale up") programs that have rigorous evidence of success, the nation will make more progress in reducing its social problems.
- Continuous high-quality evaluations of social programs as they are being implemented will increase the likelihood that they can continue to be effective and to reduce the level of the nation's social problems.
- By allocating some funds to develop promising intervention programs that are not (yet) supported by rigorous research, more and more effective model programs can be developed and progress against social problems will be enhanced.

One or more of these assumptions may turn out to be incorrect, but the least that can be said about the initiatives is that within the next few years, a massive amount of research evidence on the success of scores of social programs will begin to pour in. But already at this stage, when the implementing legislation has been enacted, around $5 billion in funds has been appropriated, all six initiatives are in various stages of implementation, and evaluations are in place, it seems safe to say that there has seldom if ever been such a broad use of social science evidence to formulate social policy and implement and evaluate social programs. Typically, social scientists and others who believe in trying to influence policy formulation through the use of evidence are fighting to get their evidence considered in the public square. In Knott/Wildavsky terms, as we will see, the Obama initiatives meet the definitions of transmitting research, understanding the implications of research, using research to guide policy development, using research to shape the policy debate, using research to shape the policy itself, and using research to shape the implementation of the policy. Once the six initiatives had been adopted and the funding allocated to scores of new programs, all but the final stage of the Knott/Wildavsky standards – showing the policy based on the research has a positive impact on the social problems addressed – have been met.

Moreover, the initiatives forced the use of research by a broad array of actors involved in the processes of policy proposing, policy debate, policy enactment, preparation for policy implementation by federal agencies and their reviewers who decided which specific programs to fund, program operators who are implementing the programs, and the individuals (usually research specialists at universities) and research firms that are planning and conducting the many evaluations required by the initiatives. Again, the scope of actors in the policy process who are being required to adopt the administration's emphasis on rigorous evidence is remarkable. Still, we are writing this chapter with the understanding that no one can claim that the initiatives are successful in Knott/Wildavsky terms because it is not yet known whether they are having positive impacts. We also write with the understanding that, as appears almost always to be the case with federal and state programs, subsequent administrations and Congresses might elect to repeal one or more of the initiatives or simply let them die a natural death by not renewing their funding. Already, the House of Representatives has eliminated funding for several of the initiatives during the annual appropriations process, although funding was restored by the Senate and eventually accepted by the House. On a similar but more positive note, subsequent administrations or Congresses may want to continue the initiatives but modify them based on how they are turning out after 5 or 6 years of implementation. We return to this issue below.

10.2 Evidence Framework

A hallmark of the Obama evidence-based initiatives is the emphasis on funding model programs that have rigorous evidence of impacts on social problems. As our interviews (for details, see below) with many administration officials showed, the programs met the evidence standards for that initiative. The selection of intervention programs by the applicants and the strength of the evidence supporting the claim that the programs had impacts became an important criterion in the agency decision about whether to fund the applicants. By contrast, the TPP and Home Visiting initiatives employed work groups of senior staffers at HHS to conduct elaborate "evidence reviews" to identify model programs that were judged, according to carefully defined criteria (see Table 10.2), to qualify as "evidence based." In the end, working with the research firms Mathematica and Child Trends, the administration identified 28 model TPP programs (Mathematica Policy Research and Child Trends 2010) and seven model home visiting programs (Paulsell et al. 2010) that their evidence reviews determined to be evidence based. Thus, for these two initiatives, the administration itself decided whether program models were evidence based and then directed most (but not all) of the funding for these two initiatives to these programs per the legislative stipulation.

Returning to Table 10.2, it may seem somewhat surprising that only two of the underlying statutes (for Home Visiting and SIF) required or prominently mentioned evidence from RCTs in order for programs to qualify for funding. However, in addition to these two, the statute for the TPP initiative required evidence from "rigorous evaluation" but without a statutory definition of what this term meant. Undeterred, the administration used the funding announcement for the TPP to require that to qualify for funding, most programs would have to be supported by evidence from the "high"- or "moderate"-rated designs which were then defined as RCTs in the former case and less rigorous RCTs or quasi-experimental designs in the latter case. Similarly, the funding notice for the i3 initiative required most programs that qualified for funding to be supported by evidence from RCTs or quasi-experimental designs. Thus, three of the six initiatives (TPP, Home Visiting, and i3) had a requirement that applicants meet some level of evidence to receive funding. In the case of i3, each tier of funding had a required degree of evidence that the applicants were required to meet. In the cases of TPP and Home Visiting, the statute stipulated that 75 % of the funds were to be spent on programs supported by rigorous evidence.

This leaves only the WIF and Community College initiatives that had no requirement that most money be spent on programs supported by evidence from RCTs or quasi-experimental designs. In both cases, as we mentioned above, what might be called the King Canute exception applies to the requirement for evidence. King Canute could not hold back the tides with his commandment just as the administration cannot command evidence from random-assignment evaluations to suddenly appear. Rather, the administration had determined that helping workers qualify for jobs with good wages was an important goal, especially for a Democratic administration. A widespread complaint among many Democrats and some Republicans is that too many workers either can't find employment or find themselves stuck in low-skill and therefore low-wage jobs. But after lots of discussion between OMB, the White House, and the Department of Labor (DOL), the administration determined that there was not much evidence from RCTs for training programs that could successfully upgrade the skills of low-income workers and young workers with little education who were preparing to enter the labor market and there was even less rigorous evidence about the role of community colleges in preparing workers for good jobs. So the Department of Labor is not requiring RCT evidence or even evidence from quasi-experimental designs to qualify for funding in these two initiatives. However, the funding announcements emphasize the importance of applicants using programs that have strong evidence and award additional points for programs that are supported by strong evidence. In our interviews with both senior officials at the Department of Labor and at OMB, it was clear that the administration wanted to require rigorous evaluations by grantees, some with random-assignment designs, in order to thereby begin to build rigorous evidence about both types of labor market programs.

10.3 Methods

The information for our study was based on interviews, documents from congressional and administrative agencies, and newspaper and magazine accounts of the events we trace. Our interviews included congressional staffers, administration staffers, and staffers from interest groups based in the nation's capital. We began by interviewing people we had worked with in the past whom we knew to have played a role in one or more of the six initiatives. Then during each interview, we asked if there were other people who had played a role in the initiative we should interview. Following this technique for identifying people to interview, often called the snowball technique (Biernacki and Waldorf 1981; Tansey 2007), we identified 179 potential interviewees. Of these, we interviewed 133; most of the information we report here is taken from these interviews. We interviewed three people about two of the initiatives, bringing the total number of interviews to 136. Of the 46 people we tried to contact but did not interview, we could not locate 2 people; 34 people agreed to the interview but repeated attempts to schedule the interview failed; and 10 people refused to participate, most of them because they said their role in the Obama initiatives had been tangential. The interviews were conducted between August 2011 and July 2013. We focused each interview on the particular Obama initiative on which the interviewee had worked (teen pregnancy, Home Visiting, i3, etc.). Broken down by initiative, 15 interviews were addressed to i3, 44 to Home Visiting, 27 to TPP, 22 to SIF, 11 to WIF, 10 to the Community College initiative, and 7 that were devoted either primarily to IES or to more than one initiative.

Each interview followed a standard protocol of about 40 questions. The protocol differed slightly depending on whether the interviewee worked for the administration, Congress, or an advocacy group. We queried interviewees about how often and under what circumstances their organization used social science evidence, what individuals or organizations they consulted with when they had a question about evidence, whether they were familiar with the research literature on the social problem addressed by the specific initiative, who they talked with as they pursued their work on the initiative, the most persuasive arguments in favor of or against passage and implementation of the initiative, and similar issues related to evidence and their role in the initiative. On nine occasions, we developed special questions for people we knew had played an especially important role in the formulation, enactment, or administration of an initiative.

In addition to interviews, we examined documents about the initiatives produced by the House, the Senate, congressional agencies (especially the Congressional Research Service), and the administration. There were surprisingly few House and Senate documents that provided information about the legislation that produced the initiatives. Upon reflection, however, the reason for the lack of abundant information from House and Senate documents is that most of the initiatives were passed as part of huge legislative provisions and as a result received little public attention, a fact that might have helped the initiatives and their vehicles get through Congress. As shown in Table 10.1, the TPP passed as part of an omnibus appropriations bill (Library of Congress b), Home Visiting as part of the Affordable Care Act (Library of Congress e), i3 as part of the American Recovery and Reinvestment Act (ARRA) (Library of Congress a), SIF as part of the reauthorization of the Corporation for National and Community Service (Library of Congress f), WIF as part of an omnibus appropriations bill (Library of Congress c), and the Community College initiative as part of the bill that amended the ACA (Library of Congress d). Thus, none of the initiatives passed as stand-alone bills, and most were part of huge and very controversial bills such as the ARRA or the ACA.

By contrast with the sparseness of congressional documents, the respective administration departments had abundant information on their websites about their role in developing the evidence standards, formulating and publishing the funding announcements, providing information about organizations that received funding, and providing information about the evaluations that were an important part of each initiative.

10.4 Findings

10.4.1 Overview

We turn now to a detailed discussion of the i3 initiative. We have three purposes in conducting this review, based primarily on our interviews and on documents made publicly available by the Department of Education (DE). First, we want to review how the administration managed to get the i3 initiative enacted into law. Although there are important differences in the legislative pathways of the six initiatives, there is considerable overlap in the legislative strategy and tactics followed by the administration. Our thinking, and indeed our reason for conducting our entire project, is that it is possible that some future administration may decide to continue the type of evidence-based initiatives that the Obama administration has undertaken. If so, they will need to enact legislation to secure funding for whatever initiatives they decide to undertake. Knowledge about the Obama experience in passing legislation, for better and for worse, can provide insights about legislative strategy. Second, the procedures followed by the DE to define what it meant to be evidence based, to solicit both proposals that were based on the strongest possible evidence and proposals to fund promising programs with potential for being effective, can also provide useful examples for future administrations. In addition, the specific decisions made by the Obama administration about how to define evidence and the tiers of evidence approach that allowed them to distinguish gradients in the quality of evidence are important in their own right to the social science community that must constantly wrestle with whether evidence and evaluation can lead to program improvement. Third, it seems doubtful that the Obama administration has made all the right choices in either its legislative strategy or its decisions on defining and using evidence to ensure that grant funds are being spent on programs that have the best chance of successfully attacking the nation's social problems. Should some future administration or Member of Congress decide to amend the Obama laws and administrative procedures in ways that might improve the respective evidence-based initiatives, a history of how one of the initiatives originated and was implemented could prove useful.

10.4.2 Origins of the i3 Initiative

On June 8, 2009, OMB director Peter Orszag published a much-discussed blog on the administration's use of evidence. He wrote that the administration would "design new initiatives to build rigorous data about what works and then act on evidence that emerges." He went on to write that the administration would create social initiatives that had "evaluation standards built into their DNA" (Orszag 2009).

Nor was there much doubt that Orszag and his colleagues at OMB and the White House had the ability, will, and technical know-how to implement what both the president and Director Orszag said would result in the federal government spending its money on more effective social programs. The Obama administration was full of scholars and researchers, many with previous government experience, who believed that RCTs were the most reliable design for determining whether social programs work. In addition, career staff at OMB, one of Washington's most powerful and influential organizations and the main driver for designing and implementing policy in most administrations, included a host of advocates for RCTs who had extensive experience in supporting and conducting them. Finally, the Institute of Education Sciences (IES), the relatively new government agency that had revolutionized the field of educational research by funding RCTs on education practices (see ies.ed.gov), brought a wealth of experience and expertise on research designs to the Obama enterprise. As the administration's i3 initiative began to take shape, IES would play an important role.

Turning specifically to the i3 initiative, as shown by our interviews with presidential advisor Jon Schnur and others, as well as a published account of the early days of the administration's efforts on education by Steven Brill (2011): Even before he was inaugurated, President-elect Obama had a team working on what grew into one of the biggest education initiatives in federal history. During one meeting in the transition period, the President-elect met in the transition office on 6th Street, ten blocks from the White House, with Schnur and a group of incoming administration officials including future Secretary of Education Arne Duncan, future White House Chief of Staff Rahm Emanuel, future White House Domestic Policy Chief Melody Barnes, and Heather Higginbottom a senior White House advisor on education and other issues. Their purpose was to discuss the new administration's education agenda. With the country mired in the depths of the worst recession since the Great Depression of the 1930s, the administration, along with virtually all Capitol Hill Democrats, now in the third year of their majority in both the House and Senate, planned to follow the Keynesian course and enact a huge spending bill, which eventually weighed in at over $800 billion. The ARRA was designed to stimulate the economy by spending billions of federal dollars. But that was not its only purpose. Emanuel, the president's Chief of Staff, set the tone for the bill with the famous – or infamous, depending on your politics – declaration that "You never want a serious crisis to go to waste" (Seib 2008), meaning that Democrats should, for example, use the stimulus bill to expand domestic social programs, which they saw as vital to fixing the country's long-term social problems.

Which brings us back to the president's meeting in the transition office. According to Schnur, the president said that he wanted his education strategy to be driven by three principles: developing policies and practices that would produce better educational outcomes for children, especially poor children; featuring policies and practices that had the potential to attract support from Members of Congress and others; and developing and defending their proposals in a way that avoids "poking anyone in the eye." Obama's principles set the tone for Duncan, Schnur, and others at the Department of Education and OMB to develop the i3 legislation.

The president and his advisors knew they had to move fast to get their education provisions in the ARRA because the administration and the Democratic leadership on Capitol Hill intended to push the bill through Congress at the speed of light. In the end, after lots of negotiation among themselves, the administration decided to pursue two major and innovative education initiatives, which became Race to the Top (RTT) and Investing in Innovation (i3). Again based on our interview with Schnur and confirmed by several interviews with congressional staffers, the latter was to be a version of an idea Schnur had originally developed with George Miller, Chairman of the House Committee on Education and Labor, and Miller's staff. Restored to the chairmanship of that committee after Democrats took control of the House in the elections of 2006, the powerful and widely respected Miller was determined to have a substantive bill to reauthorize NCLB, which was on the congressional calendar for the 2007–2008 session. The essence of the proposal Schnur and Miller developed was to establish, as part of the NCLB legislation, what Schnur called a "grow what works" fund in which the federal government would give money to education agencies that could show that they were conducting a program that had impacts on student performance, especially in closing the achievement gap between racial and ethnic groups. This provision was a major step toward creating evidence-based policy because the LEAs had to have at least achievement data showing improvements to qualify for funding. However, the "grow what works fund" did not have a definition of the kind of evidence that had to be collected to show that achievement gaps were being closed.

Miller worked with Buck McKeon from California, the senior Republican on the Committee, to develop a bipartisan bill that contained many of their ideas for reauthorization, including the "grow what works fund" (see Section 1117). A discussion draft of the bill was released to the public on August 28, 2007, and a hearing was conducted on the bill on September 10, 2007. But that was as far as NCLB reauthorization got during the 2007–2008 Congress. As it turned out, Section 1117 had a longer lifespan than the NCLB reauthorization, primarily because Barack Obama was swept into office with huge fanfare in the presidential election of 2008 – and his administration was focused on educational innovation and expanding what works.

A second important meeting to plan the new president's education initiatives was held in the Oval Office on January 29, a little more than a week after his inauguration. Schnur, Emanuel, Duncan, and other presidential advisors, including top political strategist David Axelrod, were present. As the group discussed the president's education initiatives, Axelrod questioned the political wisdom of tying funding to evidence rather than following the usual practice of using formula grants to make sure every state got at least some money (Brill 2011, p. 5). Axelrod was referring primarily to the RTT funds, but the same point applies to i3. Funding only programs that were innovative and that had evidence of success had been a major focus of the Miller/Schnur initiative since that 2007 bill that Miller introduced with McKeon. Now that President Obama was hearing questions in the Oval Office about the political viability of the administration's plan to establish a firm link between evidence that programs work and funding, an important moment had arrived. If the president had agreed to back off the evidence-funding link at the beginning of the administration, i3 might have been a very different initiative, which could in turn have had impacts on the other evidence-based initiatives, all of which depended on competitive grants as an essential part of their structure. But the president immediately nixed the criticism. According to Schnur, the president was very clear that he wanted to pursue the initiatives while maintaining a strong link between funding and good evidence that programs produce impacts on student learning. The president told the group that funding based on performance was the central idea of both RTT and i3.

10.4.3 Enacting the i3 Initiative

Given the speed at which the administration had to move to get their RTT and i3 provisions in the ARRA, administration officials began to communicate with Hill staffers as soon as they had met with the president to decide on the broad outlines of the i3 initiative. The administration was intent on completing the drafting in time to include both RTT and i3 in the stimulus bill because doing so would greatly increase the chances that both provisions would pass Congress, enveloped as they would be by the huge size and hundreds of provisions in the ARRA. Major action on the stimulus legislation was controlled by the Appropriations Committees in the House and Senate. The chairman of the House Appropriations Committee, David Obey of Wisconsin, always made it a practice to draw a sharp line between authorizing legislation, which was the job of the various authorizing committees, and appropriation legislation to fund already authorized programs, which was the job of the Appropriations Committee and its 12 powerful subcommittees. But the stimulus bill was in danger of including several provisions that had never been authorized by the committees of jurisdiction, including Obama's far-reaching provisions on education. Congress and the president were moving so fast, pushed ahead by the economic crisis, that Congress did not have time to fool around with regular and time-consuming congressional procedure. Obey, like other Democratic leaders, wanted to enact the ARRA as speedily as possible to get the money out to states and to local government where it would do the most good and perhaps contribute to an economic revival.

Despite his concern about speed, Obey was nonetheless reluctant to enact such important legislation in an appropriations bill. As Alice Johnson Cain, Miller's senior education policy advisor, told us, the administration relied on George Miller, chairman of the committee with responsibility for education, who was close with Obey, to encourage him to include non-authorized provisions in the stimulus legislation. Miller assured Obey that his majority on the Committee on Education and Labor would gladly support RTT and i3 and would have passed them out of committee if they had had time. Our interview with Jon Schnur also showed that Rahm Emanuel, the president's Chief of Staff, weighed in with Obey, assuring him that RTT and i3 were major parts of the president's agenda and that Democrats in Congress should support their new president. In the end, Obey relented and both the RTT and i3 were included in the stimulus bill.

The entire text of the i3 provision in ARRA was less than one page. Based on our interview with Schnur, and consistent with interviews with several congressional staffers, drafting the final language was a collaborative process. A senior Obey staffer wrote an initial draft and passed it around the appropriate channels for discussion and comment. There were conversations with officials at the Department of Education, as well as with Senator Kennedy's staff (Kennedy's Health, Education, Labor, and Pensions Committee had jurisdiction over the RTT and i3 provisions in the Senate) and with Alice Johnson Cain of Chairman Miller's staff. In fairly short order, everyone agreed on the language. Miller strongly supported the provision because he had previously endorsed the innovation fund concept after working with Schnur on the discussion draft of NCLB.

Under the heading "Innovation Fund," found in Section 14007 of the bill, the provision simply specified the types of entities that could apply for funds, stated that agencies had to have a record of reducing the achievement gap between students from different backgrounds, and specified that eligible organizations had to partner with a nonprofit organization (including foundations). Another provision clarified that the purpose of the fund was to allow these LEAs with evidence of closing achievement gaps to "expand their work and serve as models for best practices" and "to identify and document best practices that can be shared, and taken to scale based on demonstrated success" (United States Congress 2009).

This language does not establish strong evidence standards. But the administration welcomed the opportunity to define them later and avoid worrying about how to get the exact language they wanted in legislative text. Besides, it was simply not clear in January of 2009, at the very beginning of the Obama administration, that even the most experienced people at OMB knew exactly what language on evidence they wanted. Far better to get general language in the statute, figure out the exact language they wanted later, and then put the final language in the announcement that i3 funds were available. In fact, with the perspective provided by tracing the history of all six evidence-based initiatives, we came to believe that a strength of the initiatives was that the administration was able to create teams of senior officials, competent program specialists in the agencies, and officials throughout the administration with a knowledge of social science research and sometimes in-depth knowledge of certain areas of research to create definitions of evidence that seem solid, durable, and perhaps a model for future initiatives. It is doubtful that anyone, even the influential and sophisticated senior staffers at OMB, could have created such definitions in January 2009. At the very least, the definition of evidence had to be vetted by senior people at OMB and the executive agencies to ensure that everyone bought into the definitions. Our interviews on all the initiatives, but especially our interview with Jim Shelton, a senior DE official put in charge of the i3 initiative by Secretary Duncan, showed that working out the evidence definition and other details of the i3 funding announcements involved long hours and lots of discussion both within and between DE and OMB.

The ARRA passed the House on January 28, 2009, by a vote of 244–188 with no Republicans supporting the bill (Calmes 2009). Action then moved to the Senate, which passed its own version of the stimulus on February 10 by a 61–37 vote (Herszenhorn 2009). A compromise version then passed both Houses on nearly party line votes and was signed into law by President Obama on February 17, 2009, less than a month after his inauguration (Stolberg 2009). The i3 initiative had cleared its first hurdle.

10.5 Transforming the i3 Initiative

10.5.1 More Money for More Evidence

To begin the process of making i3 into an evidence-based program, in March 2009 OMB called a meeting that included the administration officials who would create and implement i3. Robert Gordon, one of the top political officials at OMB; Kathy Stack, a senior career official at OMB; and Allison Cole, also a career official at OMB, were there. Joining them were Jim Shelton and others from the Department of Education. Shelton, who had been appointed by Secretary Duncan to head the i3 initiative, became, along with Robert Gordon, the most important influence in giving shape to i3. Our understanding of the administration's decisions on i3 reviewed in this section is based on interviews with nine administration officials who worked directly on the initiative, but especially Cole, Gordon, and Shelton.

An important theme that received extensive attention during the initial meeting was the tiers concept – that different sizes of grants could be given out based on distinct criteria. As Shelton discussed i3 and the concept of tiers, the idea seemed to apply primarily to the size and scope of the grants. But Shelton also said that evidence would be an important component of the tiers, at which point Cole suggested that the tiers of evidence could be tied to the standards for measuring the rigor of research evidence developed by IES for its What Works Clearinghouse. Further discussion led to the idea that the amount of money given to applicant programs could reflect the strength of evidence showing that the program produced its intended results. To put the matter succinctly: More money for more evidence. Cole, a top OMB authority on education, had served a stint at the Institute of Education Sciences (IES), arguably the single unit of the federal government with the most substantial commitment to generating rigorous evidence and the best procedures for doing so (Institute for Education Sciences 2011). The group in attendance, especially Shelton, who had already been thinking about how to incorporate evidence into the selection criteria for the grants, decided that the IES standards provided a good template for i3.

In the end, i3 included three tiers of evidence: strong evidence based on one well-designed and well-implemented study at several sites or more than one well-designed and well-implemented study implemented at a single site. The studies can be RCTs or well-conducted quasi-experimentals (called the "scale-up" tier by the administration); a second tier of programs that were supported by good but not top tier evidence based on random-assignment designs with flaws or quasi-experimental designs (called "validation"); and a third tier that included programs that seemed promising based at least on a reasonable hypothesis (called "development"). In this and subsequent meetings and discussions, the precise definition of the standards of evidence that would apply to each tier of funding became a major focus of the administration's goal of developing a way to ensure that most of the grant funds went to programs that had evidence of success from rigorous evaluations but that nonetheless allocated some money for innovative programs without strong evidence of success.

After receiving nearly 350 comments from the public on the proposed rule for i3 grants, which was released on October 9, 2009, the administration prepared the final version of the i3 rule, which was announced publicly on March 12, 2010 in the *Federal Register* (Office of the Federal Register 2010). A table from the final rule gives the administration's descriptions of the evidence requirements for three tiers of funding. A slimmed-down version of this table is provided in Table 10.3. To qualify for each of the three levels, applicants had to propose conducting programs that were based on evidence of varying degrees of quality that the program would have an impact on students, with the highest level of evidence required for the scale-up tier, the next highest for the validation tier, and the lowest level for the development tier. Although it could be argued that the distinctions between the three tiers of evidence are somewhat arbitrary, they are nonetheless about as clear as the current status of social science research will permit. The scale-up tier requires either more than one randomized study or quasi-experimental study showing positive impacts or

Table 10.3 Evidence required for three types of i3 grants

Research characteristics	Type of grant: Scale-up	Validation	Development
Strength of research	Strong	Moderate	Preliminary
Internal and external validities	High internal validity and high external validity	High internal validity and moderate external validity or moderate internal validity and high external validity	Theory and practice suggest the potential for efficacy for some participants and settings
Strength of evidence from research	(1) More than one well-designed and well-implemented experimental study or quasi-experimental study or (2) one large, well-designed and well-implemented randomized controlled, multisite trial	(1) One well-designed and well-implemented experimental or quasi-experimental study, with small sample sizes or other conditions that limit generalizability; (2) one well-designed and well-implemented experimental or quasi-experimental study with lack of equivalence between intervention and comparison groups but no other flaws related to internal validity; or (3) correlational research with strong statistical controls for selection bias	(1) Evidence that the proposed practice, strategy, or program has been attempted previously, albeit on a limited scale, and yielded promising results and (2) a rationale for the proposed practice, strategy, or program based on research findings or reasonable hypotheses

Source: Based on Table 3 in *Federal Register* 75, no. 48, March 12, 2010, p. 12069

one randomized study or quasi-experimental study implemented in multiple sites showing positive impacts. The validation tier requires at least one randomized or quasi-experimental study but allows certain flaws in design or execution that prevent it from reaching the scale-up tier. Examples of flaws include small sample sizes or a lack of equivalence between the experimental and control groups at the beginning of the study. The development tier applied to interventions that have yielded promising results. Development grants can be based on a practice, strategy, or program that has a rationale grounded in research findings or even in reasonable theories. The point is to get innovative and promising interventions on the production line for eventual scale up if rigorous evidence begins to show significant impacts. Applicants for the scale-up tier could receive up to $50 million, applicants for the validation tier up to $30 million, and applicants for the development tier up to $5 million (Office of the Federal Register 2010). In the end, the administration was so serious about funding programs that met the respective tier of evidence that they conducted a separate review by IES researchers to make sure the evidence provided by the applicants met the evidence standard of the tier for which they had applied.

In reflecting on these tiers, it is useful to recall the administration's goal in making evidence of effectiveness a primary determinant of whether grant programs are funded and at what level. The administration believed that the impacts of programs – and there are already hundreds of federally funded programs on education, delinquency, teen pregnancy prevention, nutrition, medical care, child protection, employment and training, and many more – can be substantially increased if program operators are using program models that have been tested and found to produce positive impacts by rigorous evidence. The vision of senior officials in the Obama administration is that more effective programs will reduce the magnitude of the many social problems afflicting the nation and that developing programs supported by rigorous evidence is the way to get there.

In addition to defining levels of evidence, another difficult issue also finds at least a partial solution in the tiers of evidence approach. The administration was well aware that education is not exactly the queen of the evidence-based sciences. In fact, as recently as 1999, the National Academies declared that knowledge from educational research was surprisingly thin. "In no other field is the research base so inadequate," the Academies wrote in an official report (National Research Council 1999). Since 1999 the field of educational research has undergone some catching up, due in large part to the creation of the Institute of Education Sciences (IES) by legislation enacted in 2002 and aggressively implemented by the Bush administration, in particular by Grover J. "Russ" Whitehurst, the first Director of IES (Institute of Education Sciences 2008). Under Whitehurst's leadership from 2002 to 2008, IES funded at least 70 studies that used some elements of random assignment in their designs, so knowledge based on reliable evidence in the field of education is growing. However, given the time it takes to plan and execute a large-scale, random-assignment study, our knowledge of effective educational practices and programs is building at a moderate pace. The point is that if the designers of i3 had insisted on spending all the money on programs that have strong evidence of success from gold standard studies, not many LEAs and nonprofits would have been able to apply for the grants, and those that did would have been severely restricted in the programs or educational practices for which they could seek support. The tiers allow both programs with decent but not gold standard evidence and programs or educational practices based on some evidence or even reasonable hypotheses to have hopes that they could be funded.

Still, as our interview with Jim Shelton showed, the administration was conflicted about how strong the evidence standards should be, especially for the scale-up tier, which had the highest level of funding. Senior officials, especially Shelton from DE and Robert Gordon from OMB, were concerned that strong evidence standards would give an advantage in the competition for i3 funding to organizations that had had the resources to pay for high-quality evaluations of their program. On the other hand, a major goal of all the evidence-based initiatives, including i3, was to build the capacity to conduct RCTs and to send a strong signal to organizations conducting educational interventions that RCTs were the expected evaluation standard. In the end, Shelton, Gordon, and others came to believe that having the tiers of evidence would allow organizations that had not been able to evaluate their programs with expensive RCTs to qualify for the validation and development tiers, allowing the scale-up tier to require very strong evidence.

To further emphasize the importance of evidence, applicants were required to have an evaluation plan. The "evidence" in "evidence based" has two distinct meanings for the Obama administration. Not only is the quality of evidence a major criterion for getting programs funded, but the administration also insists on using evidence to evaluate the program as it is begin implemented, both to see if it had its intended impacts and to provide what the rule called "performance feedback" that would permit "periodic assessment of progress toward achieving intended outcomes" (Office of Federal Register 2010, p. 12081). Thus, applicants had to include a detailed plan for evaluating their program using a high-quality design. In addition, according to Shelton, after the initial round of funding, the administration awarded a 5-year grant to Abt Associates (2013), a research firm skilled in program evaluation and rigorous designs, to help i3 evaluators (each i3 program must have an independent evaluator) plan and conduct their evaluations. A total of 117 i3 evaluations are currently taking place, of which at least 40 are RCTs. In addition, many of the remaining evaluations are employing quasi-experimental designs. If this is a sign of how i3 will influence the evaluation of major education programs in the future, it seems reasonable to think that evaluation will play a more important role in future decision making by LEAs and perhaps even become a standard part of their way of doing business.

In addition to the rules of evidence and the evaluation plan, the announcement in the Federal Register stipulated the educational issues that applicants must pursue to qualify for funding. An overarching goal was that all proposals had to focus on high-needs students. In addition, all proposals had to show that the applicant had a record of closing the achievement gap between students of diverse backgrounds or of increasing student achievement or graduation rates. Applications also had to address at least one of what the administration called the "absolute priorities" of the i3 program.

10.5.2 Reviewing the Applications

The administration made a strong effort to help potential applicants understand and successfully complete the application process, which was bound to be a difficult and complex undertaking for LEAs and nonprofits. The magnitude of money at stake – around $650 million – was enormous, meaning that there would probably be many applications to process. As it turned out, there were 1,698 applications: 19 for scale-up grants, 355 for validation grants, and 1,324 for development grants. In addition, it was a challenge to explain the guidelines on the types of evidence (see Table 10.3 above) so that applicants could understand the grant tiers for which the evidence supporting the program they proposed to conduct made them eligible. The grant reviewers from IES who focused on the evidence (see below) likewise had to be able to distinguish the types of evidence needed for each tier and had to make sure the applicants met the requirements. Developing the best evidence guidelines in the world

Table 10.4 Selection criteria and points for i3 reviewers

	Grant type		
Selection criteria	Development	Validation	Scale-up
A. Need for project and quality of project design	25	20	15
B. Strength of research; significance and magnitude of effects	10	15	20
C. Applicant experience	25	20	15
D. Quality of evaluation	15	15	15
E. Strategy and capacity to bring to scale	5	10	15
F. Sustainability	10	10	10
G. Quality of management plan and personnel	10	10	10

Source: Department of Education, *Overview of the i3 Review Process*, July 26, 2010

would be futile unless the reviewers understood them and applied them accurately to incoming grants.

In the face of these challenges, the administration designed a grant application process that had five phases. In the first phase, the Department of Education selected and assigned more than 330 "highly qualified" official peer reviewers and provided them with training on how the reviews were to be conducted. The department then began the review process by classifying the nearly 1,700 applications according to the type of grant and the absolute priority pursued by the applicant and then assigning them to reviewers. In the second phase, the peer reviewers assessed the proposals assigned to them in accordance with guidelines supplied by the department. Table 10.4 provides a summary of the seven criteria by which reviewers judged the proposals and the points that could be awarded for each of the three types of grants for each of the seven criteria. Five of the criteria (A, C, E, F, and G) were considered by reviewers who were subject matter experts; the remaining two criteria were reviewed by evaluation and evidence experts. Reviewers submitted their scores and comments to the department's computer system. The computer adjusted for the effect of any reviewer or panel bias as measured by scores that were consistently higher or lower than the other reviewers or panels. In the third phase, department staffers confirmed several aspects of the applications of the highest-scoring proposals before they were made public. Among other items, staffers affirmed that the winning applicants were LEAs or partnerships between LEAs and nonprofits; that the practices, strategies, or programs proposed by the applicant would benefit high-need students; and that the evidence met the level required by the funding tier for which they applied. It is worth emphasizing that the staff review of whether the proposal met the evidence requirement for the requested level of funding, performed by IES staffers who had been trained in What Works Clearinghouse Standards, was an important step to be sure that all the winning applicants did in fact meet the level of evidence required for the type of grant for which they applied. Getting LEAs and their private-sector partners to use evidence to obtain federal dollars is what the administration hoped would begin changing the nature of federal grant making in education and, equally important, would cause LEAs and their partners to realize that the federal government was now making more decisions about who gets grant funds based on rigorous evidence and high-quality evaluations. If you want fundamental changes in the way organizations do business, you've got to use strong incentives – and few incentives are stronger than $650 million in payoffs for good evidence. The route to federal funding in i3 – and the other five Obama evidence-based initiatives – was through rigorous evidence.

The fourth phase of the review process was to announce the applicants with the highest scores, which was done on August 5, 2010. The projects with highest scores were assured of getting grants if they could obtain the 20 % match from the private sector. The administration awarded 4 scale-up grants (21 % of the proposals in this evidence category), 15 validation grants (4 % of the proposals), and 30 development grants (2 % of the proposals). All the programs selected for funding in all three evidence tiers attracted the matching funds they needed to qualify for the federal dollars. The fifth and final phase was for the department to announce the grantees and then, subsequently, to monitor implementation of the grantees' proposals. To provide a concrete idea of the types of proposals that were funded, Table 10.5 gives a summary of two winning proposals from each of the three tiers of grants.

10.5.3 Why the i3 Initiative Is Important

In retrospect, the i3 initiative is remarkable in at least four respects. First, at $650 million, i3 was a major education initiative by any standard. Second, as we have seen, the i3 initiative awarded funds to local education agencies (LEAs) and non-profit organizations as competitive grants. Making all the money competitive rather than distributing it on a formula basis was roughly equivalent to the administration sticking its finger in the eyes of LEAs and their private-sector partners, many of which were not funded, in large part because they did not meet the evidence standards. In addition, some LEAs that normally would have received funds under formula grants probably did not even apply. Now both LEAs and their partners had to compete for the money by showing that they were using evidence-based programs and that they had the capacity to evaluate their program if it should be funded.

Third, the administration was intent on involving the nonprofit sector in education reform. Many new administration officials, including two of the top officials in the Department of Education (Anthony Miller and Jim Shelton), had backgrounds in the private sector. They, along with Secretary Duncan, also considered the non-profit sector – especially foundations – a vital ally in the fight to reform public school programs based on rigorous evidence. In the spring of 2009, several presidents of major foundations requested a meeting with Secretary Duncan to discuss the new administration's emerging education priorities and education goals. They also wanted to discuss the proposed 20 % matching requirement for i3 grantees. The Secretary used the occasion to fully explain the administration's goals for the i3 initiative to the foundation leaders and to urge them to play an important role in the initiative. According to our interviews with Shelton, Miller, and other senior officials who worked for Duncan, his hope was that foundations would become infected by the

Table 10.5 Overview of selected i3 awards

Project	Grantees/partners	Grant amount/length	Intervention
Scale-up			
Reading Recovery	Ohio State University and consortium of 18 other university partners in various states	$45.5 million for 5 years	Short-term literacy intervention focused on one-on-one tutoring for lowest achieving first graders, scale-up network for university training centers to target low-performing schools, goal of training 750 teachers per year to serve a total of around 500,000 students
Success for All	Twelve public school districts across the country, Colorado Department of Education, Johns Hopkins University, Pennsylvania Department of Education	$49.2 million for 5 years	Whole-school turnaround program for Title I elementary schools; provides training materials for staff for cooperative learning, reading, tutoring, and support services; goal to add 1,100 schools to national network, expand training capacity, and operate more effectively; $50,000 paid to schools to help implement Success for All model
Validation			
Model Classroom Innovation	Children's Literacy Initiative and Camden City Public Schools, Newark Public Schools, School District of Philadelphia, Chicago Public Schools	$21.7 million for 5 years	Model Classroom program for raising teacher quality around student literacy achievement; train k-3 teachers in high-impact, evidence-based literacy instructional practices; goal to train 456 teachers in 38 selected public schools, reaching 45,600 students per year
Virginia Initiative for Science Teaching and Achievement (VISTA)	George Mason University, 47 school districts, 6 universities, Virginia Department of Education	$28.4 million for 5 years	Science teacher professional development to improve instruction and student performance; comprehensive professional development model for k-12 science teachers to train more than 800 teachers in elementary school and secondary schools, reaching more than 80,000 students
Development			
CollegeYES	Alliance for College-Ready Public Schools, International Society for Technology in Education, Kijana Voices	$4.9 million for 5 years	College access and success throughout the Alliance College-Ready network of charter schools in the LA area; includes aligning curriculum with Common Core College/Career standards, improving advisory courses, and using technology to help students develop skills; professional development among teachers to serve as advisors on college readiness and preparation; integrates technology projects into courses
Every Child Ready	Apple Tree Institute for Education Innovation, Apple Tree Early Learning Public Charter School, DC Prep Academy, Early Childhood Academy, FOCUS	$5 million for 5 years	Preschool intervention model that integrates special education students into general education classrooms; includes full-day instructional program; students are monitored, data used to ensure progress; instruction is differentiated on progress, with additional individual support as needed for children; goal to help children arrive at kindergarten with skills they need to succeed

Source: Department of Education, *Highest-Rated i3 Applications*, retrieved from http://www2.ed.gov/programs/innovation/2010/applications.html

evidence-based virus and begin to demand high-quality evaluations of the intervention programs they funded with their own money. The broader vision of the Secretary and his leadership team was the need for high-quality evaluations of the wide range of social programs supported by foundations. In this regard, foundations, with their billions of dollars of spending on social programs, could play a decisive role in promoting evidence-based programs.

Again according to our interview with Jim Shelton, an important idea to facilitate foundation involvement in i3 emerged from the meeting. As mentioned above, the administration planned to require projects that won the i3 competition to secure matching funds equal to 20 % of their grant amount. Most of this money would have to come from foundations. The foundations decided on an efficient way to get information from the organizations that planned to apply for i3 funds about the nature of the program they were proposing, namely, to post this information in a central location online. The foundations, which would control the website, could then review specific proposals, simultaneously get information about the sponsoring organizations, and then use this information to decide if they wanted to explore the possibility of providing matching funds for programs in which they were interested. The foundations subsequently created a website (FoundationRegistryi3.org) to facilitate their learning about the i3 proposals and the organizations making the proposals. The website eventually had nearly 700 i3 proposals that the foundations could review (of a total of nearly 1,700 applicants; Smith and Peterson 2011). The CEO of the Gates Foundation said that the registry "pave[d] the way for a new approach to leverage technology for philanthropic collaboration – increasing access, efficiency and effectiveness to drive greater impact in the field." In the end, twelve of the nation's biggest foundations committed $500 million to match the $650 million in i3 funds made available by the Department of Education (Bill and Melinda Gates Foundation 2010). The foundations included Gates, Annie E. Casey, Carnegie, Ford, Mott, MacArthur, Lumina, Walton, Kellogg, and others.

A final reason the i3 initiative is so important is that it set a pattern for the Obama administration's series of initiatives on evidence-based policy. Without i3, the administration's goal of placing evidence at the heart of its policymaking would have been a much different and less robust enterprise. In many ways – including the definition of evidence, the cooperative relationship between the administering agency and OMB, the tiers concept, and the methods of reviewing grants – the i3 initiative set the mold for subsequent evidence-based initiatives in the Obama administration.

10.6 Conclusion and Implications

Leaving aside for a moment whether future administrations will want to continue the approach to evidence-based policy developed by the Obama administration and reviewed here, the first thing we can learn from the history of the i3 initiative is that it features the major elements around which future evidence-based initiatives could be built. These elements include the focus on a serious national social problem; competitive rather than formula grants to induce competition and require the use of evidence; the tiered definition of evidence that achieves a compromise between rigorous evidence, moderate evidence, and innovation even when there is little evidence; and the requirement that programs conduct high-quality evaluations and follow-up with midcourse adjustments if the evaluation reveals poor outcomes. These, albeit with important variations in some of the initiatives, are the hallmarks of the Obama strategy for improving the quality and impact of social intervention programs and for elevating the odds that government spending on social programs will begin to actually reduce the magnitude of social problems on a national scale. We think the Obama approach to using federal dollars to leverage the use of social intervention programs supported by rigorous evidence and to evaluate the programs as they are being conducted may turn out to be a successful strategy for attacking national social problems, but there should be no claim at this point that we know the strategy will be effective or even an improvement over current policy. Before we conclude that the Obama evidence-based approach is superior, we need to see that the social problems now being addressed by the initiatives – child rearing by poor mothers; teen pregnancy; several preschool and K-12 education issues; a host of community-level social problems; and employment, training, and employment issues – are actually impacted by the six initiatives.

Even if a future administration agreed with the Obama emphasis on trying to advance evidence-based policymaking, there is much to learn from some of the problems the Obama team encountered along the way. The first problem, which we have come to understand based on our interview with officials at MDRC, on years of experience working with program operators, and on extensive experience with members of the United States Congress, will be an issue for all evidence-based initiatives. The problem is the inevitable tension between a researcher's vision of rigorous evidence and a program operator's view of what constitutes good evidence. Some program operators, as well as their board members and the politicians who support them, seem to be satisfied with heartwarming anecdotes about children who have done well in their program. Other program operators think that simply collecting evidence of good outcomes such as high test scores, high rates of school completion, or lower arrest rates is enough to show that their program works. But compared to what? Data on outcomes without a good control group to compare outcomes to receive low priority in the Obama evidence-based initiatives. The RCT is the gold standard in the Obama evidence-based world. There are other types of evidence that could qualify for funding under the Obama initiatives, but the Obama gold standard is very similar to that of the National Academies, IES, and other organizations that set standards for good evidence (Coalition for Evidence-Based Policy 2013). Indeed, an implicit goal of the Obama initiatives is to influence foundations, LEAs, community-based programs, and other actors in the world of social intervention programs to learn more about rigorous evidence and to use experimental designs to evaluate programs as often as possible.

On this point, our discussions with both program operators and child advocates suggest that there is now something like a cultural struggle taking place between program operators and their supporters on the one side and researchers, program evaluators, prominent evaluation firms, and senior officials in the Obama administration on the other. The primary issues are what constitutes good evidence of program impacts, who is responsible for collecting the evidence, who will pay for it, and – an especially touchy issue – what happens to programs that fail to produce impacts? The vision of officials in the Obama administration is that with each passing year more and more federal dollars for social programs will go to programs that are backed by solid, preferably RCT, evidence and that funded programs will undergo continuous assessment, also as often as possible by RCTs, to determine their ongoing effects.

As much as the Obama administration favored RCTs, all of the initiatives recognized that acceptable evidence comes from other types of designs as well. None of the initiatives funded only programs that already had evidence of impacts from RCTs. In fact, even the highest tier of i3 funding allowed evidence from quasi-experimental designs such as regression discontinuity and interrupted time series. In addition, several of the initiatives had a bottom tier of funding that required only "promising" evidence, thereby allowing funding for programs that had no rigorous evidence at all. Neither the WIF nor the Community College initiatives required evidence from RCTs, because, as our interviews with both OMB and Labor Department officials showed, the administration recognized that there was little RCT evidence available in these areas.

Program operators cite a host of good reasons why they are hard-pressed to use RCTs to evaluate their programs. Perhaps the most important is that they're so busy trying to run their operation and make sure they're running a quality program that they have neither the time nor the resources to conduct expensive and time-consuming random-assignment evaluations. This is a worthy criticism, and it is easy to be sympathetic to the many problems faced by program operators just to keep their programs going. Our interviews with both MDRC program evaluators involved with several SIF programs and with officials from the Corporation for National and Community Service (CNCS), who had extensive experience meeting with program operators, revealed that many program operators lacked knowledge about program evaluation and had never been involved in conducting a rigorous evaluation. We suspect, based on our interviews about the i3 initiative, that the same may be true of many LEAs and their consultants and organizations they work with. The CNCS solution as they administered the SIF initiative was to sponsor conferences with program operators for the specific purpose of teaching them about program evaluation and the use of rigorous designs. As part of this education process, CNCS developed an impressive manual aimed at helping programs develop their evaluation plans (Center for National and Community Service 2013). We did not interview program operators, but senior officials at CNCS told us that program operators understood the importance of evaluation and worked hard to create good evaluation plans for their own programs.

Another problem with the evidence-based initiatives is that good evaluations, and there are many now taking place in both i3 and the other initiatives, are virtually certain to show that many of the programs do not produce impacts (Manzi 2012a). The administration has hired Abt Associates to help the network of 117 i3 programs design and conduct their evaluations, which will almost certainly have the effect of improving the quality of the evaluations. The better the evaluations, the more likely they are to show that some programs do not produce significant impacts. As Jon Baron of the Coalition for Evidence-Based Policy has pointed out, of 90 interventions evaluated by randomized control trials (RCTs) paid for by IES since 2002, 88 % were found to have weak or no positive effects. Similar results are produced by RCTs of clinical interventions in medicine (Coalition for Evidence-Based Policy 2013). Even in business studies, Jim Manzi reports that between 80 and 90 % of studies of new products or strategies conducted by Google and Microsoft found no significant effects (Manzi 2012a, b).

Our interviews with administration officials, including those working on the i3 initiative, suggest that the local programs are going along with the Obama emphasis on evaluation. Similarly, our discussions with Abt officials working on the i3 evaluation team and with MDRC officials working on the SIF evaluation team suggest that local programs are cooperating with the evaluations and playing an active role in their design and conduct. But what will be the response of program directors and their staffs when the evaluations show their program is not producing significant impacts? In our view, this is a crucial issue that will play an important role in the success and lasting power of all the Obama evidence-based initiatives. If evaluation is to help programs improve, it must provide continuous information to program personnel so they can make improvements in their program in response to findings that show modest or no impacts. This issue is now being played out in hundreds of local programs being supported by the Obama initiatives, 117 of which are part of i3. As preliminary evaluation results begin to emerge, one hopes that both the administration and the various evaluation experts the administration has hired to work with local programs will help program operators accept the results as an indication that they need to improve their programs and that the administration will help them do so. One of the most important outcomes of the i3 initiative will be lessons in how to help local operators, including LEAs, learn to use rigorous evaluations as a major component in their efforts to improve their programs. In our view, an important part of a comprehensive, evidence-based strategy will be continuing the funding of programs with initially discouraging evaluations. Part of the federal evidence-based culture should be that federal agencies will work with programs, and continue their funding, as long as they are using evidence to improve their outcomes and are showing some progress.

It is useful to close on a cautionary note. What the Obama administration is attempting to do is breathtaking. By building funding for social programs based on high-quality evidence, the administration is aiming to reorder the factors that normally dominate the politics of decision making in the nation's capital. Normal politics, both in authorizing programs and in appropriating money, is dominated by the views of the president and powerful Members of Congress, by lobbying groups outside Congress, by governors and other state officials, and perhaps most of all by the philosophical assumptions of the two political parties. Now the Obama administration would insert a powerful new consideration into the allocation of funds. The driving force would be reliable evidence of whether a program is having its intended effects. It would be naïve to think that evidence will ever be the only or perhaps even the most important factor in allocating money for social programs, but it is possible to believe that the scope for evidence of program effectiveness could be greatly expanded if i3 and the other evidence-based initiatives produce impacts on the nation's social problems. The evidence on the success of the Obama evidence-based initiatives is not yet in. A lot is riding on the impacts of this new way of doing business. Impressively, the administration has allocated funds for the evaluation of the i3 programs and for their other five evidence-based initiatives. At the very least, the Obama administration has the courage of its convictions, thereby guaranteeing that the nation will soon know if the evidence-based initiatives are having their intended impacts and whether taxpayers are at last getting their money's worth.

References

Abt Associates. (2013). *Investing in innovation: Evaluating the i3 program.* Abt Associates. Retrieved from http://abtassociates.com/Projects/2010/Investing-in-Innovation--Evaluating-the-i3-Program.aspx

Biernacki, P., & Waldorf, D. (1981). Snowball sampling: Problems and techniques of chain referral sampling. *Sociological Methods Research, 10*(2), 141–168.

Bill and Melinda Gates Foundation. (2010). *Twelve major foundations commit $500 million to education innovation in concert with U.S. Department of Education's $650 million 'Investing in Innovation Fund.'* Retrieved from the Gates Foundation website http://www.gatesfoundation.org/Media-Center/Press-Releases/2010/04/12-Foundations-Commit-to-Education-Innovation-with-US-Department-of-Education

Brill, S. (2011). *Class warfare*. New York: Simon & Schuster Paperbacks.

Calmes, J. (2009, January 28). House passes stimulus plan with no GOP votes. *The New York Times*. Retrieved from http://www.nytimes.com/2009/01/29/us/politics/29obama.html?hp&_r=0

Center for National and Community Service. (2013, May). *Social innovation fund: Content requirements for sub grantee evaluation plans*. Washington, DC: Author.

Coalition for Evidence-Based Policy. (2013). *Randomized controlled trials commissioned by the Institute of Education Sciences Since 2002: How many found positive versus weak or no effects*. Retrieved from http://coalition4evidence.org/wp-content/uploads/2013/06/IES-CommissionedRCTs-positive-vs-weak-or-null-findings-7-2013.pdf

Corporation for National and Community Service. (2013, May). *Social innovation fund: Content requirements for subgrantee evaluation plans*.

Goodson, B., Wolf, A., Bell, S., Turner, H., Finney, P. (2010). *The effectiveness of a program to accelerate vocabulary development in kindergarten (VOCAB)*. Washington, DC: National Center for Education Evaluation and Regional Assistance. Retrieved from http://ies.ed.gov/ncee/edlabs/regions/southeast/pdf/REL_20104014.pdf

Herszenhorn, D. (2009, February 10). Senate approves stimulus plan. *The New York Times*. Retrieved from http://www.nytimes.com/2009/02/11/washington/11web-stim.html

Institute of Education Sciences, U.S. Department of Education. (2008). *Rigor and relevance redux: Director's biennial report to congress*. Retrieved from http://ies.ed.gov/director/pdf/20096010.pdf

Institute of Education Sciences, U.S. Department of Education. (2011). *What works clearinghouse: Procedures and standards handbook version 2.1*. Retrieved from http://ies.ed.gov/ncee/wwc/pdf/reference_resources/wwc_procedures_v2_1_standards_handbook.pdf

Knott, J., & Wildavsky, A. (1980). If dissemination is the solution, what is the problem? *Knowledge: Creation, Diffusion, Utilization, 1*(4), 537–578.

Library of Congress. (a). American Recovery and Reinvestment Act of 2009. Retrieved from http://thomas.loc.gov/cgi-bin/bdquery/z?d111:h.r.00001
Library of Congress. (b). Consolidated Appropriations Act, 2010. Retrieved from http://thomas.loc.gov/cgi-bin/bdquery/z?d111:h.r.03288
Library of Congress. (c). Department of Defense and Full-Year Continuing Appropriations Act, 2011. Retrieved from http://thomas.loc.gov/cgi-bin/bdquery/z?d112:h.r.1473
Library of Congress. (d). Health Care and Education Reconciliation Act of 2010. Retrieved from http://thomas.loc.gov/cgi-bin/bdquery/z?d111:h.r.04872
Library of Congress. (e). Patient Protection and Affordable Care Act. Retrieved from http://thomas.loc.gov/cgi-bin/bdquery/z?d111:h.r.03590
Library of Congress. (f). Serve America Act. Retrieved from http://thomas.loc.gov/cgi-bin/bdquery/z?d111:h.r.01388
Manzi, J. (2012a). *Uncontrolled: The surprising payoff of trial-and-error for business, politics and society*. New York: Perseus.
Manzi, J. (2012b, December). *Science knowledge and freedom*. Speech presented at Harvard's Program on Constitutional Government, Cambridge, MA.
Mathematica Policy Research and Child Trends. (2010). *Identifying programs that impact teen pregnancy prevention, sexually transmitted infections, and associated risk behaviors: Review protocol version 1.0*. Retrieved from http://www.hhs.gov/ash/oah/oah-initiatives/teen_pregnancy/db/eb-programs-review-v2.pdf
Mosteller, F. (1995). The Tennessee study of class size in the early school grades. *The Future of Children 5*(2), 113–127. Retrieved from http://www.princeton.edu/futureofchildren/publications/docs/05_02_08.pdf
National Research Council. (1999). *Improving student learning: A strategic plan for education research and its utilization*. Retrieved from http://www.nap.edu/catalog.php?record_id=6488
Office of the Federal Register (2010, March 10). *Final rule and notice*. Retrieved from http://www.gpo.gov/fdsys/pkg/FR-2010-03-12/pdf/2010-5147.pdf
Orr, L. L. (1998). *Social experiments: Evaluating public programs with experimental methods*. Thousand Oaks: Sage.
Orszag, P. (2009, June). *Building rigorous evidence to drive policy*. OMBlog. Retrieved from http://www.whitehouse.gov/omb/blog/09/06/08/BuildingRigorousEvidencetoDrivePolicy
Paulsell, D., Avellar, S., Sama Martin, E., & Del Grosso, P. (2010). *Home visiting evidence of effectiveness review: Executive summary*. Washington, DC: Office of Planning, Research and Evaluation, Administration for Children and Families, U.S. Department of Health and Human Services. Retrieved from http://homvee.acf.hhs.gov/HomVEE_Executive_Summary.pdf
Seib, G. (2008, November 21). In crisis, opportunity for Barack Obama. *The Wall Street Journal*. Retrieved from http://online.wsj.com/article/SB122721278056345271.html
Smith, K., & Peterson, J. (2011). *Supporting and scaling change: Lessons from the first round of the investing in innovation (i3) program*. Retrieved from http://bellwethereducation.org/wp-content/uploads/2011/07/Supporting-Scaling-Change-i3.pdf
Stolberg, S. G. (2009, February 17). Signing stimulus, Obama doesn't rule out more. *The New York Times*. Retrieved from http://www.nytimes.com/2009/02/18/us/politics/18web-stim.html
Tansey, O. (2007). Process tracing and elite interviewing: A case for non-probability sampling. *PS: Political Science and Politics, 40*(4), 765–772.
Tuttle, C. C., Gill, B., Gleason, P., Knechtel, V., Nichols-Barrer, I., Resch, A. (2013). *KIPP Middle Schools: Impacts on achievement and other outcomes*. Mathematica Policy Research. Retrieved from http://www.kipp.org/files/dmfile/KIPP_Middle_Schools_Impact_on_Achievement_and_Other_Outcomes1.pdf
United States Congress. (2009, January). American Recovery and Reinvestment Act of 2009. Retrieved from http://www.gpo.gov/fdsys/pkg/BILLS-111hr1enr/pdf/BILLS-111hr1enr.pdf

Part III
Defining, Acquiring, and Using Research Evidence – Looking Across and Beyond

Chapter 11
Building the Infrastructure to Improve the Use and Usefulness of Research in Education

Vivian Tseng and Sandra Nutley

We often hear calls to increase the rigor and relevance of education research in the United States. Many would agree that rigor has increased considerably over the past decade (National Research Council 2012; Institute of Education Sciences & National Science Foundation 2013). Improving the relevance of research has been more challenging. In part, this is because the criteria for judging relevance have not been clearly defined—*relevant to whom and for what?*

As we write this chapter, Congress has begun hearings to reauthorize the Education Sciences Reform Act of 2002. Research relevance is a top concern (Sparks 2013). What is unclear is to whom research should be relevant. Education—and education research by extension—has many stakeholders. The Act includes a long list of would-be research users: teachers, administrators, librarians, other practitioners, parents, policymakers, voluntary organizations, professional associations, the media, the general public, and of course the researchers themselves. Tailoring education research to the needs of so many different actors is a big lift given their wide variety of information needs. We need a clear focus on key research users and the functions research serves for their work.

Each chapter in this book presents an exciting case that builds understanding of the uses of research in education decision-making in the United States. Collectively, they cover the ways research has influenced some of the key issues of this era—the Common Core State Standards, charter schools, school vouchers, teacher merit pay, the Investing in Innovation (i3) Fund, and the No Child Left Behind Act of 2001. These authors represent a new generation of scholars working, with support from the William T. Grant Foundation, to understand the uses of research in policy and practice.

V. Tseng (✉)
Vice President, Program, William T. Grant Foundation, New York, NY, USA
e-mail: vtseng@Wtgrantfdn.org

S. Nutley
Director, Research Unit on Research Utilization,
University of St. Andrews, St. Andrews, Scotland, UK

K.S. Finnigan and A.J. Daly (eds.), *Using Research Evidence in Education: From the Schoolhouse Door to Capitol Hill*, Policy Implications of Research in Education 2,
DOI 10.1007/978-3-319-04690-7_11,

Early knowledge utilization work generated broad principles. Carol Weiss (1977) argued that research more frequently plays an "enlightenment function" influencing how policymakers orient themselves to issues rather than determining their decisions. Nathan Caplan's (1979) "two communities" theory attributed the lack of research use to the separation of research and policy by different values, reward systems, and languages. Building on these ideas, contemporary scholars more closely examine when and how research is used. They reveal the contingent nature of research use, gleaning how research informs problem formulation in some instances, decision-making in others, and more subtle learning in still others.

In this synthesis chapter, we draw out themes from this rich body of work. We begin with a discussion of the research users and their uses of research. Then we consider what these studies suggest for building a stronger infrastructure for connecting research with policy and practice. Next, we consider what the United States might learn from some other countries about developing a more research-informed education system. We close on a hopeful note: Progress is being made. And so long as we continue to learn as we go—from this body of work and others—we may just close the notorious gaps between education research, policy, and practice.

11.1 The Research Users

This book focuses on a key subset of research users—the decision-makers in Congress; state and local school boards; and federal, state, and local education agencies. Focusing on these policymakers and administrators makes a great deal of sense. Over the past decade, the No Child Left Behind (NCLB) Act, Race to the Top, state accountability policies, and the Common Core State Standards pressed for greater use of research evidence in decisions about curricula, turning around low-performing schools, teacher evaluation, and improving student test scores. They sought to cultivate a diverse cadre of research users. Asen and Gurke's chapter examines local school boards' use of research within the context of NCLB. Daly, Finnigan, Moolenaar, and Che look at district administrators', principals', and teachers' definitions and uses of evidence to improve low-performing schools, while Barnes, Goertz, and Massell focus on state education agencies. Federal actors in the Office of Management and Budget, the Department of Education, and Congress are the focus of Haskins and Margolis' study of the use of evaluation findings in program funding decisions. By focusing on this diverse group of research users, we can better understand the various functions research serves in different decision-making contexts.

The intermediaries that sit betwixt and between research and policy are another important set of research users to consider. They are not the legislators, appointees, or agency staff who hold formal policymaking roles. Nor are they part of the traditional research community consisting of higher education and policy research organizations. Some intermediaries seek to be neutral brokers, bringing research to bear on the concerns of key decision-makers. Others are more advocacy oriented, strategically drawing on research to advance their reform agendas. Scott and her colleagues examine the ways advocacy groups, think tanks, and foundations use research to promote charter schools, vouchers, teacher merit pay, and student pay for performance. McDonnell and Weatherford describe the ways the National Governors Association and the Council of Chief State School Officers mobilized support for the Common Core State Standards by promoting them as "research- and evidence-based." Honig and Venkateswaran describe yet another type of intermediary, which focuses less on disseminating research and more on assisting administrators in applying it to their day-to-day work.

Federal research agencies and their contracted organizations are not intermediaries per se, but they play mediating roles in bringing research to policy (Barnes et al. 2014, Chap. 8). Although the Institute of Education Sciences is primarily a research funder, its charge includes disseminating research to state and local decision-makers. For example, the Institute's What Works Clearinghouse and Regional Education Labs and the Department of Education's Comprehensive Assistance Centers package research for state and local decision-makers.

11.2 The Uses of Research

With such a diverse range of research users, it is not surprising that research is used in different ways by stakeholders with varying goals, interests, and roles. The authors complicate the common conception of research users as merely rational actors who have questions, go in search of research to answer them, and then apply it to their decisions (Nutley et al. 2007). In none of their cases does research use easily boil down to a single moment or an isolated decision. It is not a simple process whereby research "facts" are passed from researchers to research users and then applied in a linear decision-making process. Instead, research use is contingent, interactive, and iterative. It involves people individually and collectively engaging with research over time, bringing their own and their organization's goals, motivations, routines, and political contexts with them. Research also enters the policy process at various times—as problems are defined (and redefined); ideas are generated; solutions are identified; and policies are adopted, implemented, and sometimes stalled.

The depictions of research use across the chapters vary depending on the different users and their decision-making contexts; nevertheless, certain themes emerge about the functions research serves, what research use looks like, and the ways research uptake has been encouraged and enabled.

11.2.1 Using Research to Frame Problems and Solutions

Asen and Gurke make the cogent point that "research evidence does not speak for itself, and even if it could speak, research evidence would not speak with one voice" (Chap. 5, pp. 53–68). Instead, political actors frame research in order to substantiate their positions and to persuade others to support them. McDonnell and Weatherford show that advocates of the Common Core State Standards promoted research showing that U.S. students rank surprisingly low in international comparisons of achievement. These advocates coupled those findings with information about national standards in higher-achieving countries to strategically frame the case for common standards across states. Scott and colleagues illustrate how advocates and think tanks on both sides of the charter school debate emphasized certain studies and not others in order to bolster their positions. When they discussed the same studies, they often argued for competing interpretations of the findings (see Jeffrey Henig's *Spin Cycle,* 2009). In all these cases, research truths are not simply applied to a decision to pursue one course of action over another. Instead, these cases involve policy actors operating in a political system.

11.2.2 Using Research as Individual and Organizational Learning

Research use is also a learning process that involves gaining and applying knowledge over time (Nutley et al. 2007). Just as classroom learning is not simply a matter of transferring information from a teacher to a student, using research is not merely about transmitting findings from research producer to user. Instead, using research—like learning in general—is a process by which individuals revise their internal representations of the world in light of new information. It is an active and dynamic process, shaped by experience and mediated socially and cognitively.

In their chapter, Honig and Venkateswaran propose a linear progression from understanding research findings to their use in driving changes in district central offices. They are particularly interested in higher-order levels of learning—or research use—that go beyond incremental shifts and result in more profound changes in administrators' work. While learning processes are likely to be more iterative and cyclical than a linear model might suggest, there is considerable merit in exploring these processes. This is especially important at an organizational level given that most decisions are made by groups, not by individuals. Organizational learning is more than the sum of changes in individuals' knowledge and practices. Organizations are more complex entities with varying degrees of analytic capacity and with routines and cultures that can facilitate or obstruct learning (Fazekas and Burns 2012; Finnigan et al. 2012; Honig and Venkateswaran 2014, Chap. 4; Coburn et al. 2008). By conceptualizing research use as learning over time rather than a static event, a more complete picture of the process emerges.

11.2.3 Converting Research into Usable Applications

Several chapters highlight efforts to improve research uptake by converting research-based knowledge into usable applications. In some instances, research findings are embedded in tools for practice such as curricula, practice guides, observation protocols, and assessments (Coburn and Stein 2010). Barnes and her colleagues describe state education agencies' conversion of research findings into school improvement frameworks and tools to support districts and schools. Measures of teaching consist of items and scales for assessing the instructional practices that are predictive of student outcomes. Evidence-based programs incorporate prior theory and research on strategies that improve practice. Adopting these tools for teacher evaluation, professional development, and school improvement is one way to embed research in the educational system.

McDonnell and Weatherford describe the research bases for the Common Core State Standards. Although research was not the only form of evidence used, various studies and syntheses were significant in developing the standards for what students are expected to learn in different grades. A particularly influential body of research had examined children's learning progressions in math and English Language Arts. Other research came from faculty surveys and analyses of the relationship between student performance on admissions tests and grades in lower division coursework. The findings came from diverse sources (academic journals, books, and reports) and were published by various actors (the National Research Council, federal agencies, professional associations, Achieve, ACT, and the College Board).

At their best, these tools and other applications are not only informed by prior research; they are subject to refinement based on further research and development to improve them. Moreover, studying the choices districts, schools, and teachers make in implementing the tools can generate crucial knowledge of how to enhance the tools and to align resources and supports to ensure that they are used to maximum effect.

11.2.4 Tying Research to Funding Decisions

Programs, practices, and tools that are based on research can be promoted by tying incentives to their adoption. Haskins and Margolis focus on the use of evaluation findings to allocate federal dollars through the Investing in Innovation (i3) Fund. In this case, research consists of evaluation evidence aimed at determining whether intervention programs produce their desired impacts. The i3 program emphasized the application of rigorous research designs to determine "what works." Intervention programs are arranged hierarchically according to the degree of confidence people should have in them based on the study designs used to test their impacts. In the first i3 announcement, the top-tier programs were defined as having multiple randomized controlled or quasi-experimental trials, or one randomized controlled trial in multiple sites, showing positive impacts. The second tier consisted of programs where evaluation studies were said to be less robust (e.g., quasi-experimental designs), and the bottom tier consisted of programs where evaluation studies drew only on weaker designs (e.g., pre- and post-tests). The strength of the research evidence was then used to decide on funding levels. Top-tier programs were eligible for grants of up to $50 million, the second tier for $30 million, and the third tier for $5 million.

11.3 Building the Infrastructure to Connect Research with Policy and Practice

In addition to illustrating the various ways research is used and promoted, the chapters point the field toward ways of better connecting research with policy and practice. Drawing on these cases and concurrent efforts in the field, we suggest four ways to shore up the infrastructure for those connections: build relationships and trust, shore up capacity, create conditions for evidence integration, and develop partnerships.

11.3.1 Build Relationships and Trust

All the chapters implicate personal and organizational relationships as key pathways by which policymakers and practitioners acquire research and evaluate its trustworthiness. Despite the importance of relationships, the field too infrequently leverages the power of networks as a way to enhance research dissemination and use. Barnes, Goertz, and Massell suggest that state education agencies have a cadre of people and organizations that they turn to for research. These sources include regional education boards and professional membership associations who have a history of working with the agencies, are familiar with their local context and staff, and are seen as credible. Identifying these key information brokers is a good start. The next step is forging strong ties between them and researchers to ensure that high-quality research informs the advice and technical assistance provided to agencies. Engaging with these brokers has the added benefit of exposing researchers to policymakers' information needs—knowledge that can help them improve the relevance of their work.

Daly et al. (2014) hone in on information brokers as key leverage points. They use social network analyses to map the relationships within a school district, evaluate the strength of the various social ties, and identify where the ties are particularly weak. They find, for example, that principals of low-performing schools are the most isolated—from each other, from colleagues in higher-performing schools, and from district administrators. The educators with the greatest need for assistance, ideas, and information to support reform efforts have the least access to them. These types of analyses can help district administrators and researchers visualize the social systems they are trying to impact and target resources to the people and places where research brokerage is weakest.

A focus on relationships brings trust to the foreground and indicates a need to build greater trust to support research use. A growing body of work reveals the mistrust practitioners and local policymakers have of research and research purveyors. Decision-makers judge not only the trustworthiness of research evidence but of the people presenting it (Granger et al. 2013). Finnigan, Daly, Molenaar, and Che find a pervasive distrust of research among educators in their study. For example, practitioners believe that "research" and "evidence" are often manipulated. As one educator put it:

> You can find research to support anything... People are now using research to say that all the problems are the teacher, and if you can correct the teacher, all our problems go away, which is ridiculous.... The point is research can be slanted to support many different viewpoints. It doesn't mean it's correct. (Daly and Finnigan 2011)

Asen and Gurke show that in high-conflict, low-trust settings, decision-makers tend to distrust any rationale other parties offer for their positions, and that includes research. In one district, for example, school board members' distrust of the administration contaminated their perceptions of information as "spoon-fed for us from the district." Distrust of the district administrators transferred to the researchers they cited, with the assumption that both operated with a political agenda. On the flip side, Asen and Gurke argue that higher levels of trust among decision-makers can facilitate better understanding of research and more informed uses of it. Trust is malleable, and it can be built over time with deliberate effort.

11.3.2 Shore Up Capacity

Using research well at school, district, state, or federal levels requires adequate time, knowledge, and skills. It takes organizational leadership as well as the cultures, structures, and resources that are conducive to research use (Coburn and Turner 2012). The evidence-based initiatives launched under the Obama administration were possible because staff in the Office of Management and Budget had expertise in research design as well as the motivation and leadership skills to make things happen. The i3 initiative could draw on the standards of evidence already developed through the What Works Clearinghouse of the Institute for Education Sciences (Haskins and Margolis 2014). Policymakers also need the political savvy to persuade others (Asen and Gurke 2014; McDonnell and Weatherford 2014). As the National Research Council report on using social science comments:

> Success at promoting science depends on grasping the complexity of the policy world, and on understanding the assumptions underlying divergent policy framings, expert judgments, and consensus-building techniques, as well as standard analytic methods and approaches... [There is a need to] recognize the limits of the persuasive power of scientific reasoning, the substantial institutional barriers and cultural resistance to new scientific knowledge, and the role of moral and ethical beliefs. (National Research Council 2012, p. 6)

Capacity-building is also needed on the research side of the equation. Scott and her coauthors (2014) point to the irony that intermediaries and legislative staff view university-based research as more credible than research produced by think tanks and advocacy groups. But they also see it as too expensive to produce, not timely, and too narrow to be useful. As much as policymakers and practitioners need the capacity to interpret and use research, researchers need the knowledge, skills, and time to produce more useful work and to interact fruitfully with would-be research users.

They also require institutional and professional supports to conduct research that addresses persistent problems of policy and practice. The current academic system rewards researchers for publishing in academic journals. While the peer review process helps to ensure the scientific quality of research, it does little to address the usefulness of research to policymakers and administrators. Incentive systems could reward researchers for the impact of their work in those arenas. Moreover, if future generations of scholars are to be more apt than their predecessors at conducting relevant research and communicating it clearly, they will need better training than is currently available. They will require skills for collaborating with policymakers and practitioners in designing relevant research, writing for them, and helping them understand what existing research suggests for improving their work.

11.3.3 Create Conditions for Productive Evidence Integration

As the preceding chapters show, bringing the best available research evidence to the table is only the beginning. It is relatively rare for research findings to provide clear-cut solutions that can simply be adopted and implemented across a range of contexts. More often, research findings suggest a direction of travel, but specific actions are negotiated locally (see also Finnigan et al. 2013; Honig and Coburn 2008; Nelson et al. 2009). In this process, research knowledge interacts with other sources of knowledge including that from local data analyses, organizational history, and practice experience (Asen et al. 2012). Conditions must be in place so that decision-makers can weigh and integrate different types of evidence and discern their implications for the specific problems at hand.

The Common Core State Standards movement suggests ways policymakers can foster productive integration of research and other types of evidence, according to McDonnell and Weatherford. Advocates wanted the Standards to be based on research but knew that research was not sufficient in and of itself to inform the development of the Standards nor their adoption and implementation by states. They developed a process that allowed for "grafting" together research and other types of evidence (T. Lindhorst, Personal communication, July 12, 2013). For example, research on learning progressions was useful for drafting the math standards for K–2 but was not available for the upper grades. In order to develop K–12 math standards, the writers pulled in other types of evidence. They relied on researchers to provide their professional judgment on what learning progressions would look like in the upper grades—judgment that was extrapolated from their knowledge of existing studies. The Standards writers also incorporated the judgment of teachers and state education agency staff—a process that strengthened the Standards and fostered broader stakeholder support for their adoption and implementation. The American Federation of Teachers and National Education Association provided feedback on the wording of the Standards, identifying areas that would be confusing to teachers and suggesting ways to clarify them. In this case, a collaborative approach across professional specialties and interests facilitated the productive integration of research with other types of evidence.

11.3.4 Develop Long-Term Partnerships

Partnerships between researchers and state or local education agencies are another promising way to strengthen the production and use of research. Researchers, policymakers, and practitioners work in separate spheres with differing incentives, goals, language, demands, and time frames (Caplan 1979). They have few opportunities for sustained engagement across these worlds. Researchers and policymakers might interact after studies are completed and findings are ready for distribution. Lack of significant interaction at the outset, however, obstructs researchers' ability to adapt study designs, measurement plans, and sampling choices so that they will address decision-makers' information needs. Even collaborative research projects are typically quite delimited, taking the form of one-off studies or circumscribed consultations.

Coburn et al. (2013) make the case for long-term partnerships that strive for sustained, joint commitments and enable partners to tackle larger questions and explore issues in greater depth. The collaboration is maintained via frequent and regular interactions. These exchanges provide researchers with a better understanding of the problems districts face, the evolution of their system goals and work, and the constraints and opportunities for making change. For practitioners, the interactions foster greater trust that researchers will share their findings in a timely and useful fashion and help them apply the research to their work.

It is an exciting time for these education partnerships, as support grows at the federal level and organizations experiment with various approaches and strategies for fostering useful work. At the federal level, the Institute for Education Sciences has issued a Request for Applications to support research-practice partnerships, and their contracts for Regional Education Labs require working through regional research alliances. The National Science Foundation is focused on partnerships in which researchers and practitioners codesign educational innovations. A crucial need is connecting the lessons learned across these partnerships. Successful partnerships—like marriages—are not made overnight. They confront the challenges of developing research agendas that meet multiple stakeholders' needs, navigating the different time frames between research and practice, maintaining trust even when research findings can damage districts' public images, and preserving collaboration during frequent changes in district leadership. Some partnerships are developing smart strategies to address these challenges, but mechanisms are needed to aggregate and share these strategies broadly.

11.4 The United States in Comparative Perspective

While various vantage points are represented in this book, the focus is on domestic education policy. In this section, we take a look at the use of research in select nations to seek insight into factors that may otherwise be overlooked or taken for granted within the U.S. context. Understanding differences across countries can also provide fresh ideas for facilitating stronger links between research, policy, and practice.

Around the world, the United States is best known for its "what works" approach to evidence-based policy and practice and is regarded as having taken a more top-down approach to research use than have many other countries (OECD/CERI 2007; Fazekas and Burns 2012; Nutley 2013). The following is a common characterization of the United States:

> The clearest and most wide-sweeping attempt to mandate the use of rational learning modes is provided by the No Child Left Behind Act of 2001 in the United States… By mandating the use of rational learning modes, the producers of such knowledge gained power and prominence and overshadowed other forms of learning. (Fazekas and Burns 2012, pp. 22 and 27)

Mason (2013) also underscores the U.S. federal government's role in setting the course of education policy over the last decade. She describes how decisions made at the federal level have profoundly affected the demand for particular types of education research and the ways this research is supplied. In Canada, by contrast, there have been no significant federal initiatives for education, and the approach within Canadian provinces has been primarily bottom-up and facilitative rather than top-down and orchestrated (Qi and Levin 2013).

The approach in the United Kingdom has tended to fall somewhere between the United States and Canada. The United Kingdom has centrally funded many initiatives to improve the supply of education research and its use in policy and practice, but these initiatives have not always been well planned or coordinated (Gough 2013). There are signs that the United Kingdom may be traveling further in the direction of the United States in its approach to research use. In 2013, the U.K. government announced four new "what works" evidence centers on local economic growth, aging, crime, and early intervention. These centers have come together with the existing National Institute for Health and Care Excellence (NICE) and the recently formed Education Endowment Foundation (EEF) to create a "what works" network. The aim of the network is to improve the use of high-quality evidence in decision-making at national and local levels.

This effort to link what works centers in different policy areas is an interesting approach. The United States has a myriad of what works initiatives in education, crime, mental health, child welfare, violence prevention, and other areas, but they are not well connected. A "network" infrastructure to coordinate what is learned across different efforts is a promising idea. In addition, the U.K. what works centers also aim to go beyond acting as clearinghouses for evidence by helping decision-makers invest in services that can deliver the best outcomes for citizens and value for money for taxpayers. They are tasked with identifying research and capability gaps and are expected to work with partners to fill these gaps. Each center is to produce and apply a common set of standards for comparing the effectiveness of interventions. The early signs are that these standards may reflect U.S.-style hierarchies of evidence, but there is recognition that matrices of evidence might be useful given the need to answer more than just "what works" questions in order to facilitate decision-making (Nutley 2013; Nutley et al. 2013). This includes assessing the quality of evidence for addressing questions about what is important for whom and who needs to be involved in the decision-making process.

The use of a top-down versus bottom-up approach to improving research use seems to be related to the extent to which knowledge (research) mobilization is viewed as primarily about the dissemination and implementation of research or about the coproduction of knowledge at a local level. In the United States and United Kingdom, what works initiatives are mainly focused on the former. Canada and Singapore, meanwhile, seem to be more attentive to the latter (Qi and Levin 2013; Teh et al. 2013). Singapore, for example, has shifted the locus of knowledge production to schools so that they are collaborating with university researchers to coproduce their research agenda, conduct the research, and learn from it (Teh et al. 2013). In this scenario, the mobilization challenge is less concerned with the vertical dissemination of research knowledge from a central hub to peripheral locations and more intent on ensuring horizontal knowledge exchange and learning between schools and districts. This Singaporean initiative seems more consistent with recent interest in research-practice partnerships in the United States. Research and school district partners jointly determine the research agenda based on local problems of practice, and the challenge is aggregating lessons learned across localities. Further understanding these various efforts around the world is useful as nations and localities seek to balance bottom-up and top-down approaches—providing the scope to focus on local needs, synthesize lessons centrally, and share learning across communities.

11.5 Conclusion

As we write this chapter, the U.S. policy context that put research evidence front and center in education reform is shifting. The No Child Left Behind Act is retreating into the past. Investing in Innovation funding is being debated and it is unclear how the approach of tying program funding to evaluations will evolve. The Common Core State Standards movement is also shifting; attention is now focused on maintaining political support and ensuring strong implementation. As these political and policy contexts change, opportunities emerge for greater maturity in our efforts to improve research and uses of it by various decision-makers in the policy process.

The chapters in this book suggest some promising strategies and a few cautions as we move forward. We should avoid viewing research use in overly simplified ways. Research is not the next silver bullet for education reform, and simply mandating its use will not get us to our ultimate goals of better teaching and learning. Instead, research helps us understand problems and think about potential solutions. Research must be integrated with different types of evidence and adjudicated alongside values, interests, and local circumstances. The chapters also caution us against stereotyping the approach to research use in the United States as completely top-down and based on rational learning models. But, in so far as this stereotype has some merit, they warn us about the limitations of such an approach.

If we are committed to using research to enrich problem framing, decision-making, and individual and organization learning in education, the next decade should focus on building trust, capacity, strong relationships, and the conditions for productive evidence integration.

References

Asen, R., Gurke, D., Connors, P., Solomon, R., & Gumm, E. (2012). Research evidence and school-board deliberations: Lessons from three Wisconsin school districts. *Educational Policy, 26*, 33–63.

Asen, R., & Gurke, D. (2014). The Research on Education, Deliberation, and Decision-Making (REDD) project. In K. Finnigan & A. Daly (Eds.), *Using research evidence in education: From the schoolhouse door to Capitol Hill.* New York: Springer.

Barnes, C., Goertz, M., & Massell, D. (2014). How state education agencies acquire and use research knowledge for school improvement. In K. Finnigan & A. Daly (Eds.), *Using research evidence in education: From the schoolhouse door to Capitol Hill.* New York: Springer.

Caplan, N. (1979). The two-communities theory and knowledge utilization. *American Behavioral Scientist, 22*, 459–470.

Coburn, C., & Stein, M. (2010). Key lessons about the relationship between research and practice. In C. Coburn & M. Stein (Eds.), *Research and practice in education: Building alliances, bridging the divide* (pp. 201–226). Lanham: Rowman & Littlefield Pub, Inc.

Coburn, C., & Turner, E. (2012). The practice of data use: An introduction. *American Journal of Education, 118*, 99–111.

Coburn, C., Bae, S., & Turner, E. (2008). Authority, status and the dynamics of insider-outsider partnerships at the district level. *Peabody Journal of Education, 83*, 364–399.

Coburn, C., Penuel, W., & Geil, K. (2013). *Research-practice partnerships: A strategy for leveraging research for educational improvement in school districts.* New York: William T. Grant Foundation.

Daly, A., & Finnigan, K. (2011). *Defining, acquiring, and using research evidence: early findings from underperforming districts and schools.* Paper presented at the use of research evidence meeting, Los Angeles.

Daly, A., Finnigan, K., Moolenaar, N., & Che, J. (2014). The critical role of brokers in the access and use of evidence at the school and district level. In K. Finnigan & A. Daly (Eds.), *Using research evidence in education: From the schoolhouse door to Capitol Hill.* New York: Springer.

Education Sciences Reform Act, 20 U.S.C. § 9501. (2002).

Fazekas, M., & Burns, T. (2012). *Exploring the complex interaction between governance and knowledge in education* (OECD education working papers no 67). Paris: OECD. http://dx.doi.org/10.1787/5k9flcx2l340-en

Finnigan, K., Daly, A., & Stewart, T. (2012). Organizational learning in schools under sanction. *Education Research International, 2012*(16), 1–10.

Finnigan, K., Daly, A., & Che, J. (2013). Systemwide reform in districts under pressure: The role of social networks in defining, acquiring, and diffusing research evidence. *Journal of Educational Administration, 51*(4), 476–497.

Gough, D. (2013). Knowledge mobilisation in education in England. In B. Levin, J. Qi, H. Edelstein, & J. Sohn (Eds.), *The impact of research in education: An international perspective.* Bristol: The Policy Press.

Granger, R., Tseng, V., & Wilcox, B. (2013). Connecting research and practice. In E. T. Gershoff, R. S. Mistry, & D. A. Crosby (Eds.), *Societal contexts of child development pathways of influence and implications for practice and policy.* New York: Oxford University Press.

Haskins, R., & Margolis, G. (2014). Obama's promise: Using evidence to fight the nation's social problems. In K. Finnigan & A. Daly (Eds.), *Using research evidence in education: From the schoolhouse door to Capitol Hill.* New York: Springer.

Henig, J. (2009). *How research is used in policy debates: The case of charter schools*. New York: Russell.

Honig, M., & Coburn, C. (2008). Evidence-based decision making in school district central offices: Toward a policy and research agenda. *Educational Policy, 22*, 578–608.

Honig, M., & Venkateswaran, N. (2014). Leaders' use of research for fundamental change in school district central offices: Processes and challenges. In K. Finnigan & A. Daly (Eds.), *Using research evidence in education: From the schoolhouse door to Capitol Hill*. New York: Springer.

Institute of Education Sciences (IES) & The National Science Foundation (NSF). (2013). *Common guidelines for education research and development*. Washington, DC: IES and NSF.

Mason, S. (2013). The federal challenge to university-based education research in the United States: Turning research into policy and practice. In B. Levin, J. Qi, H. Edelstein, & J. Sohn (Eds.), *The impact of research in education: An international perspective*. Bristol: The Policy Press.

McDonnell, L., & Weatherford, M. S. (2014). Research evidence and the common core state standards. In K. Finnigan & A. Daly (Eds.), *Using research evidence education: From the schoolhouse door to Capitol Hill*. New York: Springer.

National Research Council. (2012). *Using science as evidence in public policy*. Committee on the Use of Social Science Knowledge in Public Policy, K. Prewitt, T. Schwandt, & M. Straf, (Eds.). Division of Behavioral and Social Sciences and Education. Washington, DC: The National Academies Press.

Nelson, S., Leffler, J., & Hansen, B. (2009). *Toward a research agenda for understanding and improving the use of research evidence*. Portland: Northwest Regional Educational Laboratory.

Nutley, S. (2013). Reflections on the mobilisation of education research. In B. Levin, J. Qi, H. Edelstein, & J. Sohn (Eds.), *The impact of research in education: An international perspective*. Bristol: The Policy Press.

Nutley, S., Walter, I., & Davies, H. (2007). *Using evidence: How research can inform public services*. Bristol: Policy Press.

Nutley, S., Powell A., & Davies, H. (2013). *What counts as good evidence?* Provocation paper for the Alliance for Useful Evidence. London: Alliance for Useful Evidence. http://www.alliance4usefulevidence.org/assets/What-Counts-as-Good-Evidence-WEB.pdf

OECD/CERI. (2007). *Evidence in education: Linking research and policy*. Paris: OECD Publishing.

Qi, J., & Levin, B. (2013). Knowledge mobilisation in education in Canada and the role of universities. In B. Levin, J. Qi, H. Edelstein, & J. Sohn (Eds.), *The impact of research in education: An international perspective*. Bristol: The Policy Press.

Scott, J., Lubienski, C., Debray, E., & Jabbar, H. (2014). The intermediary function in evidence production, promotion, and utilization: The case of educational incentives. In K. Finnigan & A. Daly (Eds.), *Using research evidence in education: From the schoolhouse door to Capitol Hill*. New York: Springer.

Sparks, S. (2013, August 27). Ed. Dept. Research Reauthorization Gains House Attention. *Education Week*. Retrieved from http://www.edweek.org

Teh, L., Hogan, D., & Dimmock, C. (2013). Knowledge mobilisation and utilisation in the Singapore education system: The nexus between researchers, policy makers and practitioners. In B. Levin, J. Qi, H. Edelstein, & J. Sohn (Eds.), *The impact of research in education: An international perspective*. Bristol: The Policy Press.

Weiss, C. (1977). Research for policy's sake: The enlightenment function of social research. *Policy Analysis, 3*, 531–546.

Chapter 12
Conclusion: Using Research Evidence from the Schoolhouse Door to Capitol Hill

Kara S. Finnigan and Alan J. Daly

Decision-making based upon evidence has been promoted at all levels of the educational system, yet we have little current research that helps us understand evidence use at any of these levels. In fact, scholars have argued that we lack a solid empirical base in understanding what is meant by "evidence" and how that "evidence" is acquired and used for reform (Honig and Coburn 2008; Nelson et al. 2009; Nutley and Davies 2008; Tseng 2012). The chapters in this book provide both substantive and methodological contributions to this area. Despite the different levels, theoretical lenses, research targets, and methodological approaches, these chapters converge on a few important ideas. While in Chap. 11 Tseng and Nutley synthesized the prior chapters by linking specifically to the important points in each, in this final chapter we consider the overall meta-themes from the set of studies in terms of converging ideas and important directions. We outline these themes as a way to push collective understanding on importance and use of research evidence at all levels of the educational system.

Note: Both authors contributed equally to this chapter.

K.S. Finnigan, Ph.D. (✉)
Warner School of Education, University of Rochester,
414 LeChase Hall, Rochester, NY 14627, USA
e-mail: kfinnigan@warner.rochester.edu

A.J. Daly, Ph.D.
Department of Education Studies, University of California,
San Diego, La Jolla, CA, USA
e-mail: ajdaly@ucsd.edu

K.S. Finnigan and A.J. Daly (eds.), *Using Research Evidence in Education: From the Schoolhouse Door to Capitol Hill*, Policy Implications of Research in Education 2,
DOI 10.1007/978-3-319-04690-7_12,

12.1 Limited Access to Evidence

While educators are swimming in data compared with only a decade ago, these chapters indicate that data is only one type of evidence that helps to frame a problem and uncover solutions. It was not that long ago when schools and teachers would complain that they did not have access to data that could inform their instructional practice and that all too often they never had the opportunity to see the data from their students until they had moved on to the next grade. Recently, educated teachers and administrators would be shocked to know that classes like "data-based decision-making" did not exist a decade ago given the widespread and frequent discussions about data in our educational system.

Student performance data, however, is only one type of evidence, and, as these chapters indicate, other types of evidence are valued, but perhaps not as widespread and used for decision-making. Educators hold a variety of definitions of what counts as evidence as they consider educational issues or problems, ranging from empirical studies, to local evaluation reports, and to expert opinion to popular press (Coburn et al. 2009; Finnigan et al. 2013; Nutley and Davies 2008). This is not only true at the school level but out to the district, to states, and even to the federal government. This fact just underscores the notion that while all levels of system can agree that research is important and needed, these levels vary widely on whether they value and use this research or other types of evidence in decision-making. Documenting the complicated nature of evidence use, as has been done in the chapters, is the first step to moving toward greater coherence.

The limited access to evidence found in the chapters was in part due to the nature of the structure of educational organizations, often being siloed and disconnected, as well as cultures that did not support evidence use in a systematic and distributed manner. For example, principals of underperforming schools were disconnected from the data advice network in their larger school district, and those in formal positions to "broker" access to evidence were not always serving these roles. This may help to explain why districts and schools facing sanction under NCLB continue to draw on existing approaches that may or may not be rooted in an empirical base (Finnigan et al. 2012; Mintrop and Sunderman 2009). Moreover, it suggests the importance of the social side of the research evidence equation.

Traditional academic research and more rigorous evaluations are ironically viewed as both the most credible form of evidence and at the same time being viewed with skepticism because of the amount of time and resources involved, as well as who produces this work. These types of evidence are often viewed as being too "ivory tower," meaning disconnected from the work of practice due to academic language and publication venues. This is a fundamental paradox in that research intended to impact policy and practice often rarely enters the hands of the policy-maker or practitioner.

As federal and state policy requires the use of "research-based evidence," researchers presumably produce high-quality research evidence that would be of great use to educators, who also want to use best practices grounded in research evidence, and yet at each step along the way there seems to be definitional, translational, and usability issues. In fact, while researchers usually hope that their work will impact the field, those on the ground, e.g., practitioners and policymakers, have limited time, training, and capacity for interpreting and translating the results into actionable steps. Moreover, the research that is produced is often framed from the researcher perspective rather than from educator/policymaker vantage point, and as such there is a large supply of research, but often the supply is at best tangentially related to the strong demand from the field (Nutley et al. 2007; Porter 2007; Tseng 2012). With better connections between the demand and supply side, research evidence could have a greater potential to support the important work of improving educational systems.

For years, scholars and educators have argued for the need to bridge these gaps between research, policy, and practice. Many have called for academic researchers to do more "translational" research to make sure their work gets into the hands of practitioners and policymakers and more recently for research partnerships to jointly shape research. However, both of these potentially high-leverage strategies require changing long held beliefs about roles as well as substantial reallocation of resources. Some academics do get their work into the mainstream media through blogposts, social media, or other mechanisms, but even then that work may not be valued from a university perspective and thus may actually inhibit researchers from making their work more widely accessible to diverse audiences. As larger systems continue to focus on "impact factors" that measure influence on other scientist and not "practice impact," it will be difficult to move further into translational work. Hence, as we consider the next steps forward in the study of research evidence, we must also consider the larger "incentive" structures in educational systems, such as universities, that do not necessarily reward translational activity or other more accessible venues for moving work out into the field.

Despite the fact that universities do not typically value more "alternative" diffusion venues, these dissemination tactics, which are likely more nimble and responsive to research demands, are central to the work of many intermediary organizations. However, the research in this text indicates such organizations may have other agendas beyond dissemination. Beyond the translation and partnership approaches, governmental and foundation funders of research may benefit from facilitating the process of dissemination through a variety of mechanisms from websites to policy forums, as the WT Grant Foundation has done with much of the work funded under their Use of Research Evidence initiative (which supports the work in this volume). Universities and think tanks could also facilitate the research dissemination process by taking it upon themselves to institutionally build resources, supports, and incentives into communicating results from their scholars and analysts using the same technologically driven approaches as the intermediary organizations as a form of outreach to practice and policy communities.

12.2 Strategic Use

Although prior scholars have identified a variety of uses of evidence from instrumental to conceptual approaches (see, e.g., Nutley et al. 2007; Weiss 1977), the chapters in this book suggest that most of the use of evidence at all levels of the educational system is strategic or symbolic – to sway opinions or confirm ideas.

In many cases, "the research says…." was a common refrain even though individuals couldn't point to specific studies or data. Particularly at early points in advocating a position at the local, state, or federal level, evidence is more often used strategically to gain buy-in or support, rather than instrumentally as part of a learning process to diagnose problems and uncover solutions.

Perhaps this narrow use of evidence is not surprising for two reasons. The first is that evidence is promoted as the answer. As Peter Orszag, director of Office of Management and Budget at the time, pointed out in 2009:

> Rigorous ways to evaluate whether programs are working exist. But too often such evaluations don't happen. They are typically an afterthought when programs are designed – and once programs have been in place for awhile, evaluating them rigorously becomes difficult from a political economy perspective.
>
> This has to change, and I am trying to put much more emphasis on evidence-based policy decisions here at OMB. Wherever possible, we should design new initiatives to build rigorous data about what works and then act on evidence that emerges – expanding the approaches that work best, fine-tuning the ones that get mixed results, and shutting down those that are failing.

In that way even if the evidence is limited or inconclusive, it becomes used as part of arguments for supporting or removing a particular policy or practice because of the high level of importance placed upon evidence-based decision-making. A second and related reason is of legitimacy – if one can offer evidence, particularly a compelling anecdote or a rigorously designed study, then one may be more likely to be able to persuade others of the importance of a particular approach because it has been sanctioned or legitimized by this external "expert" source. At both the district and national level, this allowed individuals to support their proposed course of action and move beyond an ideological debate.

12.3 Evidence as Learning

The chapters also point to a major challenge in moving beyond strategic or symbolic uses of evidence – that individuals need prior knowledge and experience that they can build upon as well as a "readiness" to engage in a learning process around evidence. The idea of "learning" around evidence is one of the most compelling notions in this book. We have typically thought of "evidence" as an input, but an input to what? As the chapters in this text either directly state or hint at, evidence is an input to a learning process that is influenced by individual experiences, the context in which one resides, and the social interactions around the evidence. In this way evidence is just part of a process that both acts with and on the evidence. Hence, while at the outset evidence may be a research report or expert opinion, or even student data, thought of from a learning orientation, it is just one element, albeit important, to a larger process that involves learning. This of course implies the leadership and conditions necessary to be in place to support this approach, and as the authors in the text point out, this is best achieved through a combination of both internal and external partnerships.

In order for learning to be realized, we have to pay better attention to the interconnected and interdependent system in which evidence is used. Developing the types of learning communities at all levels of the educational system to strengthen the capacity of educators and policymakers to make judgments about the various types of evidence seems critical. Individuals bring different expertise to situations, and it would be useful to develop collaborative processes to facilitate what Marsh (2007) refers to as "joint work" to enable the co-interpretation and co-construction of different types of evidence into actionable steps for policy or practice. This implies that the necessary social conditions also be in place for the work to occur. While much of the literature attends to training and fidelity, one main theme across these chapters has to do with the collegiality necessary for knowledge development and transfer (Lazega 2001).

While calls for professional learning communities have become common in education circles, these are rarely discussed beyond teachers, yet administrators in local or state departments of education or policymakers at all levels of the system would benefit from the same collaborative thinking to jointly use and interpret multiple types of evidence to tackle complex problems. However, these professional learning communities – or what we refer to as "knowledge communities" – would need to be authentic partnerships that understand that evidence is not just the purview of the university but actually is a much broader and nuanced idea. This broadened understanding of what counts as evidence, along with allocated time to grapple with and interpret different types of evidence, through a learning process, not only requires a paradigm shift but also leads us to our next theme – trust – which is critical to evidence use.

12.4 Building (or Rebuilding) Trust

Trust and relationships are central to many of these chapters, as strong relationships, including both vertical and horizontal ties, facilitate the flow of ideas and practices throughout the educational system. The role of networks has been implicated as both supports and constraints in the process of organizational change, learning, and improvement. This literature suggests that the structure of social networks can support organizational goals by facilitating the flow of information among individuals and overcoming problems of coordination, as scholars such as Lazega and Pattison (2001) and Tsai and Ghoshal (1998) have pointed out. Research further suggests that strong reciprocated relationships within and across a network have been associated with initiating and sustaining change (McGrath and Krackhardt 2003; Tenkasi and Chesmore 2003).

Trust plays a role in several aspects of evidence use. First, people make determinations about the evidence based upon the person providing the evidence. In other words, the same type of evidence brought by a trustworthy or untrustworthy source will have a different result in a person's response to that evidence, i.e., whether it resonates or they are skeptical of it, for example. This is particularly interesting, as it suggests that the emotional connection to an individual, as exemplified by trust, can actually override the rational evaluation of a piece of evidence. As such we must be mindful of not only the fact that individuals have social relationships but the quality of the relationship between those individuals matters as it may be consequential for the use of evidence. For symbolic evidence use, therefore, a trusting source is key to convincing people of a particular approach or strategy.

Second, trust is important to evidence use because of the politics of data use. In fact, our work suggests that there is a degree of vulnerability that exists when educators or policymakers actually find out "what the data says." Because of our political context, it is difficult to have a nuanced conversation of the evidence, if, for example, the results are not all positive. At that point, having a trusted colleague to help dig deeper into understanding the various types of evidence and considering appropriate instructional, structural, or policy changes depending upon the issue at hand is important. What the work in this book indicates is that institutional support around evidence use is critical and those who serve in supporting roles by facilitating access to evidence and facilitating interpretation and action steps should not necessarily be those who serve in supervisory roles or, if they are, then attention must be paid to underlying relationships given a high level of distrust across our educational systems (Daly and Finnigan 2012).

So how do you rebuild trust given the current climate of accountability and systems of compliance at the local and state level? The lessons in this book would suggest leadership is critical. First, as much literature regarding the rebuilding of trust suggests (e.g., Tschannen-Moran 2004), it is incumbent upon leaders to set the stage for a trusting environment. Leaders who are able to model being vulnerable, open, and respectful and operate with high integrity are more likely to engender those characteristics in their context. As to evidence specifically, leaders who work to rebuild trust must first consider what evidence they consider valuable and whether this is similar to the types of evidence that others consider useful. As the work in this book suggests, a leader has to bridge and connect to others not just to provide access to evidence but in the co-interpretation of this evidence. Leaders who can successfully acknowledge and validate various types of evidence, including experience and observation, are better able to honor expertise and knowledge production at all levels of the system. This process of acknowledgement and valuing sends clear messages about one's importance in an organization and, as the work in the book suggests, supports the rebuilding of trust and creating buy-in at all levels.

Trust can also be rebuilt by facilitating the exchange of research and other types of evidence through the types of "knowledge communities" discussed above. Through this rebuilding of trust, access to evidence can be increased and use of evidence can be strengthened. Furthermore, by shifting to an orientation of systems of support in the building of capacity around evidence use (away from compliance and monitoring), trust can be rebuilt. Building on this point, one of the main lessons from this work is that evidence use occurs in a robust network of interconnected relationships, whether one focuses on the school, district, state, or federal government, as we discuss more below. This interconnected system of relationships is critical to the use of evidence, and as such, greater attention should be paid to both the quantity and quality of relationships between and among research users.

12.5 Importance of "Research Mediators" and Policy Coalitions

As several chapters suggest, the prominence of evidence use across the educational system has resulted from several forces including bully pulpit statements and funding allocations from the federal government, new sources of funding from both governmental and foundation sources, and state accountability systems. This push, combined with an often disjointed relationship between the research producers and the research users, has allowed for new groups to emerge or position themselves as the "interpreters" of evidence. As mentioned above, academic research may lack visibility and accessibility as a result of both what is rewarded in the system, but also the result of funding cycles and institutional priorities. Not only do researchers tend not to be involved in the active promotion and dissemination of their work, but their institutions also do not necessarily allocate resources toward these activities, despite the benefit of moving the work into the policy or practice sphere. In essence, much of the talk of moving research into policy and practice relies on individual researchers to either rework their final products or reach out directly to groups, but, in reality, institutional resources on both the researcher and user end could be more productively reallocated toward more "translational" activities.

Better using institutional resources in a coherent and focused manner for moving research into practice and policy appears a high-leverage strategy that takes into account the systemic nature of the work. However, this will require a retooling on the part of institutions. For universities recognizing the importance of translational work through incentivizing that type of work and using communication systems to move the work outward and on the research user side, providing the capacity building to be able to incorporate and evaluate evidence as it moves into the system. In both instances different skill sets and capacities must be built, but as it stands now the pressure is generally on individuals to figure out how to move their work into the practice or policy communities with limited institutional support.

In many ways intermediary organizations have quickly moved to fill this gap between producers and users in the broader system. In particular, foundations have become centrally involved in evidence production. External groups not only provide research but make sense of it and offer practical advice, filling a much needed niche. Intermediaries have taken on important roles in the packaging of research and the management of perceptions to "sell" policymakers or practitioners on a set of findings, as well as to validate whether evidence is credible. Of course while filling a larger "need" of the system to bridge researcher to user, another "need" was being filled as many of these organizations spent considerable resources moving their own agendas forward, many unchecked. In perhaps a similar but different capacity, district staff have filled gaps between producers and users of evidence. These brokers also serve in intermediary positions, but they are internal to the organization vs. external to the organization.

This emergence of intermediary organizations in both the production and interpretation and evidence illustrates the shifting roles of these groups, as well as the importance of further research into their roles. In essence, these interpreters or brokers – or what we call "research mediators" – have come to play a critical role in the flow of ideas and practices because they filter what is known about research and can also facilitate integrating evidence into the practice of others if they are well trusted as discussed previously. In examining these groups, it will be important to consider their role as policy advocates, for example, by considering which types of evidence they promote about particular issues and the degree to which they advocate for policies or practices solely along ideological lines.

Beyond the individuals and groups that serve as "research mediators," connecting producers and users of evidence, policy coalitions, which included foundations, think tanks, and advocacy groups, emerged in the chapters as important in both symbolic and instrumental uses of evidence. To capitalize on the diverse networks of individuals that these policy coalitions connect, it may be worthwhile to consider either creating these or building upon groups that already exist to make meaning of and disseminate evidence around a particular topic, like mathematics reform, or a particular challenge in our educational system, like how to improve the lowest performing 5 % of schools. Extending these policy coalitions to include researchers and practitioners, i.e., academics and teachers or administrators, rather than just connecting these two groups, would be an important next step. Another next step from an institutional perspective is to convene consortia of producers and consumers of evidence – along with these policy coalitions – to create common dialogue and recognition that the production of knowledge does not reside in one part of the system but across the system in various sectors and levels. As we see from the work in this book, perhaps a positive result of the accountability pressures is that it has resulted in new connections or stronger connections given the stakes are so high. The interconnectedness of the system leads us to our final theme – the importance of a systemic approach to educational issues and improvement.

12.6 Education: An Interconnected System

As United States Secretary of Education Arne Duncan said a few years ago now in his testimony to Congress, NCLB "has created a thousand ways for schools to fail and very few ways to help them succeed" (Duncan 2011). Our interest in evidence stems from our commitment to a more equitable educational system, and as we began to conduct our own research on the lowest performing schools, we saw first-hand the interconnectedness of the various parts, for example, in the movement of principals into and out of these schools as a result of accountability policies as we discuss in our recent work (Daly and Finnigan 2014; Daly et al. 2014; Finnigan and Daly 2012, 2014; Finnigan et al. 2012). In bringing together the chapters of this book that focus from the schoolhouse to Capitol Hill, we were interested in moving our understanding of educational issues forward by joining these disconnected parts.

The contributors of this book each provide unique lenses on the issue of evidence use in education, and in combination these provide us with an important reminder that is becoming ever so clear in this moment in history: the interdependence of all of the moving parts of the US educational system. The implementation of the Common Core across the country may be the first time that we have explicit evidence of the consequences of an occurrence at any particular level of the system, e.g., as parents "opt out" of assessments, or a state department of education provides curricular units that are implemented locally, or a foundation grant ends there is a sort of ripple effect that is felt in other parts of the system and the system, as a result, makes adjustments and self corrects (or doesn't).

We are not the first to argue the utility of using complex adaptive systems (CAS) theory to understand the *entire* system of education (see, e.g., Maroulis, et al. 2010; Sabelli et al. 2012). This body of research, however, demonstrates quite clearly that it is important to look beyond the more traditional governmental layers involved in K-12 education such as local and state educational agencies and the federal government, extending to "outside" groups from higher education, to foundations, think tanks, advocacy groups, and municipal governments. Given that a central premise of this book was to examine whether, how, and under what conditions evidence is used by practitioners and policymakers, CAS can help us to understand the linkages between the macro- and micro-systems for not only the types of evidence that are produced but also to increase access and allow for co-interpretation across the system. These dynamic linkages among the various subsystems and levels are critically important to take into account and frequently overlooked in trying to bring about educational change (Lemke and Sabelli 2008). Absent an understanding that this work is about an interdependent system in which the success of one part of the system is dependent on the other, we are not likely to see the type of transformations necessary to be responsive to the needs of the twenty-first century.

It strikes us then that part of the reason that we have created a thousand way for schools to fail is because we continue to think about these issues as a school problem – with our policies based in underlying assumptions that relate to what individual teachers or administrators or students in those schools are not doing rather than considering what the system is not doing to improve performance in these schools. In the end, then, to some degree we are all implicated in the failure, as Gloria Ladson-Billings (2006) suggested when she argued that we need to consider the "educational debt" that we owe to students of color and living in poverty. If we have systems that are interconnected but do not use these connections wisely to provide support, co-construct new knowledge around various types of evidence, and allow for the flow of ideas and practices based upon this new knowledge to move into and out of schools serving these students, then it seems like misplaced blame to argue for a "death penalty" for failing schools as New York Governor Cuomo recently did. In essence, all of the groups in the larger system have allowed the inequities (that happen to align closely along racial and socioeconomic lines) to exist and even thrive so it is unclear why the educators within these schools are blamed for the failure of the larger system.

In conclusion, although in education we have spent a lot of time talking about the importance of evidence, we have not spent as much time considering how evidence will be interpreted to develop new knowledge that can then serve to improving opportunities and outcomes for children. In essence, we have done a good job of creating a lot of hippos but haven't spent time helping the hippos to dance. Hippos in this sense refer to big important ideas from research. In and of themselves these ideas are important but are often so weighty they do not "dance" easily into practice or policy. We rarely take the time to collectively teach hippos to dance; rather, we wait and hope that somehow they will don dancing slippers and find their way into the ball of educational practice and policy. Sometimes this happens, but more often than not hippos do what hippos do, that is to float, eat, and only move when necessary or provoked. As we face continued and unprecedented challenges in improving educational outcomes and reducing the inequities in our educational system, developing better ways for research evidence to be interpreted and taken up into practice – or helping the hippos to dance – will be critical.

References

Coburn, C. E., Honig, M. I., & Stein, M. K. (2009). What is the evidence on districts' use of evidence? In J. D. Bransford, D. J. Stipek, N. J. Vye, L. M. Gomez, & D. Lam (Eds.), *The role of research in educational improvement* (pp. 67–86). Cambridge: Harvard Education Press.

Daly, A. J., & Finnigan, K. (2012). Exploring the space between: Social networks, trust, and urban school district leaders. *Journal of School Leadership, 22*(3), 493–530.

Daly, A. J., & Finnigan, K. S. (2014). *Challenges, changes, and churn: A longitudinal social network perspective of urban district leadership*. Presented at the annual meeting of the American Educational Research Association, Philadelphia, PA.

Daly, A. J., Finnigan, K. S., Jordan, S., Moolenaar, N., & Che, J. (2014). Misalignment and perverse incentives: Examining the politics of district leaders as brokers in the use of research evidence. *Educational Policy*. doi:10.1177/0895904813513149.

Duncan, A. (2011, March 31). Winning the future with education: Responsibility, reform and results. *Oral Testimony to Congress*. Retrieved March 31, 2011, from http://www.ed.gov/news/speeches/winning-future-education-responsibility-reform-and-results

Finnigan, K. S., & Daly, A. J. (2012). Mind the gap: Learning, trust, and relationships in an underperforming urban district. *American Journal of Education, 119*(1), 41–71.

Finnigan, K. S., & Daly, A. J. (2014). *The social side of change: Understanding the substantive and methodological challenges resulting from leadership churn*. Presented at the annual meeting of the American Educational Research Association, Philadelphia, PA.

Finnigan, K., Daly, A., & Stewart, T. (2012). Organizational learning in schools under sanction. *Education Research International*, Article ID 270404, 1–10. doi:10.1155/2012/270404.

Finnigan, K. S., Daly, A. J., & Che, J. (2013). Systemwide reform in districts under pressure: The role of social networks in defining, acquiring, and diffusing research evidence. *Journal of Educational Administration, 51*(4), 476–497.

Honig, M. I., & Coburn, C. (2008). Evidence-based decision making in school district central offices: Toward a policy research agenda. *Educational Policy, 22*(4), 578–608.

Ladson-Billings, G. (2006). From the achievement gap to the education debt: Understanding achievement in U.S. schools. *Educational Researcher, 35*(7), 3–12.

Lazega, E. (2001). *The collegial phenomenon: The social mechanisms of collaboration among peers in a corporate law partnership*. Oxford: Oxford University Press.

Lazega, E., & Pattison, P. (2001). Social capital as social mechanisms and collective assets: The example of status auctions among colleagues. In R. Burt (Ed.), *Social capital: Theory and research* (pp. 185–208). New York: Aldine de Gruyter.

Lemke, J. L., & Sabelli, N. (2008). Complex systems and educational change: Towards a new research agenda. *Educational Philosophy and Theory, 40*(1), 118–129.
Maroulis, S., Guimera, R., Petry, H., Stringer, M. J., Gomez, L. M., Amaral, L. A. N., & Wilensky, U. (2010). Complex systems view of educational policy research. *Science, 330*, 38–39.
Marsh, J. A. (2007). *Democratic dilemmas: Joint work, education politics, and community*. Albany: State University of New York Press.
McGrath, C., & Krackhardt, D. (2003). Network conditions for organizational change. *Journal of Applied Behavioral Science, 39*(3), 324–336.
Mintrop, H., & Sunderman, L. G. (2009). Predictable failure of federal sanctions-driven accountability for school improvement – And why we may retain it anyway. *Educational Researcher, 38*(5), 353–361.
Nelson, S. R., Leffler, J. C., & Hansen, B. A. (2009). *Toward a research agenda for understanding and improving use of research evidence*. Portland: Northwest Regional Educational Laboratory.
Nutley, S., & Davies, H. (2008). *Using research to provide stronger services and programs for youth: A discussion paper for the William T Grant Foundation*. Unpublished manuscript.
Nutley, S., Walter, I., & Davies, H. (2007). *Using evidence: How research can inform public services*. Bristol: Policy Press.
Porter, S. (2007). Making connections between research and practice. *Eye on the LSI, 4*, 3–5.
Sabelli, N., Lemke, J., Cheng, B., & Richey, M. (2012). *Education as a complex adaptive system: Report of progress*. Menlo Park: SRI International.
Tenkasi, R., & Chesmore, M. (2003). Social networks and planned organizational change. *Journal of Applied Behavioral Science, 39*(3), 281–300.
Tsai, W., & Ghoshal, S. (1998). Social capital and value creation: The role of intrafirm networks. *Academy of Management Journal, 41*(4), 464–476.
Tschannen-Moran, M. (2004). *Trust matters: Leadership for successful schools*. San Francisco: Jossey-Bass.
Tseng, V. (2012). The uses of research in policy and practice. *Social Policy Report, 26*(2), 3–16.
Weiss, C. H. (1977). Research for policy's sake: The enlightenment function of social research. *Policy Analysis, 3*(4), 531–545.

Author Index

K.S. Finnigan and A.J. Daly (eds.), *Using Research Evidence in Education: From the Schoolhouse Door to Capitol Hill*, Policy Implications of Research in Education 2,
DOI 10.1007/978-3-319-04690-7, © Springer International Publishing Switzerland 2014

Y

Z